INDIANS OF CANADA
Cultural Dynamics

INDIANS OF CANADA
Cultural Dynamics

John A. Price
York University

Sheffield Publishing Company

Salem, Wisconsin

For information about this book, write or call:

Sheffield Publishing Company
P.O. Box 359
Salem, Wisconsin 53168
(414) 843-2281

Cover: "Tribute to the Great Chiefs of the Past" by Daphne Odjig.
Reproduced courtesy of The McMichael Canadian Collection,
Kleinburg, Ontario

Printed in the United States of America

7 6 5 4 3 2

Contents

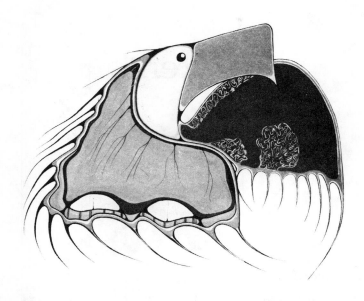

Thunderer Spirit by James Simon. Reproduced courtesy of The McMichael Canadian Collection, Kleinberg, Ontario.

The Embrace by Daphne Odjig. Reproduced courtesy of The McMichael Canadian Collection, Kleinberg, Ontario.

Foreword

This book is a survey of the dynamics of Indian life in Canada. It looks at ecological adaptations, historical persistence and acculturation, cultural evolution, and the background to current Indian-White relationships. The first three chapters give perspectives for the entire country. Chapter 1 reviews racial characteristics and the unfolding picture of prehistoric archaeology. Chapter 2 describes the work on the fifty Native languages. Chapter 3 discusses cultural patterns and the use of theoretical models in understanding the differences between societies.

The core of the book is five regional chapters. Each of these chapters presents (1) traits of the region or *culture area,* (2) sketches of one or two well-known societies within each area, and (3) one or more examples of prominent themes of research within the area. This book is meant to be an introduction for the general reader to the cultural heritage of Canadian Indians and Inuit, and for students who are curious about Native studies. The book touches on a variety of topics. An extensive, chapter-by-chapter bibliography is given at the end for those interested in deeper exploration into the areas, societies, or research themes of the book.

The five core chapters are ordered according to the evolutionary complexity of the aboriginal societies within the five culture areas. The Arctic and Subarctic culture areas described in chapters 4 and 5 had simple *band* level societies who lived by hunting, fishing, and, occasionally, plant gathering. The Iroquoia and historical Plains areas described in chapters 6 and 7 had more advanced *tribal* level societies: village farmers in the first case and horseback buffalo hunters in the second. The Pacific area, described in chapter 8, had highly evolved fishing *chiefdoms*. Following is an outline of these chapters:

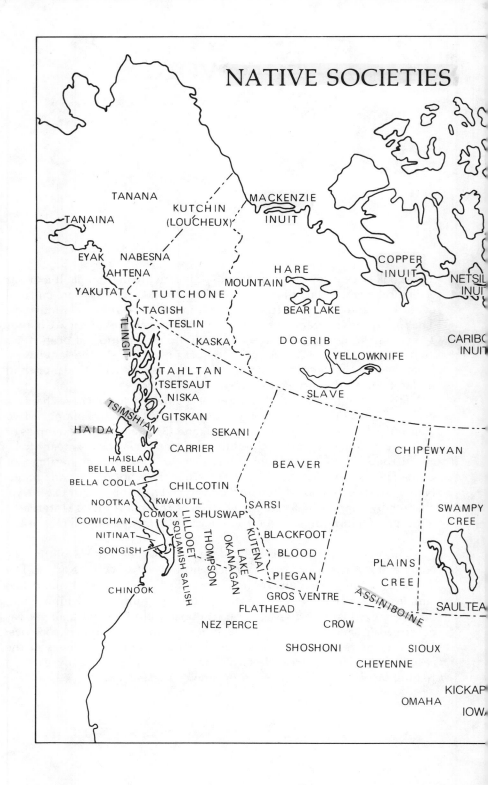

NATIVE SOCIETIES

TANANA

TANAINA

KUTCHIN
(LOUCHEUX)

MACKENZIE
INUIT

EYAK   NABESNA

AHTENA

YAKUTAT   TUTCHONE

COPPER
INUIT

NETSIL
INUI

HARE

MOUNTAIN

TAGISH

BEAR LAKE

TESLIN

KASKA

TLINGIT

DOGRIB

YELLOWKNIFE

CARIBO
INUIT

TAHLTAN

TSETSAUT

NISKA

SLAVE

TSIMSHIAN

GITSKAN

HAIDA

SEKANI

CHIPEWYAN

CARRIER

HAISLA

BELLA BELLA

BELLA COOLA

BEAVER

CHILCOTIN

NOOTKA   KWAKIUTL

COWICHAN

COMOX   SHUSWAP

SARSI

SWAMPY
CREE

NITINAT

SONGISH

LILLOOET

SQUAMISH SALISH

THOMPSON

OKANAGAN

LAKE

KUTENAI

BLACKFOOT

BLOOD

PLAINS

CREE

CHINOOK

PIEGAN

GROS VENTRE

FLATHEAD

ASSINIBOINE

SAULTEA

NEZ PERCE

CROW

SHOSHONI

SIOUX

CHEYENNE

KICKAP

OMAHA

IOWA

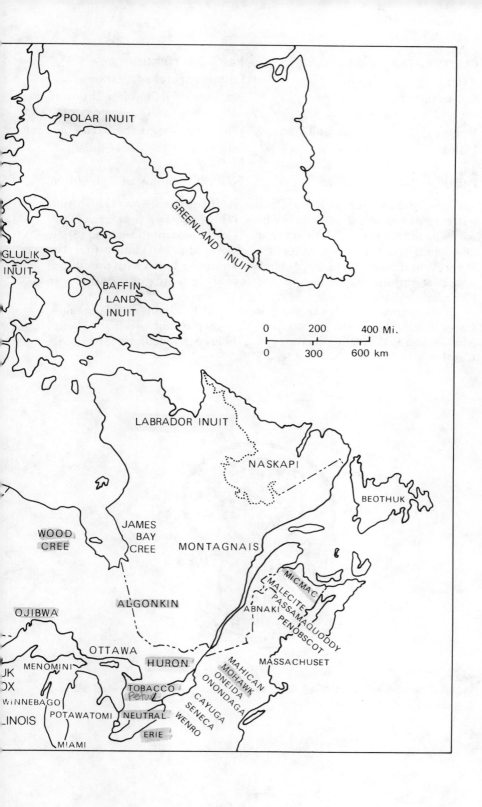

POLAR INUIT

GREENLAND INUIT

GLULIK
INUIT

BAFFIN
LAND
INUIT

0   200   400 Mi.

0   300   600 km

LABRADOR INUIT

NASKAPI

BEOTHUK

WOOD
CREE

JAMES
BAY
CREE

MONTAGNAIS

MICMAC

MALECITE
PASSAMAQUODDY
ABNAKI
PENOBSCOT

OJIBWA

ALGONKIN

OTTAWA

MENOMINI

UK
OX

WINNEBAGO

ILLINOIS

POTAWATOMI

MIAMI

HURON

TOBACCO
Petun

NEUTRAL

ERIE

MASSACHUSET

MAHICAN
MOHAWK
ONEIDA
ONONDAGA
CAYUGA
SENECA
WENRO

CULTURE AREA	CASE STUDIES	RESEARCH THEMES
Artic	Inuit	Environmental adaptations
Subarctic	Northern Algonquians	Acculturation of isolated hunters
Iroquoia	Huron and Iroquois	Warfare among tribal farmers
Plains	Blackfoot	Influence of the horse on a hunting society
Pacific	Kwakiutl	Political economy of a chiefdom

The final chapter is on modern issues. It comments on (1) historical patterns of Indian-White relationships, (2) the Indian Act of Canada, (3) patterns of current anti-Indian racism, (4) urban adaptations, and (5) the development of modern voluntary associations. It shows that the theoretical themes of the third chapter can be combined with the culture area descriptions to give insights into events that are going on today in Canadian Indian societies.

Suggestions by Patricia Shaw improved the chapter on languages. Carol Randall of York University Cartography did the maps. Janice McBain and Eadie Henry did the typing. This book is dedicated to my wife Caralee.

Windigo Spirit by Saul Williams. Reproduced courtesy of The McMichael Canadian Collection, Kleinberg, Ontario.

CHAPTER 1

Race and Prehistory

CANADA DOES NOT have a very long or complex human prehistory, compared with other large areas. For one thing, humans entered the New World late in history, probably only about 30,000 years ago. Thus, no fossils of earlier forms of humans have been found in the New World; all are *Homo sapiens*. For another thing, Canada was not very hospitable for humans until after the last ice age ended several thousand years ago, and there is little history of early hunting cultures in Canada. Further, the cultural revolution of the domestication of plants and the accompanying development of complex societies took place in Mexico. Canada was therefore on the far periphery of that important historical tradition.

Only in relatively recent developments—by the Inuit in the Arctic and the people of coastal British Columbia—were Canadian Natives central to major cultural innovations in prehistory, though several minor cultural innovations took place at least partially in Canada: the copper technology of the Old Copper Culture of the Great Lakes area, the environmentally related innovations of the Subarctic cultures, and the florescent participation of the Iroquoians in the eastern agricultural tradition.

The Eastern and Western Hemispheres remained separate and largely isolated until ocean-going ships were developed, perhaps by Polynesians, Japanese, or Phoenicians, and certainly by Vikings. Prior to that, the only connection between the hemispheres was across the Bering Straits between Siberia and Alaska. This was frozen over in the winter and the Inuit who lived in the area could walk across, visiting between the Inuit settlements in Siberia and Alaska.

Racial Characteristics

The cold climate, meager sources of food, and inland glacial barricades during the past ice age meant that there was very little traffic in people, new ideas, or objects of trade between the hemispheres. Several diseases developed in the Old World populations for which the New World Natives had no immunity when Europeans finally arrived: smallpox, typhus, measles, and malaria. The cold and isolated Bering area was a disease filter (Stewart 1973). The Old World developed milk drinking cultures. Genetic changes occurred in the people in those pastoral societies that allowed people to continue to digest mild sugars beyond childhood. Today New World Native adults, by contrast, usually have trouble digesting milk sugars.

New World Natives apparently came from a broadly Mongoloid racial stock, and had enough time to form a separate American Indian sub-race. Native Americans usually have the following physical traits (Hughes and Kallen 1974):

1. Straight black hair.
2. Very little facial or body hair; rarely baldness.
3. Brown skin.
4. A broad face with some prominence of cheek bones.
5. A tendency toward the Mongoloid eyefold.
6. In the ABO blood system, a very high frequency of O (up to 100 per cent in some populations) and a very low frequency of B. There was some recent diffusion of B into the Native populations of western Alaska from Siberia. The Blackfoot are unusual in having a high frequency of A.
7. A general absence of the rh- blood factor.
8. Certain obscure traits as dry rather than sticky earwax, the ability to taste as bitter the chemical PTC, and fingerprints with frequencies of loops and whorls similar to those of Asians.

The Inuit are more similar to the classically defined Mongoloid type than are other Native Americans, and are thought to have arrived in the New World only in the past 5,000 years. The basics of Inuit culture developed in northern coastal Alaska and Canada around Arctic marine mammal hunting. This development allowed the Inuit to fill out an almost unoccupied ecological niche along the coasts from Siberia to Greenland and down the Aleutian chain of islands. The Diego blood antigen is generally present in Indian populations and absent among the Inuit. In one survey, 98% of the Beaver and Cree Indians could taste PTC, but only 59% of the Labrador Inuit could taste it.

There are other physical differences between Indian populations, comparable to the variations of stature, head shape, skin color, etc., of Europeans. For example, the B.C. coastal Indians have the most facial and body hair of the Indians in Canada. The Inuit and the B.C. coastal Indians are short, and the Iroquoians tend to be tall. The Huron men were taller than the Frenchmen who described them in the 1600s. The average height of Iroquois men in the early 1900s was about 5'8". The Mackenzie and B.C. Indians tend to be round-headed (brachycephalic) and the rest are medium (mesocephalic) or, rarely, long-headed (dolichocephalic).

Dark skin has evolved, seemingly as a partial protection from ultraviolet solar radiation. The short stature and stocky build of the Inuit conserve heat for an Arctic people whereas the tall, thin build of the more southerly Huron-Iroquois disperses body heat. The Mongoloid eyefold (and the Scandinavian eyefold in Europe) evolved perhaps to protect the eye from cold.

In spite of the above, racial traits do not have powerful adaptive advantages for survival. Racial variations seem to have risen primarily from the pervasive influence of a specific set of ancestors and the fluctuating cultural patterns in the sexual preferences of mates. Thus we would explain the small amount of facial and body hair among the Native people as a combination of long-term genetic patterning from their ancestors and a preference for sexual partners with little or no facial and body hair. It is significant that, to the eastern Indians, the most shocking part in the ugliness of the Europeans was the facial hair of the men.

Across Beringia and down the Mackenzie Corridor

When humans first entered the New World the Bering area was probably dry land, free from glacial ice. In cold periods of the ice ages large amounts of the moisture in the world's environment were locked up in glaciers and ice sheets. The ocean levels decreased by up to 300 feet, and the shallow continental shelf areas of the world became dry land. The Bering Straits became a broad plain now called Beringia, an inter-hemispheric land bridge. Ice age mammals crossed Beringia in both directions, and humans undoubtedly hunted them there after 28,000 B.C. during the last ice age, known as the Wisconsin Ice Age.

As predators of large mammals, humans required a very large amount of space per person. There is reason to suggest that the Old World was becoming overpopulated for humans as big game hunters by 28,000 B.C. There were populations of hunters moving into marginal areas of the Old World that were new to human occupation, particularly Australia and northward close to the margins of the glaciers across Europe and Asia. Certainly in the latter continents cultural adaptations had to be made for survival in the cold and damp climates near the glacial ice sheets. Entry into the New World seems to have been simply population expansion of the Old World. "Migration" in reference to these movements should be taken to mean a flow based on population growth, rather than the movement of single bands of people over long distances.

Over the millenia, in response to fluctuations in temperature, ice sheets, and ocean levels, Beringia was alternately dry land and shallow seas that iced over in the winter. The continental ice sheets also expanded and decreased, sometimes closing off human travel inside Alaska and Canada. Between 22,000 B.C. and 10,500 B.C., during the height of glaciation, the only passage was the Mackenzie Valley, and even that was usually closed off. The optimal entry times were just before and just after the height of glaciation: 24–22,000 B.C. and 10–8,000 B.C., when the climate was sufficiently cold for Beringia to be dry, and warm enough to permit a large, ice-free corridor through Alaska and Canada.

There appear to have been two migration routes through Alaska; one north of the Brooks Mountain Range along the Arctic Ocean slope and the other through central Alaska up the Yukon River Valley. There are early archaeological sites in both areas, but the Yukon Valley was warmer, had more game animals, and seems to have been the major route. These routes converged in an ice-free corridor that passed through the Mackenzie Valley in the Northwest Territories and then through Alberta and Saskatchewan. Huge continental glaciers were on both sides of the corridor: The Cordilleran centered over the Rocky Mountains, and the Laurentide, about 9,500 feet thick at its maximum, centered over Hudson Bay.

Archaeological Finds

The oldest generally accepted archaeological find in the New World was in Canada; it uncovered a collection of fleshing tools and other artifacts made from caribou bone in a site near the Old Crow River in the Yukon. The tip of a caribou shinbone was neatly cut in a toothed or serrated pattern, probably for scraping skins. These and associated bones of extinct mammoth elephants are dated by the radioactive carbon technique to between 27,000 and 23,000 B.C. The only other find so far in Canada that might predate the glacial closure of the Mackenzie Corridor is the skeleton of a child found under glacial till near Taber in southern Alberta, possibly more than 22,000 years old. Only two other skeletons, both from Los Angeles, California, have been found that seem to date back to this era: one from the La Brea Tar Pits that dates to 21,600 B.C., and one from Laguna Beach that dates to 15,000 B.C.

The few other archaeological finds from this period are mostly pre-projectile forms of stone tools, especially tools to cut meat and to scrape skins for clothing. From the find of wooden spears with fire-hardened points that date back to earlier periods in the Old World and from the use of wooden spears in historically known hunting societies, we can infer that these hunters used wooden spears. Also, some crude stone projectile points were found in Sandia Cave, New Mexico, that seem to date to about 20,000 B.C.

The hunting technique at the time was probably similar to that of other predators and to hunters such as the aboriginal Australians and the Bushmen of South Africa. Two or three hunters might stalk any large animal and spear it, but they usually succeeded only when the animal was slowed down in a bog or if it was an infant, or aged, sick, or lame. Even then the hunters had to fend off predators and scavengers. There were more dangerous predators to man in North America in the ice age than there are today, including the dire wolf, the saber-toothed tiger, and the giant panther (the largest predatory land mammal), as well as the present species of cougar and jaguar. Larger hunting bands sometimes organized drives of herding animals, such as the horse or buffalo, over cliffs or into a ravine to be dispatched with spears. These large kill sites, however, have shown up in the North American archaeology only after 10,000 B.C.; that is, after the final opening of the Mackenzie Corridor.

The phase after the Mackenzie Corridor opened up is variously called the *mammoth hunters,* for one of the spectacular animals (a woolly elephant) they hunted; *Llano culture,* implying the Great Plains region where most of them lived; and *Clovis,* for the most popular form of stone projectile point that they used to tip their spears. The Clovis is a chipped flint point that in the classic form is 7–12 cm in length and has three features that aid in hafting it: flutes chipped out on both sides, basal thinning, and a concave base. Although the large populations of Clovis hunters were in the Great Plains, finds of the distinctive Clovis points indicate that these hunters were scattered in small numbers across the continent. Such points have been found at Engigstciak, Yukon, and at Edmonton, Alberta. An adze made from an elephant bone was found 50 miles northeast of Winnipeg. A Clovis culture, found in a site at Debert, Nova Scotia, was dated to about 8,600 B.C. At that time there was still a continental glacier over most of *northern* Ontario, but there are over a dozen scattered finds of Clovis points in *southern* Ontario, south of the glacial edge. The eastern Clovis peoples were in a subarctic climate and probably hunted caribou more than mammoths and mastodons.

In the Great Plains east of the Rocky Mountains a specialized variation of Llano flourished between 9,000 and 7,000 B.C. This was the *Folsom* culture, named for a special form of Clovis point in which the side flutes were removed in single large flakes, possibly by a special technique of preheating before the large flakes were taken off. At the time the Plains probably had the largest human population in the New World, but very few of the Folsom people lived in Canada. In the Folsom period the population of mammoths declined sharply, probably because of over-hunting and a warming and drying climate. The Folsom people shifted to buffalo for game. Folsom points have been found near Mortlatch, Saskatchewan, and near Cereal and Edmonton, Alberta.

Notes: Name of Tradition, years (date), basic characteristics in sum.

def'n:- Paleolithic, mesolithic, Neolithic Ages

Asian-American Similarities

There is some typological evidence of migrations during and after the second period of optimal crossing conditions between Asia and North America, from 10,000 to 8,000 B.C. Stone-tool-making traditions occurred simultaneously in northern Asia and North America. One consists of blades and lens-shaped bifacially chipped projectile points that occur in Japan, in the Amur River Valley, in the Kamchatka Peninsula, at Healy Lake and Flint Creek in Alaska, and is called Cordilleran tradition in Canada and the U.S. The other is the Paleoarctic tradition of microblades made from wedge-shaped cores that is found in the Yenisei River Valley, in northern Japan, the Kamchatka Peninsula, and Alaska. A blade industry in the Aleutians looks like one found in Hokkaido, Japan. An industry from British Mountain (Engigstciak, Firth River, northern Yukon) of blades, bifacial knives, and single-sided points is similar to an industry found near Irkutsk, Siberia. A continuing influence of these Asian blade traditions shows up primarily in the Arctic Small Tool tradition, which is ancestral to the pre-Inuit cultures, and secondarily in the Northwest Microblade tradition, which seems to have contributed (along with the northern Plano) to the Subarctic Dene cultures; their influences remained largely in the north, while many other tool traditions were developed throughout the New World.

Later similarities show up in Siberian and North American knives, adzes, spoons, harpoons, hair combs, and burial practices such as the use of rock cairns, applying red ochre to the body, and having dog burials. There are data that suggest that one form of pottery-making with a stamped or cord-marked surface diffused into the eastern Woodlands areas about 1,000 B.C. from Siberia. Good cases for diffusion the other way, into Siberia, can be made for an early bifacially flaked bi-point, the stemless projectile point, and sandstone shaft straighteners. There are also similarities in such specialized practices as hunters speaking to the spirit of an animal they killed, special treatment of its bones, practices such as fasting, bathing, and public dancing for female puberty ceremonies, and procedures of shamanistic curing.

Shift to the Mesolithic

By 6,000 B.C. the warming of the earth and the retreat of the glaciers brought, for about 3,000 years, an altithermal with a warmer and drier climate than exists today. That climate was beneficial to such species as horses, camels, the giant ground sloth, and the dire wolf. However, the climatic warming and the overkill by hunters led to a decline in the number of large mammals. Since the last ice age some 33 genera, over one hundred species, of large mammals became extinct in North America

(Martin and Wright 1967). Native people probably contributed to these extinctions by (1) increasing human populations at the expense of animal populations, (2) specializing in the hunting of one kind of game once the techniques of killing that particular form of game had been mastered, and (3) destroying the environment through such techniques as driving game by starting fires.

Some large animals have not been effective at defending themselves against primitive human hunters. For example, the musk-oxen evolved with an apparently genetically-based defence against the large northern wolves, but the defence was ineffective against humans. When attacked, musk-oxen formed a tight half-circle and faced the predators. The calves squeezed in between the larger animals for protection and the bulls charged forward in a short attack and then backed up into the line again. This provided protection against wolves, but humans just speared them one at a time. If the musk-oxen had not lived in such inaccessible and scattered pockets in the Arctic, they too would have become extinct.

A similar large-scale loss of species occurred in Australia, correlating with the spread of human populations there though without the element of large-scale climatic changes. In both North America and Australia, the overkill theory for these extinctions is supported by the fact that the extinctions came at the very end of the ice age, *after* several hundred thousand years of climatic changes. Both cases involve large mammals that evolved away from humans and that developed without defences against the most dangerous of all predatory animals.

Corresponding with a rise in the human population and the extinction of one species after another was a fundamental shift toward a broadened and intensified use of all available food resources in each environment, the Paleolithic to Mesolithic shift. In the Paleolithic large mammals were hunted while in the Mesolithic a great variety of new tools were invented to abstract whatever food resources were available: fish, shellfish, plant foods, and sea mammals.

Hunting continued in Canada until historic times. However, depending on the environment, it was supplemented or even largely replaced by other food sources. Predominant food production shifted to fishing along coastal British Columbia and to agriculture in southern Ontario and in the St. Lawrence River Valley. There were also several localized developments, such as shellfish gathering on Prince Edward Island and wild rice gathering around the Great Lakes. Atlantic shellfish gatherers developed the earth-oven style of clambake we still use today. Hunting remained predominant in the rest of the country, particularly of sea mammals in the Arctic; caribou, moose, and water fowl in the Subarctic; and buffalo in the Plains of Alberta and Saskatchewan. In evolutionary terms, the British Columbia fishing and the Ontario–St. Lawrence agriculture were the foundations of fundamentally more complex cultures—a Mesolithic to Neolithic shift. The hunters, on the other hand, remained at the Mesolithic level until the time of European contact. After the Europeans reintroduced the horse, it was applied to buffalo hunting and enabled such a productive form of hunting in the Plains that these hunters were shifting to a Neolithic level of culture in the century before the Europeans permanently settled in the Plains, roughly 1770–1870 for the Blackfoot and Assiniboine in southern Alberta and Saskatchewan.

Early Mesolithic Hunters: Plano, Old Copper, and Archaic

The hunting tradition of 7,000–5,000 B.C. that developed out of Clovis, and its Folsom variation, is called *Plano.* There is a Plano site at Acasta Lake, N.W.T., dated to 5,000 B.C., which was a Subarctic tundra environment with caribou. Another Plano site is at Sheguiandah, Manitoulin Island, Ontario. This site includes a rock quarry where projectile points and cutting tools were made for several thousand years. Plano sites have been found in Cereal, Red Deer, and Edmonton in Alberta; near Thunder Bay, Ontario (the Brohm site dates to 6,000 B.C.) and at Killarney, Ontario, near the shore of Lake Huron. The Cereal, Alberta, site has the Alberta point, a heavy projectile point with a stemmed base, and the Cody complex of long leaf-shaped points and the shouldered Cody knife. Plano projectile points tend to be thin and leaf-shaped or lanceolate with fine rows of "ripple" flaking.

The *Old Copper* culture began around 5,000 B.C. as a Plano culture around Lake Superior. It later added tools made from native copper to its kit of tools. Thus we find a Plano culture site at Thunder Bay, Ontario, with a copper spear point. In later sites copper artifacts have been found in the form of harpoons, adzes, celts, knives, and awls. During 2,000–1,000 B.C., extensive mining of seams of copper in small pits was accomplished with stone mauls and by throwing cold water over, and cracking, fire-heated rock.

Copper tools were traded out of the Lake Superior area throughout eastern Canada. This introduction of copper tools, and the introduction of polished stone tools, are used to define the beginning of the *Archaic* cultures. Ceremonial burials existed earlier in the Plano, but in the Archaic there was the introduction of regular village cemeteries. The Archaic lasted from 5,000 B.C. to 1,000 B.C., and had regional variations of the Shield Archaic in the Hudson Bay area and the Laurentian Archaic in southern Ontario, Quebec, New York, and Vermont.

The people of the Laurentian Archaic hunted deer, elk, beaver, and bear. They used the spear-thrower, a leverage arm hooked to the end of the spear for greater thrust in throwing. There are also archaeological indications of killing and processing small animals, shellfish gathering, the preparation of forest plants, and fishing (hooks, spears, and gaffs). Long, ground-slate bayonets were used in Newfoundland to spear seals and walruses around 1,500 B.C. They had cemeteries, covered the bodies with red ochre, and placed burial goods with the body. Some burial goods originally came into the area through long chains of trade, such as conch shells from the Gulf of Mexico, nearly 1,000 miles away. By 1,500 B.C. they had dog burials.

The Shield Archaic extended from Nova Scotia across the Maritimes, Quebec, and Ontario to the Keewatin District of the N.W.T. Sites tend to be at the narrows of lakes and rivers which were crossings for caribou, a major animal in the Shield Archaic diet. There was likely a variety of uses for tree bark, such as containers and mats. They probably developed the birchbark canoe, because the sites were on waterways and the canoe was universally used in the area; and snowshoes and the flat toboggan to cope with the deep snows in this area. Sleds, by contrast, have runners, are used over thin snows or ice, and seem to derive from Asia.

The Archaic cultures represent the first large populations in eastern Canada and they developed many elements of culture that still persist among Indians. The Shield Archaic is the major ancestor to the historically known northern Algonquian cultures such as the Cree, Montagnais, Naskapi, Micmac, and probably Beothuk. The Ojibwa, who live south of the Cree, also speak a language in the Algonquian family of languages, but in such traits as wild-rice gathering are closer to the Laurentian Archaic.

Woodland

The term *Woodland* has been used by archaeologists for the transition period between the Archaic and the historic societies in the east. Archaeologists pay an inordinate amount of attention in their classifications to the well-preserved objects, such as pottery. In this case both the Huron and Ojibwa are classified as Woodland, because they had a similar kind of crude molded pottery. However, the Hurons had huge agricultural villages and one of the greatest population densities in Canada while the Ojibwa were simple hunters with one of the lowest population densities in Canada.

It is useful to use the term Woodland for those Mesolithic hunting societies that were influenced by Neolithic agricultural societies. That way we say something about the whole culture in our terminology. A minor introduction of pottery, some elaboration of burial practices such as burial mounds and imported grave goods, and the smoking of tobacco in pipes, are the essential features of the Woodland influence on the Archaic hunters. However, these societies were still simple hunting and gathering societies, and too nomadic to make an extensive use of pottery. Though excellent for soups or stews over a fire, pottery is heavy and breakable; many other lighter materials are good for containers: animal stomachs for liquids, and woven basketry and folded bark trays for solid goods.

In Ontario five different early Woodland cultures have been distinguished, primarily on the basis of pottery styles (Wright 1972). Meadowood (1,000–500 B.C.) was in New York and adjacent parts of Quebec and Ontario. Point Peninsula (700 B.C.–A.D. 1,000) was from about Toronto to Quebec and New York. The Serpent Mounds site, at Rice Lake south of Peterborough, is a large cemetery of this culture and is preserved today as an archaeological park. Saugeen (700 B.C.–?) was from Toronto north and west to Lake Huron. Princess Point (A.D. 500–1,000) was from Toronto to Windsor and around Lake Erie. Laurel (700 B.C.–A.D. 1,000) is a scattered spread of a style of pottery from Northwestern Quebec through northern Ontario into Manitoba and Saskatchewan. After A.D. 1,000 a style of pottery with a punched hole rim pattern known as Black Duck spread through much of the earlier Laurel area, apparently constituting a stylistic change in Laurel pottery. These fine distinctions and comparisons between pottery styles are useful in helping us to discover the prehistoric networks of trade, culture influence, and migrations.

Around A.D. 800 corn agriculture began to spread up from the south into southern Ontario and the St. Lawrence Valley. By the time of European contact in the 1600s there were two fundamentally different kinds of culture across Ontario: (1) the Mesolithic, Woodland, band-organized, Algonquian-speaking, Ojibwa and Cree in the north, and (2) the Neolithic, agricultural, tribally organized, Iroquoian-speaking, Huron, Petun, and Neutral in the south.

Northern Mesolithic Cultures

The first *Arctic* coastal tradition is the Arctic Small Tool tradition of 3,000–1,000 B.C. The tool kit included knives, blades, scrapers, burins, and micro-tools (tiny stone flakes) known particularly from the Denbigh Flint complex. They seem to have belonged to the Paleolithic people, who specialized in hunting walrus and caribou. Because of its isolation, the Arctic was late in starting a tradition and some earlier traits have persisted there. Along with other isolated places such as the Baja California peninsula, it retained more of the Paleolithic or early stone age and big game hunting features.

A more distinctly Inuit culture developed about 1,000 B.C. in the Bering area, diffusing eastward along thousands of miles of Canadian coasts and into the Arctic islands, Greenland, Labrador, and Newfoundland. There are important sites at Baker Lake in Keewatin District and on the island of Igloolik north of Melville Peninsula. Apparently the development of skin-covered canoes greatly facilitated transportation and sea hunting, and thus a much greater spread of humans throughout the Arctic. The main villages were on or near beaches to exploit both land and water resources. The early Inuit had tailored clothing, semisubterranean winter houses, oil lamps, ground slate and ivory tools, ice-creepers, and snow goggles. Skin tents and sleds seem to be slightly later additions. By the time of the Thule Inuit (A.D. 1,000) of Canada and Greenland the chipped-stone tools had been largely replaced by ivory and bone tools. The sleds were drawn by dogs. The Thule had harpoons with sealskin floats, sinew-backed bows, the men's crooked knife and the women's semilunar knife, whale-oil lamps, slotted snow goggles, the tambourine drum, and tools were sometimes even tipped with iron obtained by trade from mines in Siberia. The Thule styles of working bone and ivory have remained, and the carving skills survive in the commercial production of artistic stone sculptures.

The western Subarctic cultures seem to have evolved out of the combination of a Siberian migration that brought in the Northwest Microblade tradition and the older northern Plano. There are microblade sites in the interior of Alaska from 6,000 to 3,000 B.C. and from 5,000 to 1,000 B.C. in the Yukon. The Pointed Mountain site north of Ft. Liard in the southern N.W.T. has some forest orientation, indicating a more Subarctic adaptation. It dates to about 3,000 B.C. and has burins, microblades, and large projectile points. We see a northern Plano influence in the double-pointed, laurel-leaf Agate Basin points found at Moose Jaw, Saskatchewan, and the crude Angostura points that date to 2,600 B.C. at Great Bear Lake, N.W.T. We see Siberian influence in the blades in the Thyazzi site on the western shore of Hudson Bay. There seems to be continuity from those early Subarctic hunters to the historic Subarctic Dene.

A site at Klo-kut on the Porcupine River in northern Yukon shows 1,500 years of Dene-like culture. There is continuity in semisubterranean houses, serrated or stemmed stone arrowheads, barbed bone and antler arrowheads, bone projectile points and fish spears, stone and bone scraping tools, some native copper projectile points and knives, and even some preserved birchbark baskets. It also had incised designs on bone and antler. The site is unusual in that it was used for such a long time, apparently because it is near a major crossing point for herds of migrating caribou. The Chimi site on Aishihik Lake in southern Yukon is about 700 years old and has similar fish spears.

There is more variation in the Subarctic than in the Arctic, but there are still broad similarities: snowshoes, toboggans, canoes, shamanism, bear ceremonialism, fear of animistic spirits, fishing weirs, game drives. The northern Dene and Algonquian fished, hunted caribou and moose, and had base camps on lakes or large streams. Their sites were more scattered than the Inuit sites, and were usually not reoccupied as much over the centuries. The archaeological differences between the western Dene Subarctic and the eastern Algonquian Subarctic are based on differences in location and ecology. The Algonquian homeland had more moose, elk, waterfowl, and fewer caribou, and was closer to southern trade links for copper and pottery than the Dene homeland. The Algonquian Cree took advantage of these closer trade links to acquire guns and a central position in the European fur trade. Thus the Cree moved into Dene territory and tried to dominate the Dene, just as they successfully moved out into Prairies and dominated that area without resistance until they met the Assiniboine and Blackfoot.

One archaeological site indicates that the ecological adaptations of Indians and Inuit were mutually exclusive. The site is in a good fishing and caribou hunting place by the Dubawnt River, Keewatin District, N.W.T. (Wright 1975:19). It shows a changing sequence of occupations: Indians (7–1,500 B.C.), Inuit (1,500 B.C.–200 B.C.), Indians (200 B.C.–A.D. 1,700), and Inuit (A.D. 1700–1950s). Apparently the early occupation cycles correlated with climatic changes. When the area became markedly colder after 1,500 B.C. and the tree line moved southward, changes in the caribou winter ranges led to an abandonment of the area by the Indians. Inuit hunters then expanded their territory south into this area. When the weather warmed after 200 B.C. the cycle reversed, bringing back the Indians. The Indians moved south again to participate in the European fur trade, and the Inuit used the area for another two hundred years. Since the Barren Lands, where Inuit and Indians met, was a poorer environment than most coastal environments, the Caribou Inuit who moved into the area regressed toward greater simplicity (Oswalt 1978:70).

The Neolithic Tribal Iroquois

Plant gathering, shellfish gathering, and fishing societies acquired a highly localized use of the environment. They became more sedentary than the hunting societies and women played a major role in food production. Features like this *pre-adapted* the cultures of the Mississippi River Basin to an agricultural way of life. When agriculture did come from Mexico into the Mississippi Basin after 1,000 B.C. it spread very rapidly up the river valley and tributaries. There were an early cultural florescence in the Adena (800 B.C.–A.D. 200) and, later, Hopewell cultures of the Ohio Valley. These cultures are known primarily from log tombs with grave offerings: pottery vessels, pipes, incised tablets of stone, combs of bone and antler, copper bracelets and rings, etc. The burial cult became the religious and artistic focus of that tradition and set a pattern for eastern North America, spreading pottery and funeral practices even beyond agricultural societies to the simple hunting and gathering societies in Canada.

In the central Mississippi area dense populations of agriculturists built villages and towns. Around A.D. 1,000 they began building what could be called a primitive city at Cahokia, Illinois. At the same time corn agriculture was spreading into the southeastern fringe of Canada. The introduction of agriculture into Canada was so recent—about A.D. 800— that it can be linked to historically known societies that speak languages in the Iroquoian family of languages.

The diffusion of corn agriculture around Lake Erie, from Ohio to Ontario, took a very long time, some 1,600 years. There seem to be several reasons for this. First, the people of southern Ontario were hunters, not plant gatherers, shellfish gatherers, or fishermen; and were not pre-adapted to agriculture. Second, there was ample land for population expansion in the south. Third, as they moved north they met the climatic limits of corn agriculture. Fourth, the major travel, trade, and migration routes were by canoe within the Mississippian River system whereas Ontario, despite its proximity, was in a totally different system of lakes and rivers.

The pre-agricultural Woodland period in Ontario prepared it to receive agriculture. When populations increased in the south, agriculture was extended northward as far as possible into southern Ontario. Beyond that point, climatic conditions made it more practical to hunt and fish than to farm. Farming in Ontario today is still essentially limited to the same area that was used by the Indians.

Small amounts of carbonized corn have been found in a few of the pre-agricultural Woodland sites (Wright 1972). Princess Point sites in the Grand River area north of Lake Erie have some that dates to as early as A.D. 600. The Princess Point hunters were influenced by the Hopewell, or were even migrants from the Hopewell area itself. Princess Point Culture does not have any clear local antecedents; thus they could be migrants. Hopewell influence shows up in such traits as stone platform pipes, ceramics, small circular burial mounds, blade-like flake tools, and certain exotic trade goods. The pioneer efforts at farming seem to have been on the river mud flats as part of an annual migratory round of hunting, fishing, and plant gathering. Very little is known about the transition, but by about A.D. 800 corn farming in upland areas was a significant part of subsistence activities.

Princess Point people seem to have become matrilocal with settled agriculture. Because women did the earlier plant gathering, they took responsibility for agriculture. When corn became the major subsistence food, women, after marriage, had to stay and work cooperatively with their mothers and sisters; the husband would move into the wife's house. We assume that the women made pottery, because they were making it in historical times. The archaeological evidence for this matrilocal shift is an increasing localization of pottery construction techniques and artistic motifs on the pottery surfaces, an indication that the women potters stayed in their home villages.

Early Iroquois culture involved planting corn in rows of small hillocks in clearings of slashed forest and supplementing that with hunting and fishing (Heidenreich 1971). Large villages were built, up to ten acres with rows of multi-family longhouses, a style that was widespread in the agricultural societies of eastern North America. The villages usually had defensive features, indicating extensive warfare, such as location in easily defended positions on the brow of a hill and away from water routes. They usually had tall palisade walls made from upright logs.

Around A.D. 1,300 there spread the use of domestic sunflowers, an elaborate pipe complex and the use of tobacco, cemeteries in the form of large ossuaries filled with bundle burials, and cannibalism. The latter is indicated by finds of burned and broken bones of adult human males in the trash heaps. Human bones were also made into tools. From this data and from known cannibalism, it appears to be related to the cannibalism of war captives. Cannibalism reached a peak about A.D. 1500.

Pottery similarities indicate cultural continuities from Point Peninsula to the Pickering in the east (from Toronto spreading eastward to the St. Lawrence) and from Princess Point to the Glen Meyer in the west. Beans and squash were added as cultigens by about A.D. 1400, increasing the available plant protein so much that animal protein could be almost ignored in nutrition. The basic food preparation became a soup of beans, hominy corn, and small bits of meat. This food apparently contributed to a population expansion.

Around A.D. 1300–1400 there was some convergence of Pickering and Glen Meyer, with Pickering dominant—perhaps a sign of warfare. Glen Meyer sites suddenly appeared in neighboring Michigan and Ohio, suggesting a military withdrawal. After A.D. 1400 the Pickering people apparently pulled out of the Toronto area and slowly concentrated in what was known historically as Huronia, between Lake Huron and Georgian Bay.

In 1615 the Europeans contacted the Hurons concentrated in the Midland area near Lake Huron and their occasional allies the Petun or Tobacco Indians south of the Hurons. These two could be descendants of the Pickering people. Still farther south were the Neutrals around Windsor, who, along with the related Erie in western New York, could be descendants of the Glen Meyer populations.

The Iroquois disappeared from the St. Lawrence River Valley in the late 1500s, probably destroyed by the Hurons. St. Lawrence styles of pottery came into the Huron area at that time, presumably carried on by the female captives who were not killed. The St. Lawrence style of pipes did not enter the Huron area, presumably because the men, who made pipes in the Iroquoian tradition, were killed in warfare. Then over 10,000 Hurons died in a smallpox epidemic introduced into southern Ontario by Jesuit priests in 1638–1640. Finally, the New York Iroquois defeated the Ontario Huron and Petun in a concerted series of attacks between 1649 and 1654.

Rise of Neolithic Chiefdoms of the Pacific Coast

The most unusual culture in Canada, seen in a worldwide context, was the development of the spectacularly successful marine-oriented cultures of coastal British Columbia. The richness of marine resources, particularly the huge runs of salmon in the streams, was the key to the *chiefdom* level of their cultural evolution. Not only were the B.C. Indians *neolithic*, in having large concentrated populations like the Iroquois, but they went beyond the *tribal* structure of the Iroquois and developed chiefdom features. Tribes have society-wide political, economic, and religious institutions, but the chiefdom has a *class structure* and *centralized* political, economic, and religious institutions. Chiefdoms have true chiefs, people who have strong powers by virtue of their positions within the social structure, while tribal leaders have basically personal powers by virtue of their abilities.

Evidence of early hunters in the area is occasionally found; for example, leaf-shaped points that date to about 6,300 B.C. on the east coast of Vancouver Island. That hunting culture appears to be unrelated to the later fishing cultures, which made the first step from hunting to fishing in the interior Plateau on streams that lead to the Fraser and Columbia River Systems. Extensive fishing and plant gathering began several thousand years ago in Oregon, Idaho, and in eastern B.C. and Washington. There are many early fishing sites; for example, on the Snake and Salmon Rivers. After populations expanded they apparently moved downstream and eventually along the coasts after about 2,000 B.C. The move to the coast brought them into a different environment of high rainfall, dense forests, and even greater fish and shellfish resources.

A sequence of cultures in the Fraser Delta around Vancouver indicates the environmental adjustments and cultural elaborations involved in the creation of such an original culture. Unfortunately some important evidence, such as fish weirs and canoes, was made of wood and has disintegrated. Locarno Beach culture (2,000–400 B.C.) had shellfish

A Chronology of Sites and Cultures

Dates	Arctic	Western Subarctic	Eastern Subarctic	Pacific Coast	Plains	Southern Quebec and Ontario
Present	Inuit	Dene	Algonquian	Tsimshian Wakashan Salish Gulf of Georgia (Stselax)	Assiniboine Blackfoot	Neutral-Petun-Huron
1500		Chimi				Glen Meyer Pickering
1000	THULE Igloolik	Klo-kut	Blackduck			Princess Point Point Peninsula Saugeen
500	Baker Lake					
A.D.						
B.C.						
500			Laurel WOODLAND	Whalen (Whalen II) Marpole		Meadowood WOODLAND
1,000		Thiazzi Dubawnt River Great Bear Lake				
1,500				Locarno Beach		
2,000	Engigstciak					
2,500	ARCTIC SMALL TOOL	Kluane Lake Pointed Mountain NORTHWEST MICROBLADE	SHIELD ARCHAIC			
3,000					Moose Jaw	LAURENTIAN ARCHAIC
3,500						

(handwritten note near Eastern Subarctic: NORTHERN ONT.)

Years B.P.			
4,000			Edmonton Red Deer Cereal
4,500	OLD COPPER Killarney		
5,000	Acasta Lake	Sheguiandah	
5,500	NORTHERN PLANO		PLANO
6,000		Brohm	
6,500		*Cordilleran Culture (7000–5000)*	Edmonton Cereal Mortlatch
7,000			
7,500			FOLSOM
8,000			
8,500			CLOVIS (EASTERN CLOVIS)
9,000	British Mountain, Yukon	Debert, Nova Scotia	Taber, Alberta
22,000			
28,000	Old Crow, Yukon		

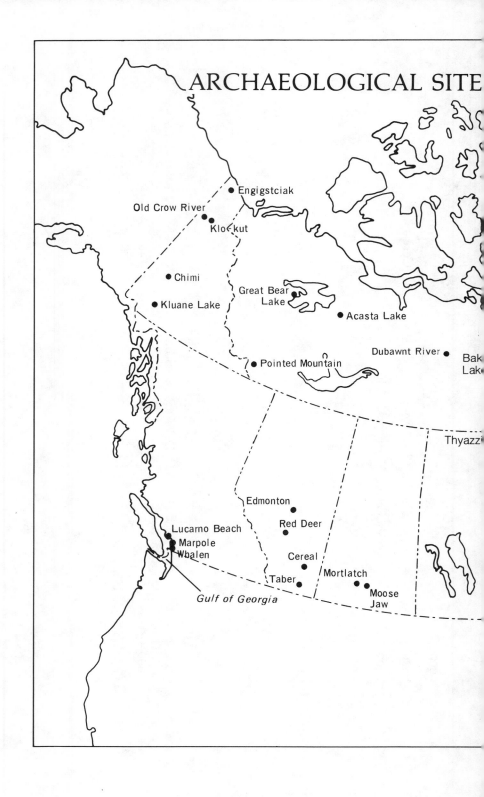

ARCHAEOLOGICAL SITE

Engigstciak
Old Crow River
Klo-kut
Chimi
Great Bear Lake
Kluane Lake
Acasta Lake
Dubawnt River
Bak Lak
Pointed Mountain
Thyazz
Edmonton
Red Deer
Lucarno Beach
Marpole
Whalen
Cereal
Mortlatch
Taber
Moose Jaw
Gulf of Georgia

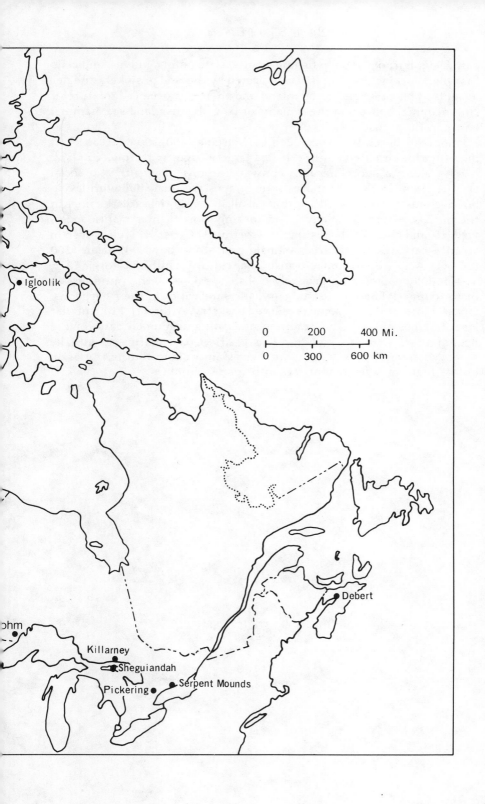

0   200   400 Mi.

0   300   600 km

Igloolik

Debert

ohm

Killarney

Sheguiandah

Pickering

Serpent Mounds

gathering, harpoons, bone fishing-points, slate points, knives, and celts for woodworking. Fishing is also indicated by the find of sinkers and net weights. The sites tend to be inland and there is a balanced mixture of land mammal bones and the remains of fish, shellfish, and sea mammal bones in the refuse areas.

Locarno Beach was succeeded by Marpole (400–200 B.C.), an even more marine-oriented culture. It had large villages with rows of plank houses along a shoreline and many indications of wealth and social stratification. In the cemeteries some graves are furnished with lavish burial goods and others with nothing at all, indicating class distinctions in the burials. There are many woodworking tools such as mauls, adzes, wedges, and chisels. The distinctive Northwest Coast art style is seen in steatite carvings of stylized animals and stone bowls. Whalen (200 B.C.–A.D. 400) was a similar transitional culture. Gulf of Georgia (A.D. 400–1800) people were probably Salish speakers with continuity to historic times. There are strong stylistic similarities in their harpoons, lances, bows, and even some preserved basketry. After A.D. 1200 tubular steatite pipes entered this tradition, indicating a minimal date for the beginning of tobacco smoking. The Pacific Coast culture eventually extended along the coast from northern California to southern Alaska, but its highest development was in British Columbia.

CHAPTER 2

——— ·◆· ———

Language

LANGUAGE CAN BE viewed as an oral-auditory system of communication that uses *symbols* of constructed meaning rather than the more natural *signals* such as crying, laughing, and burping. It does not include sign languages or writing systems, but these are discussed at the end of this chapter.

All languages use the *phonemic process* of building up meaningful units of sound (morphemes) from a limited and specific set of meaningless sound units (phonemes). All languages use a central conversational vocabulary with several hundred words and a total vocabulary of at least 2,500 stem words, from which thousands of additional words can be constructed by systematic combinations and permutations. One early dictionary of Dakota Sioux has 19,000 words.

Two phonemes seem to be present in all languages of the world: *s* and *n*. Beyond that, the sound systems are quite different from the European languages. Thus some Indian languages use *p* and *b* or *t* and *d* as the same phoneme. The *voicing* or vibration of the vocal chords may not be held to be important in these *stopped* sounds: *p*, *b*, *t*, and *d*. However, other elements in sounds might be stressed, such as nasalizing or glottalizing. For example, glottalized stops—closing the vocal chords at the same time as normal consonant articulation—are common in Indian languages. The Iroquoian languages do not use labial consonants, such as the bilabial stops *p* and *b*. Thus, the Iroquoians "can talk with a pipe between their teeth." There is quite a wide range of phonemes in Native languages. Inuktitut (the Inuit language) has only 14 in total, Cree has 9 consonants and 8 vowels (4 short, 4 long), and Chipewyan has 48 consonants and 8 vowels (4 plain, 4 nasalized). English by contrast has about 36 phonemes (that we try to write with only 26 alphabet letters).

Indian languages tend "to divide the verb sharply into an active and a neutral class, one of which is closely related to the possessive forms of the noun, while the other is treated as a true verb . . . most frequently the neutral verbs expressing a state, like *to sit, to stand*. . . . [T]erms expressing activities—like *to sing, to eat, to kill*—are treated as true predicative terms . . ." (Boas 1911:72), the latter generally having a separate set of pronouns. An exception is Nootka, which does not make a basic distinction between nouns and verbs (Driver 1969:32). Even more than such uses as -*ed*, -*ing*, and -*s* in English, Nootka expresses some highly specialized ideas by adding suffixes to the end of stem words: on the head, in the hand, on the rocks, on the surface of water. *Suffixing* is developed, but *prefixing* absent, in Inuktitut, Kwakiutl, and Nootka. Inuktitut grammar consistently uses only one process—suffixing grammatical elements. A long chain of endings is added to the stem to develop the meaning. Algonquian also makes frequent use of suffixing. Tlingit, on the other hand, uses prefixing. Tlingit is also unusual in that the pronunciation of a word in a low tone means that it occurred in the past and in a high tone means that it will occur in the future.

Infixing—inserting a grammatical element into the body of the stem word—is uncommon. The *compounding* of words, as in "railroad," is generally absent in Athapascan languages.

Many Indian languages use *reduplication*, by which a stem or part of it is repeated to denote repeated activity, plurality, or increase in size or intensity. Thus in Tsimshian *am* is "good" and *am'am* is "several (are) good." Also *gyad* is "person" and *gyigyad* is "people." In Kwakiutl *met* is "clam" and *metmat* is "to eat clams." In Nootka *hluch* is "woman" and *hluhluch-'ituhl* is "to dream of a woman."

Sapir (1921), an early Canadian linguist, discussed the idea of his time that the degree of synthesis or elaboration of the words of a language is important to the structure of a language. He said that languages were *isolating*, as, Chinese and Cambodian; *weakly synthetic*, as, English and French; *strongly synthetic*, as, Latin and Greek; and *polysynthetic*, as, a large number of the American Indian languages. Inuktitut, Haida, Sioux, Nootka, and Algonkin are all in different language families; yet are all polysynthetic. In polysynthetic languages there is an extreme elaboration of the word by affixes and symbolic changes in the stem word or radical. U.N.E.S.C.O. is a polysynthetic word in English. People find quick ways to say the things that they say most often. In Iroquois the adjectives usually are combined with their nouns to form a single word. Inuktitut is particularly polysynthetic. The Inuktitut word *aneyaarqerquwaatit* means "He begs you again to go out early." Inuktitut has over 250 possible forms for any noun because it has seven major noun cases, twelve possessive pronouns, and three numbers (singular, dual, and plural).

Jenness (1967:23) considered the Algonquian languages the most musical because of their richness of vowel sounds, avoidance of harsher consonants, and use of whispered syllables. He thought that the Salish languages were the most harsh and the Athapascan languages the most difficult to learn. These kinds of subjective judgments are, of course, ethnocentric and stereotypic, comparable to the way people feel about hearing Spanish, German, Russian, or whatever. Apparently Jenness was reacting against consonant clusters in Salish that an English speaker finds unusual and hard to pronounce.

Linguistic History

Sapir developed the case for the historically genetic relationship between Tlingit-Haida and the Athapascan languages. He argued that morphology is the relatively unchanging kernel of a language and that there was no direct historical evidence that morphology is profoundly influenced by diffusion or borrowing. Sapir argued that morphological changes were based on autonomous, drifting, evolutionary processes internal to each language system. He listed 98 similarities in structural morphemes and basic vocabulary in at least two of the three branches of the Dene phylum of Haida-Tlingit-Athapascan.

Since the Tlingit and Haida were two of the most advanced fishing cultures in the New World and the Athapascan were simple hunters and gatherers, many people were skeptical of the connection. Franz Boas, Sapir's former professor, disagreed with Sapir. Boas argued that cases of deceptive similarity can occur as a result of the diffusion of surface effects obscuring basic differences. Boas agreed to the historical relationships between these languages but said that this was only a diffusional and borrowing relationship, not a historically genetic relationship of development from a common ancestral language.

Swadesh (1951), Sapir's student, much later took up Sapir's case in a classic presentation on linguistic prehistory. Swadesh introduced time scales based on the history of the diversification of European languages into the prehistory of Indian languages. Athapascan had been in contact for a long time with Inuktitut, Tsimshian, Tlingit-Haida, Wakashan, and Salishan, but the only apparent structural resemblance between Athapascan and any of these languages is with Tlingit-Haida, and that resemblance is closer than the resemblance between French and English. These are the major similarities that Sapir pointed out.
1. The stem is usually a consonant followed by a vowel, and then perhaps by another consonant—CV(C).
2. Reduplication is absent.
3. Noun and verb are distinct.
4. There is little affixing on nouns. Prefixes are possessives and suffixes are human plurals and a diminutive.
5. Noun–noun compounds occur with an initial qualifying element.

6. The verb complex involves a single verb stem at or near the end of the sentence.
7. There are verb suffixes for modes of time and other aspects.
8. Postpositions are used in prefixes and compounds, such as "edge of" (*wan* in Tlingit and *man* in Athapascan).
9. There is relative suffixing with verbs (-*yi* in Tlingit and -*ye* in Athapascan).

Vocabulary lists were also checked for similarity and then converted into an estimate of time of separation. In Swadesh's test list 44 per cent of the words had a phonetic correspondence suggestive of common origin between Tlingit and Athapascan. By comparison, German, English, and French have 27–29 per cent of the test list in common after 5,000 years of divergence and English and German alone have about 60 per cent in common after 2,000 years of separate development. It appears that languages lose, that is totally change, roughly 14 per cent and retain about 86 per cent of their basic vocabulary words over 1,000 years. There are, in fact, some differences in the rates of change in basic vocabularies, particularly under modern conditions of rapid change, but the technique is still useful. If a roughly universal rate of divergence is assumed, the inference is that Tlingit and Athapascan have been separated for about 3,500 years. The separation between the Northern Athapascan language of Chipewyan and such southern Athapascan languages as Hupa in California and Navajo-Apache in Arizona is about 1,000 years. In another case, the separation of Greenland/Canada Inuktitut from southern Alaskan Yuit is 1,000 years and from Aleut is 4,000 years.

When you do not have written texts, the history of languages is unraveled backward. To discover their historical relationships, languages are compared as they were known at their first written description. The data from physical anthropology, archaeology, and from ethnography are also used to correlate the relationships between the history of languages and the history of culture in general. The slowest-changing feature of languages is syntax. Thus syntax is the primary indicator of historical connections.

Within the lexicon or units of meaning the words that are part of the basic vocabulary change more slowly and more predictably than the peripheral vocabulary. Basic vocabulary words are learned early in life by children; they refer to the universal experiences of humans (sun, moon, mother, father, one, two, three, water, blood, mouth, die) and are thus not related to any specific physical environment. They are associated with the simplest *and* the most complex societies. When a society migrates or expands by population growth into a new environment it would need new words for the new kinds of things in that environment, but the basic vocabulary could remain the same. English has taken peripheral rather than basic words from Indian languages. English has incorporated thousands of place names from Indian languages. From the

Algonquians English has taken such words as hominy, moccasin, mugwump (political renegade), papoose, podunk (a small town), succotash, squaw, toboggan, and wigwam, none of which are basic vocabulary words. In looking for the degree of historical similarity in languages we thus pay particular attention to the degree of similarity in both syntax and *basic* vocabulary.

Linguistic histories are also built up in chains, just as languages themselves must diversify, dividing and dividing again. Language A is related to language B and in turn B is related to C. It may not be apparent that languages A and C are related until we see how both are related to B.

Once the general picture of language similarities has been shown, it is possible to work on a theoretical model for the history of the diffusion of languages. The most general theories are (1) the age–area theory—the greater the distance of diffusion the older the time level; (2) that population movements have taken place in waves with the later waves displacing and absorbing the earlier; (3) that the more diversified a language phylum or family the older it is. According to these ideas, the purest retention of the cultural (including linguistic) features of early migrations would be the farthest away from the point of entry or in isolated cul-de-sacs, such as peninsulas and islands where displacement or absorption would be more difficult. Thus we would expect that the early languages would be best retained in South America, or perhaps by such isolates as the Guaycura at the tip of the Baja California peninsula or the Beothuk on Newfoundland. These later cases are exceptions to the rule about age being related to degree of diversification of a language phylum.

The central corridor of migration (Yukon–Mackenzie–Plains) remained very conservative in continuing as an area of hunting cultures, but must have changed in population and language over and over again. We know by archaeological data that certain areas such as the coastal Arctic were not significantly populated until recent millennia. This kind of thinking is the basis for the following historical classification of Canadian Indian languages (modified from Voegelin and Voegelin 1966). Language communities joined by dashes are considered to be dialects of the same language, as in Blackfoot–Piegan–Blood, at the time of their first written description. Their approximate aboriginal locations are given as well as the number of status Indians in Canada who have that language heritage (Department of Indian Affairs and Northern Development 1970). The popular name of the language is italicized. By the definition used here, there are 50 Native Canadian languages.

A Classification of Indian Languages by Sequence of Diffusion
1. *Beothuk* Isolate: Newfoundland; extinct.
2. *Kutenai* Isolate: Upper watershed of the Kootenay and Columbia Rivers. Their territory included an adjoining part of southern

Alberta before they were pushed out by the Blackfoot Confederacy; 446.

3. Penutian Phylum, Tsimshian Family (7,730).
   a. *Tsimshian*: Lower Skeena River and the coast and coastal islands in northern B.C.; 2,863.
   b. *Niska*: Nass River; 2,364.
   c. *Gitskan*: Upper Skeena River; 2,503.
4. Wakashan Family (8,217)
   a. *Haisla*-Kitimat: Kitimat River, Douglas Channel; 848.
   b. *Bella Bella*-Heiltsuk: Islands and coast along Queen Charlotte Sound; 1,245.
   c. *Kwakiutl*: Douglas Channel to Bute Inlet and northeastern Vancouver Island; 2,715.
   d. *Nootka*: West coast of Vancouver Island; 3,038.
   e. *Nitinat*: Nitinat River and coast in southern Vancouver Island; 371.
5. Salish Family (20,989).
   a. *Lillooet*: Upper half of the Lillooet River; 2,494.
   b. *Shuswap*: Thompson River; 3,862.
   c. *Thompson*: Around the junction of the Fraser and Thompson Rivers; 2,742.
   d. *Okanagan*-Sanpoil-Colville-Lake: Okanagan and Sanpoil Rivers and middle of the Columbia River; 1,533.
   e. *Bella Coola*: Dean Channel and Bella Coola River; 597.
   f. *Comox* (Puntlatch-Sechelt): Northern shores of the Straits of Georgia; 1,341.
   g. *Cowichan* (Halkomelem): Southern shores of the Straits of Georgia; 6,031.
   h. *Squamish*: Vancouver metropolitan area and the Squamish River; 1,232.
   i. *Songish*-Lummi-Clallam: Southeast end of Vancouver Island around Victoria and nearby places in the U.S. to the south and southeast; 1,157.
6. Macro-Siouan Phylum, Siouan Family (6,212).
   a. *Assiniboine*: Southeast Saskatchewan, Montana, and North Dakota; 1,059.
   b. *Dakota* (Teton, Yankton, Santee): North and South Dakota and Minnesota. They came into Canada in three waves in the 1800s; 5,153.
7. Macro-Siouan Phylum, Iroquoian Family (22,304).
   a. *Huron*-Petun: Between Lake Huron, Georgian Bay, and Lake Ontario; 1,041.
   b. *Neutral*-Erie: Neutrals on the north shore of Lake Erie, Niagara Peninsula, and the Niagara-Buffalo area of New York (where

they were called Wenro); Erie on the south shore of Lake Erie. Extinct as a language community today, but surviving individuals were assimilated into the Hurons and Iroquois in the middle 1600s.

   c. Languages of the Iroquois Confederacy; 21,263.

      1. *Seneca*-Cayuga-Onondaga: Western New York south of Lake Ontario.

      2. *Oneida*: North central New York.

      3. *Mohawk*: Northeastern New York.

8. Algonquian Family (153,594)

   a. *Blackfoot* (Siksika)-Piegan-Blood: Historically migrated out of Saskatchewan and into southern Alberta and northern Montana; 8,030.

   b. *Gros Ventre*: Southwest Saskatchewan and Montana.

   c. *Potawatomi*: Michigan, with entry into southwest Ontario after the Huron and Neutral defeat in the 1600s; 863.

   d. *Ojibwa*-Saulteaux-Ottawa-Algonkin; 55,890. Some 300 years of migrations and separations seem to be contributing to the evolution of these dialects into three separate languages.

      1. Ojibwa were originally across central Ontario, but spread into southern Ontario and into the prairies, where they are called Saulteaux (pronounced Sōto); 50,431.

      2. Ottawa (Odawa) are on Manitoulin Island and the shores of Georgian Bay; 1,632.

      3. Algonkin were along the Ottawa River to St. Maurice; 3,827.

   e. *Cree*-Montagnais-Naskapi; 76,488.

   Like the Ojibwa, the historical scattering of these dialect groups for three centuries is contributing to their evolution into separate languages.

      1. Cree originally lived from the southwestern third of the Labrador Peninsula westward across northern Ontario and northern Manitoba, but spread from there northward into the N.W.T. and westward across Saskatchewan and Alberta; 70,403.

      2. Montagnais live in southeast Quebec north of the St. Lawrence River; 5,765.

      3. Naskapi live in the southeastern third of the Labrador Peninsula; 320.

   f. *Abnaki*-Penobscot: Central Maine and an adjacent strip of Quebec south of the St. Lawrence River; 627.

   g. *Malecite*-Passamaquoddy: Northeast Maine and neighboring Quebec and New Brunswick; 1,744.

   h. *Micmac*: Nova Scotia, northeast New Brunswick, and the Gaspe Peninsula; 9,342.

9. Dene Phylum, *Haida*: Queen Charlotte Islands; 1,367.

10. Dene Phylum, *Tlingit* (Tagish): Alaskan panhandle and adjacent B.C.; 491.
11. Dene Phylum, Athapascan Family (22,657).
   a. Kutchin-*Loucheux*: Peel, Porcupine, and Upper Yukon Rivers; 2,334.
   b. Tanana-Koyokan-Han-Tutchone (*Nahani*): Alaska and Yukon; 1,112.
   c. *Dogrib*-Bear Lake-Hare: Western N.W.T.; 1,917.
   d. *Chipewyan*-Slave-Yellowknife: Hudson Bay to Great Slave Lake and the Mackenzie River; 8,936.
   e. *Tahltan*-Kaska: Upper watershed of the Stikine and Liard Rivers; 702.
   f. *Sekani*-Beaver-Sarsi: Peace and Athabasca Rivers; 1,706.
   g. *Carrier*-Chilcotin: Upper watershed of the Fraser and Chilcotin Rivers; 5,950.
   h. Nicola: Southern B.C. west of the Okanagan; extinct.
   i. Tsesaut: Head of the Portland Canal; extinct.
12. Eskimo-Aleut Family—Two Aleut languages in the Aleutian Islands, Yuit in southern Alaska, and *Inuktitut*: north Alaska, Arctic Canadian islands and coasts to northern Labrador, and Greenland coasts; 20,000.

Some linguists place Beothuk in the Macro-Algonquian phylum, which would indicate that it is more recent than I have shown. The placement of Tsimshian in the Penutian phylum connects this language to some 21 other ancient language families down the western margin of the hemisphere all the way to Bolivia in South America. It is a very ancient language phylum in California; and farther south some 31 Mayan languages, for example, are also in the Penutian phylum. Wakashan, Salish, and Kutenai seem to be ancient language groups preserved by environmental factors favoring isolation in the mountainous terrain of southern British Columbia. Wakashan and Salish may even be related if we go back several thousand years. These two, plus Chemakuan farther south, have often been grouped together in a "Mosan" phylum. Kutenai remained a small group with a single language because it retained a simple Plateau culture, while Wakashan and Salish became involved in the rich Pacific Coast culture, underwent massive population increases, and split into many languages. Salish, in the core area for the development of the Pacific Coast culture, divided into 16 languages (nine in Washington) while Wakashan divided into six languages. Wakashan presumably received the benefits of the Pacific Coast culture slightly later and thus did not expand as much in population or in migration into new territories, or diversify as much in number of languages.

The Pacific Coast is by far the most linguistically diverse and complex culture area in Canada, presumably because it is mountainous inland and extremely convoluted in shorelines and island environments. These are geographical features which supported much more isolation than other Canadian environments, except the island of Newfoundland. In historic times the linguistic diversity along the Pacific Coast was overcome by the use of a simple form of Chinook from Washington as a trade language. Iroquoian is another group that greatly expanded in population in the last two millennia, because it had agriculture. The Iroquoian expansion and diversification into several languages could have involved a northeastern migration from Adena-Hopewell culture in Ohio to New York and Ontario.

At least four basic waves of language diffusion seem to be indicated in Canadian languages. The oldest wave is composed of Beothuk, Tsimshian, Wakashan, Salish, and Kutenai, which all have the characteristics of local survivals of the most ancient migrations. Algonquian and Macro–Siouan, the second wave, are virtually the only language phyla in the eastern half of North America, and both have probably been there for several thousand years. Dene is fairly recent with a heartland in the western Subarctic of Alaska and Canada and a scattering of languages to the south (B.C., California, Arizona, and New Mexico) beginning only about 1,000 years ago. Navajo and Apache, the two most famous societies of the southern Dene, seem to have arrived in the U.S. Southwest as a single language community around A.D. 1400. Another indication of the recency of Dene is that it is related to certain East Asian languages. Eskimo–Aleut also has related languages in Siberia and filled out the Arctic coastal ecological niche only in the last few millennia.

We know that this linguistic history is only a model. For example, unrelated languages have come together and influenced each other in terms of sounds, words, and even grammatical features. Language families not only diversify like the branches of a tree, they can converge and become more similar again. Real linguistic history is multidimensional and involves a network of influences.

Language and Culture

Boas (1911) conducted experiments among the Kwakiutl in "language and thought." While these Indians traditionally did not ordinarily discuss abstract or generalized ideas apart from daily life and definite individuals, Boas participated in discourses on such isolated philosophical concepts as love and pity.

Sapir spent much of his life working out the internal linguistic systems of logic in languages. He showed how in Nootka by consonantal play the speaker could indicate he was speaking to or about children, fat people, short adults, the lame, the left-handed, the circumcised, the greedy, or cowards. The Nootka language influences one's perceptions of people by emphasizing certain kinds of things and ignoring others. He showed how a system of linguistic logic and a vocabulary patterned the perceptions of reality, as well as the forms of poetry and literature, of the speakers of a language. In Kwakiutl the grammatical form used to refer, for example, to a house *must* indicate whether the house is seen or not seen by the speaker.

In Tlingit one uses *he* in referring to an object that is very near and always present; *ya*, also near and present, but a little farther away; *yu*, farther yet; and *we*, out of sight.

In Inuktitut there are some twenty words for snow, much more precise than our "snow," "hail," "sleet," and "slush." They have a large set of words for ice that tells of its age, roughness, and whether or not it is drifting. Old sea ice loses its salt and can be boiled down for water. The roughness of ice is important in crossing it on sleds. Slight cracks on the thick sea ice may mean that the ice pack can break up and drift away from shore. The best snow for building igloos is old, firm, and compact without fissures that will break easily. This is comparable to the cross-country skier's distinctions of the frozenness, age, and temperature of different kinds of snows, for which there are different kinds of ski waxes. Similarly there are separate words for several kinds of seals, reflecting features such as age, size, and coloring which are important in hunting them. Linguistic patterning and distinctions shape our thinking.

One of Sapir's students, Benjamin Lee Whorf, specialized in this kind of research. Whorf analyzed the Nootka phrase *tl'imshya'isita'itlma* to illustrate Nootka logic. *Tl'imsh* is "boiling," that is cooking, *-ya* is "result" or "finished," *'is* is "eating," *-ita* is "those who engage in the activity," *'itl* is "go, in order to get," and *-ma* is "someone." It is important that in Nootka logic the categories and sequences are something like "cooked food eaters, going to get them, someone is," rather than the European logic of "he invites people to a feast." In European languages the subject is usually first and dominant, and actively carries out the action of the verb on the object of the sentence. Europeans see the subjects of their sentences in control of their worlds. The idea that the interaction of language and culture affects perception and logic is called "the Sapir–Whorf hypothesis" (Carroll 1956).

Floyd Lounsbury found, through textual analysis of things said at all kinds of social gatherings, that giving thanks is a major theme in Iroquois, which is expressed in numerous and subtle ways in the language.

In a recent example of this kind of research into ideology, Basso (1972) described the complex view of kinds of ice held by the Slave of Fort Norman. The generic term is *te*, which is used as a basic initial stem or radical in the grammar of words about ice. Subordinate to this are three conceptual conditions and thirteen specific forms of ice: solid (8 forms), melting (2 forms), and cracked (3 forms). Different conditions of solidity, thickness, transparency, and color are used to *generate* these types, particularly to tell how safe it is to travel across it. Blue ice is safe in any condition; black ice is safe only on foot and on snowshoe, but not by dogsled; slippery ice is safe only on foot; and brittle ice is dangerous under all conditions.

In a similar vein of research, Darnell (1970) discussed the socio-linguistic tendencies in Kaska speech from data collected by Honigmann. The Kaska lacked a value for verbal fluency, did not use baby talk, and used silence as a response to pain or frustration. Knowing how to hold one's tongue was a positive value, particularly for men. "Leaders were not required to be skillful speakers; children were expected to learn primarily by observation and imitation; adults avoided speech in many situations" (1970:131).

Impassioned speech tended to be equated with interpersonal hostility and silence was an appropriate response to verbal violence. Affection was rarely expressed in speech, except to infants. Potentially dangerous topics, especially those involving ambiguity, were usually avoided, such as witchcraft, pregnancy, menstruation, and sex. In historic times the use of English as a minor second language opened up some taboo subjects. English was used in giving insults and swearing and to avoid the normal restraints when drinking. Speech skills were valued in creative story telling and singing. Also, non-verbal communications are extremely important in all primitive societies. Who is that walking down the path? What are they wearing and carrying, and thus going to do? People in small communities acquire a great amount of information just by watching each other, and there is less need than in urban societies for verbal communications.

Teachers in an English-speaking school system who are teaching children of an Indian-language upbringing should try to explore the Native logical categories that the children are working with. The Nootka, for example, measure by one finger width, four finger width, hand width, hand with extended thumb, fingertip to armpit, and so forth. Peter Denny (1974), for example, studied the teaching of mathematics to Ojibwa and Cree children. Some troubles came from the fact that Algonquian languages use classifiers ("sticklike," "stringlike," "sheet-like," "berrylike," and "rocklike") when counting anything. Algonquian languages also usually use different basic shape terms, such as "round," "bent," and "straight" instead of the common shape words taught in English—"triangle," "square," and "circle," although they can say "square" and "circle."

In Inuktitut *marruuk* is 2 and *arviniliit* is 6, but *marruungnik arviniliit* is not 8 as it would be in the English logic of addition. It is 7, because it is second of the *arviniliit* series of 6, 7, and 8. While counting in tens is common in Native languages, one also finds counting in threes, fours, and fives, and combinations of these. If the mathematics teacher knows these kinds of things for the primary language of the children, the mathematics lessons can incorporate these phenomena to prevent confusing the Native students.

The Plains Sign Language

With high mobility and frequent interaction in the horse-buffalo period, the Plains tribes developed a gesture language. Tomkins (1969) described 836 signs, including synonyms, compound signs (such as *Sunday*—day, medicine), and twentieth century signs (such as *monkey*—half, Whiteman, dog). The signs are usually pantomimes of natural or cultural phenomena. Thus, for example, *cold* is indicated by clenched fists held across the chest with a trembling motion; *rain* by the fingers hanging down and pushing down from the shoulder level. Many of the signs have come into Western culture through such media as motion pictures that included Plains Indians. Thus people very commonly use Indian signs without knowing their origin and assume that they are either just natural or part of older Western cultural traditions.

Signs give some idea of the inter-societal stereotypes that became conventional symbols for the various tribes and races: Blackfoot—moccasin, black; Cheyenne—cuts fingers (in mourning); Comanche—snake; Crow—pompadour hair style; Indian—colored skin; Metis—half of body one kind, half of another; Negro—Whiteman, black; Nez Perce—nose pierced; Ojibwa—trees, people; Osage—shaved heads; Pawnee—wolf; Pueblo—make, blanket, stripes; Shoshoni—sheep, eat; Sioux—cut off heads; Ute—black, red (face paints); Whites—wearers of a hat with a brim.

Different kinds of syntax from the various languages caused some confusion when they were applied to the sign language. The following is how Tomkins signaled "Have you eaten supper?":

Question—palm up, fingers separated, turn hand by wrist action two or three times.

You—point index finger at person.

Eat—tips of fingers curved down past the mouth two or three times.

Sunset—thumb and forefinger facing down to form an incomplete circle (of the sun), hand extended to the right and over the horizon falls to the horizon.

The signs give some insight into traditional Indian perspectives and cultural practices that became fixed in an inter-societal system of communications:

Beautiful—*face*, hand passes down face; *good*, right hand moves horizontally from right front to left breast over heart.

Dance—Fingers apart and facing up, palms a few inches apart, hands move up and down two or three times.

Eaten enough—*eat*; hand rising from stomach to throat.

Fire—closed hand rises and fingers open upward repeatedly.

Friend—right hand in front of neck, palm out, index and second fingers extended upward, hand raised to head (brothers growing up together).

Hungry—hand with the palm up moves back and forth across stomach (cuts one in two).

See—index and second finger point away from eyes.

Thank you—hands together and backs up sweep down and out toward the person being thanked.

Tobacco—right fist grinds over left palm, as in preparing tobacco leaves for a pipe.

Ugly—*face*; *bad*, right fist near chest thrown out and down as fingers opened (thrown away).

There were comparable signs within other societies. For example, the Kwakiutl had a variety of signs that were used in dances, by lovers, by hunters, and by fishermen. Scratching on the wall of a house near the usual seat of a person was a sign for that person to come outside. The head was moved down and in a circle as a sign to paddle quickly. Our "peace" sign of two fingers up and slightly apart was a sign that a person was willing to make love.

Syllabic Writing Systems

In 1840 James Evans, a missionary at Norway House, developed a writing system for Cree that used syllables. This spread through the northern Algonquian languages and a similar system was developed for Inuktitut. Syllables are less efficient in reading and writing than a phonemically based alphabet, but the Evans syllabic system became a mark of pride and of Indian ethnicity; therefore there is not enough reason to replace it now. It seems destined to become a writing system of Indian poetry, literature, and history, an aesthetic rather than a technically efficient

LANGUAGE FAMILIES

TLINGIT

ATHAPASCAN

ESKIM
ALEU

HAIDA TSIMSHIAN

WAKASHAN

SALISH

KUTENAI

SIOUAN

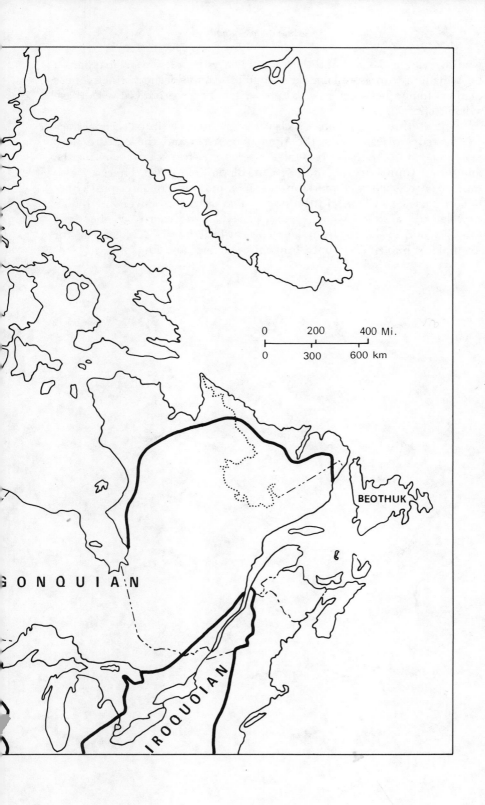

0   200   400 Mi.

0   300   600 km

BEOTHUK

GONQUIAN

IROQUOIAN

writing system. To tens of thousands of Native people the syllabary and a growing literature in syllabics are tangible symbols of the distinctiveness of their Indian heritage. Even a typewriter is now produced with these syllabic characters.

The literature in syllabics is classified by the Cree into (1) *ātayōhkēwin* or "sacred stories" about the time of genesis and the culture hero *wīsahkēcāhk,* and (2) *ācimōwin* or "tales" of old time stories, everyday events, anecdotes, funny stories, and so forth (Bloomfield 1930). There are also minor genres such as animal stories, songs, and traditional recipes. There is some use of syllabics in the poetry and stories in dozens of Indian newsletters across Canada, particularly in northern Quebec and Ontario, and among the Inuit. *Inuit Today* by Inuit Tapirisat of Canada, for example, is published in both Inuktitut syllabics and English.

CHAPTER 3

————————————◆◆◆◆————————————

Cultural Dynamics

Terminology

CULTURAL DYNAMICS refers to the processes of change, and to both the *structure* and *function* (continuing and normal operations), of cultures. In this chapter we examine three broad types of change: ecological, historical, and evolutionary. In structure and function the focus is on the parts and the manner in which they work in concert—what might be called the anatomy and physiology of culture. The concluding section on kinship systems touches on this area.

As used here, the term *ecology* refers to the patterns of adaptive relationships to the environments that humans live in. There are some minor biological adaptations, both *racial*, with changes in the genetic composition of a population over time, and *acclimatized*, with short-run accommodations. However, most adaptations are *cultural*—learned and held over time in a social tradition.

Culture is a category of behavior which includes a material, a social, an ideological, and a communications dimension. *Material culture* is observable in the physical products, tools, and constructions of humans, such as food, shelter, and clothing. *Social culture* is directly observable only in the fleeting interactions between humans, but because these interactions are so repetitive and predictive we say they are institutionalized in economics, politics, kinship, and so forth. *Ideological culture* is observable in the meanings and emotions that are conveyed through speech, writing, gestures, and arts. *Communications culture* is the learned patterns of speech, writing, gestures, and arts as media or carrier systems for meanings and emotions. We speak of small units of culture as *culture traits*.

In order to work with common baselines of cultures in comparative studies, we try to reconstruct what the Indian cultures were like prior to European influence; this is the *prehistoric* period. Following this is the *protohistoric* period, which describes the transition from European influence to written description. During this period, a few European explorers, along with trade goods and horses, traveled among the Native peoples before the Natives had been extensively described. The *ethnographic present* refers to the period during which a culture is initially described; it also refers to the grammatical use of the present tense for historical description, as in "the Blackfoot hunt buffalo on horseback."

A *society* is a human population integrated by a common culture. *Diffusion* is the spread of cultural traits across space, from one society to the next. Like historical theory, diffusion theory assumes that most cultural similarities are due to learning and imitation, and that invention is rare. Diffusion is structural in that the receiving society is selective in what it adopts, ecological in that it aids in environmental adaptation, historical in that traits tend to diffuse between societies with the same historical tradition, and evolutionary in that the adoption and abandonment of traits tend toward a cross-cultural systematic change of forms over time.

In the terms of cultural dynamics, *history* is specific and *evolution* is general. History is the sequence of events within tradition and evolution is the change of the tradition itself. Both are related to understanding what happens to cultural forms over time, and involve systems theory and predictability. It is assumed that culture is a *system*, a collection of elements interrelated to the extent that a change in one element will cause changes in the others.

History is the tendency of elements to persist in cultures. Systems have a steady state or equilibrium aspect: people do things in a way that they learned from their parents and community. We find historical persistence of similar traits among societies that were once together but migrated into different environments thousands of years ago.

Evolution proper is the systematic change of forms over time in a world-wide pattern. Traits are added, discarded, and modified in a way that is universally predictable. Change is usually orderly and not cataclysmic, with a gradual modification of existing forms and some predictable direction. This is beyond the changes to meet local environmental characteristics and the changes inherent in historical traditions. This analytical isolation of the evolutionary processes is useful in gaining insight into the nature of culture, the relationships between cultures of different evolutionary levels, and very general processes of change. In practice, however, we are usually concerned with combining the general processes with ecology (ecological evolution), history (historical evolution), or in a three-way combination (specific evolution). Also in practice, we recognize that cataclysms do occur in the forms of internal revolutions, or exterior conquest and colonialization, which radically reshape the evolution of cultures.

Idiocultures, the learned behaviors of individuals, are similar the world over in neurological complexity and other biologically patterned ways. Thus the life of the individual has strong similarities in every society in the world and in this sense does not evolve. Cultures change, but the effective world of the individual human being must remain the same and be ultimately defined by the biological nature of the individual human. While there is an immense variety of cultures in the world they are all designed for the same kind of biological being. For discussions of theories of culture that are similar to those used in this book see Anderson (1976), Price (1973, 1975, 1978), and Service (1971, 1975).

Traits of the Ethnographic Present

Some broadly defined traits are universal, such as the use of language, telling of origin stories, living in families, prohibiting incest, gift giving, and holding funeral rites. With more-limited definitions there are traits that correspond to limited historical and ecological areas, such as continents or *cultural areas,* large zones of similar cultures. Aboriginal Canada was not an integrated area: Its culture areas overlapped with Alaska, Greenland, and the U.S. There is no unique single trait common to all aboriginal Canadian Indians, though the area had a large proportion of the world's remaining simple hunting band societies at the time of the ethnographic present. The universal traits are particularly those that have survived from an early common historical horizon, and that can persist into new ecological settings and be retained through changes with the evolution of culture. Some of the obvious universals are tools such as stone knives and bows and arrows. There are also social and religious traits that come from an early time horizon and were universally still practised at the time of ethnographic description.

Food

Deadfalls, pitfalls, and snares were in use. Land mammals were occasionally hunted by driving them into water, or, in the Plains, over cliffs or into compounds. Long fences of wood (piles of stones in the Arctic) were occasionally used in driving game. Except for the Blackfoot and Gros Ventres, who did little fishing, all societies had composite fishhooks, fish spears (leisters), gill nets, seines, and fish weirs.

Meat was everywhere dried in smoke or over a fire, though there was little fuel for this in the Arctic. Stone boiling (briefly putting fire-heated stones in a water container) was in use, except in the Arctic for lack of fuel and in Iroquoia where pottery was used. The earth oven was a general western trait. The use of milling stones with a lateral grinding movement was virtually absent, but pounding foods with a stone or wood mortar and pestle was common. Salt was not intentionally gathered or eaten in any Native Canadian society though it was used in many other North American societies. Though never important as a food, dogs were eaten ceremonially in the Pacific, Plains, and Iroquoia and even specially fattened for eating in Iroquoia.

Constructions and Crafts

Hide coverings were used for houses in the Arctic, Subarctic, and Plains; bark in the Subarctic, Iroquoia; and both bark and wood planks in the Pacific. In the east, the conical-tent foundations usually had three poles; and, from the Blackfoot westward, four poles. Defensive palisades were built around villages in both Iroquoia and the Pacific, and the historic Plains adopted the circular arrangement of tents in their camps in part for defence. Iroquoia and the Pacific had multi-family houses and wooden sitting platforms.

All areas had snowshoes. Toboggans were widely used except in the Pacific, but the sled was used only in the Arctic. All had boats: finely tailored hide-covered canoes in the Arctic; bark canoes in the Subarctic and Iroquoia; a bowl-shaped, hide-covered thing called the bull boat or coracle in the Plains; and the great dugout wood canoes of the Pacific.

Clothing was made of skins, finely tailored in the Arctic and semi-tailored elsewhere, except in the Pacific where robes were woven of twisted cedar bark. Twisted and woven fur strip robes were also used, except in the Arctic and Plains where large skins were plentiful. Women usually made all the clothing. They first dressed the skins by scraping, then usually used mashed brains to soften the skins. The Inuit and some Pacific societies soaked sea mammal hides in urine to remove the excess grease. Soft and continuous-soled moccasins were used, except in a few Inuit societies. The moccasin with a separate hard sole was also used in the Arctic and Plains. Only women made basketry and it was made everywhere except in the Plains. Porcupine quill decoration was common, except in the Arctic and Pacific. Tattooing was in use in the Arctic, western Subarctic, and Pacific.

Rituals and Entertainments

All had life crisis ceremonies for birth, puberty, marriage, and death. A girl's puberty ceremony began at her first menstruation. The first large game killed by a boy was treated ceremonially and often given away to people from outside the household. The dead were placed on platforms or in trees in one form of disposal, except in the Arctic where there are no trees. First-fruits rites were held each year for the first game or fish or plants harvested. Bears were everywhere treated with special ceremony when they were killed. All societies used shamanistic curing and divination techniques. All enjoyed water vapor sweating. Bear ceremonialism, shamanism, and water vapor sweating are all boreal traits that are found in the northern parts of Europe and Asia, as well as North America.

All had dancing, drumming, singing, and story telling. The North American Natives were unusual in the world in the extent of their gambling, particularly with *hand games* in which one side hides small marked and unmarked objects made of wood or bone, and the other side guesses the location of the marked object. Dice games were popular, as was story telling with string figures. Tobacco was probably aboriginal only in southern Canada, particularly Iroquoia, Plains, and Plateau; and had more ceremonial uses than are found today.

Culture Areas

The Arctic and Subarctic areas tend to run east-west while the Iroquoia, Plains, Plateau, and Pacific areas all run north-south. All areas are cut by the U.S.-Canada border and the majority of the Plains and Plateau areas are on the U.S. side. The Arctic is an unusual culture area in that it had such a severe climate for humans that it was occupied very late in human history and by only one society, the Inuit, who are relatively homogenous. Inuit culture extends along the coastlines from the eastern tip of Siberia through northern Alaska and Canada, to Greenland. Thus the Inuit today live under the administration of the U.S.S.R., the U.S., Canada, and of Greenland, a protectorate of Denmark.

The Subarctic is the largest area, stretching from interior Alaska across the Yukon and Northwest Territories through northern Ontario and Quebec, to the Atlantic provinces. It is an area of boreal forests with long, cold winters. The population densities here were very low and the pattern of life was a semi-nomadic round of hunting and fishing within a territory by small groups. The major items of material culture usually use hide or bark.

Iroquoia is a sub-area of the agricultural eastern woodlands, where there was some hunting and fishing, but Natives depended primarily on corn, beans, and squash. They made bark canoes and covered their "longhouses" with bark. They made pottery and lived a fairly sedentary life in large, well-defended villages.

Canada has only the northern tip of the Plains, a large zone that extends along the east flank of the Rocky Mountains and into the flat grasslands from southern Alberta and Saskatchewan to Texas. The major food was buffalo, which was hunted on foot by small bands much like the Subarctic hunting of caribou, until the Europeans introduced the horse. Then there was a very rapid diffusion of new traits and the

TABLE I
Culture Area Traits

	Arctic	Subarctic	Iroquoia	Plains	Pacific
Population per 100 square km	0–10	0–60	25–150	10–60	25–375+
Level of Evolution	bands	bands	tribes	tribes	chiefdoms
Language families	Eskimo-Aleut	Athapascan Algonquian Beothuk	Iroquoian	Algonquian Athapascan Siouan	Tlingit Haida Tsimshian Wakashan Salish
Major Cooking	stone lamp toasting	roast	soups in pottery	roast	smoked fish
Houses Winter	igloo	earth lodge	bark longhouse	hide tipi	plank house
Summer	hide tent	bark/hide wigwam	bark wigwam	hide tipi	mat lodge
Transportation	kayak umiak sled	bark canoe toboggan	bark canoe toboggan	travois	dugout canoe
Intergroup conflicts	rare feuds	rare feuds	warfare with torture	horse & scalp raids	raids with slavery

evolution of a new culture in the Plains. The material culture then focused on horses and the buffalo.

The Plateau area of the western mountains has been called a *foraging area* because of the pattern there of gathering a very diverse mix of plant, fish, and animal foods. The Plateau people turned to small and scattered food sources. However, in the Canadian portion of the Plateau there was a strong orientation toward fishing the headwaters of the Fraser, Thompson, and Columbia Rivers.

The Pacific is an area of indented coastlines with fiords and steep mountains, heavy rainfall, a mild climate, dense forests, and abundant fish. The population was the largest and most sedentary of any of the culture areas. Salmon was the principal food, taken particularly in runs in the spring and summer by means of traps or weirs in the rivers. The technology made wide use of the straight-grained cedar wood for canoes, plank houses, boxes, dishes, and carvings. Cedar bark was twisted and woven into mats and robes. Finer artistic weaving used the hair of mountain goats and domestic dogs. The social organization included social grading that could be classified as ranging from nobles to commoners and slaves. This social gradation was organized through the kinship system and validation ceremonies we call potlatches.

The population density estimates in Table I were taken from Driver (1969: map 6). A more conservative but fairly reliable source on

TABLE II
Population Densities by Area

✱ chart p. 42

	Population	Territory (100 km²)	Density
Arctic	30,900	15,057	2
Subarctic — Micmac, Abnaki	7,300	3,285	2
— Ojibwa, Ottawa, Algonkin	37,300	5,188	7
— Cree, Montagnais, Naskapi	23,000	25,677	1
— Athapascan	33,930	38,944	1
Iroquoia	42,500	4,421	10
Plains	50,500	13,978	4
Plateau	47,650	6,600	7
Pacific — Salish	23,700	725	33
— Wakashan, Bella Coola	17,300	594	29
— Tlingit, Haida, Tsimshian, Haisla	28,100	1,666	17
Totals	342,180	155,079	2.2

interesting.

aboriginal populations is Kroeber (1934). His material includes the following estimates for Canada and the adjacent areas (see Table II). The northern densities of 1–2 per 100 square kilometers are among the lowest in the world while the Pacific densities are high for fishing societies.

If estimates are made about Canada proper then about 60,000 have to be taken from the total for those living in the U.S. However, Kroeber tended to underestimate the early effects of White diseases. For example, my estimate for Iroquoia is 56,000, or 32 per cent more than Kroeber's. Thus, the aboriginal population of Canada was probably somewhat over 300,000.

Plateau Culture Area

The Canadian portion of the Plateau is such a small and transitional area that it will not be given a separate chapter in this book, but there are several things that need to be said about it. It is in the mountainous and high plateau areas of southeast B.C. and it extends southward through western Montana, Idaho, and eastern Washington and Oregon. Aboriginally it was an area of (1) poor transportation and communication, (2) conservative retention of ancient cultural practices, and (3) transition between the surrounding culture areas. In Canada the Plateau societies were the Kutenai in the east, the now extinct Athapascan Nicola, and the Interior Salish societies—Lakes, Shuswap, Lillooet, Thompson, and Okanagan.

Sites with fishbone debris and occasional artifacts such as flint blades show a fishing specialization beginning in the Plateau around 11,000 years ago. Later archaeological evidence shows the use of pithouses and earth ovens, to bake fish and camas root.

Jenness (1932:351) wrote that the Lillooet were influenced by the Coast Salish tribes because they traded with them and adopted the advanced coastal type of clan system with clan ancestors that were impersonated in masked dances. Most Plateau societies had bilateral descent and patrilocal postmarital residence. The Plateau societies were also drawn somewhat into a tribal type of large-scale warfare with raids for plunder and revenge. Some groups took prisoners in war, something that simple bands rarely did. However, these were usually women and children, and they were assimilated into the society.

The Plateau societies were like tribal societies in their ownership and defence of places of primary food production: specific village-owned fish weir sites and sometimes long fences built for deer drives. They had some mix of political forms, in the band-tribe transition range of evolution, sometimes with the patrilineal inheritance of a civil village chief who led a council of village elders. Raids were organized by separate war chiefs. They usually had small but fairly stable villages of about 50–100 persons.

The winter house was circular and semi-subterranean, with a pit about four feet deep and a conical or pyramidal roof. The roof was supported by central posts. The number of posts ranged from one to four, depending on the house size, which varied according to the needs of from one to several families. The roof was covered with earth and had a combination smoke-hole and central entrance with a notched log ladder. The summer house was a small wood frame covered with woven mats.

Clothing included soft-soled moccasins, hide sandals, tailored skin clothing, and woven fur-strip robes. Basketry hats were worn, particularly by women to protect their forehead when they carried burden baskets on their back with a tumpline strap to the head. They also used fur caps in winter. They made a variety of forms of basketry: matting for bedding, cradles, deep storage baskets, flat winnowing trays, and small finely woven pouches.

The Plateau Indians lacked organized religious societies, like those of the Pacific or the Plains, and emphasized religious traits which are considered to be of an ancient historical level: shamanism, vision quest, and the girl's puberty rites. The puberty rites derived from belief that menstrual fluid is dangerous to men and that the time of the first few menstruations patterned a girl's adult life.

At the time of her first menstruation the girl dieted, especially from meat, so that hunters would not be affected by her dangerous state. She also avoided fishermen, gamblers, and shamans, men engaged in unsure activities for which they needed strong supernatural support. She should not touch her body or hair with her hands, but only with a special scratching stick. She was protected and instructed in sexual matters by an older woman other than her mother. She gathered firewood and helped women in their work, finally ending the special rituals by bathing and dressing in new clothing. In some societies there were such things as a special dance, hair cutting, ritual meals, and prayers for the girl.

Evolution

Just as we use such broad ecological types as Arctic, Subarctic, and Plains, we find that broad evolutionary categories are useful. When thoughts about evolution were quite different in the nineteenth century, people used the typology of primitive, barbaric, and civilized. These terms became too loaded in favor of complex societies and were used pejoratively against the simpler societies, on many mistaken assumptions about human nature. As we needed more neutral terms and we needed to make finer distinctions, the terms band, tribe, chiefdom, and state came into use.

The *band*, the simplest category of society, had hunting and gathering food production, a sharing kind of economics, and a style of leadership based on common residence and divisions of labor by sex, age, and ability. Indian women specialized in gathering and processing plants, so we have them to thank for the Neolithic Revolution through the domestication of plants and probably for the invention of a broad range of domestic equipment such as basketry, pottery, and the mortar and pestle. We have the men to thank for our heritage of hunting, warfare, religion, and politics.

The *tribe* developed economic, social, and political ties that are broader in scope than those of bands. Sharing continues to predominate in the intimate sectors of life, such as the household, but the calculations of reciprocity are developed as a basis of economic distribution beyond such spheres. Impersonal trade develops. Lineal kinship groups and other "pan-tribal sodalites" create social ties beyond the residential communities and give political cohesion to the society. Most tribal societies of the world were horticulturalists, with simple hand gardening, but the tribal level was also achieved by some fishing and pastoral societies.

At a more advanced level there develops a central integration of economic, social, political, and religious factors. This is referred to as a *chiefdom* because there is usually a chief and some kind of administrating group that serves as an integrating center to tax and redistribute goods and services and to organize feasts, warfare, major religious ceremonies, and long-distance trade. Chiefdoms typically have elaborate social ranking and a class system, often with some slavery; well developed arts, in part because some people are allowed to specialize as artists; pageantry; and so forth. Beyond the chiefdom the *state* level was achieved

TABLE III

A Model of the Evolution of Culture

Stage	Economic Production	Economic Distribution	Political	Religious
State	Agriculture	Administration and markets	Laws and bureaucracy	Priesthoods
Chiefdom	Horticulture, Pastoralism, or Fishing	Redistribution	Chieftainship	Public dramas
Tribe	"	Reciprocity	Pan-tribal sodalities	Religious societies
Band	Hunting, gathering	Sharing	Residential and task leaders	Curing Food Increase

with intensive agriculture, a centrally administered economy with markets, a legal structure with a large scale bureaucracy, and priestly (full-time specialists) religions that support the ideology of the state.

TABLE IV
Scalogram of 17 Traits in 9 Societies
(Carneiro 1968, with corrections)

Trait	Naskapi	Inuit	Kaska	Ojibwa (Chippewa)	Gros Ventres	Blackfoot	Salish (Clallam)	Iroquois	Kwakiutl
Leader bestows land, slaves or rank									X
Special deference to leaders									X
Full-time craft specialists									X
Supra-provincial organization								X	X
Full-time retainers for leaders									X
Death penalty decreed								X	X
Full-time political leader								X	X
Judicial process								X	X
Neolithic food level					X	X	X	X	X
Craft specialization						X	X	X	X
Significant status differences						X	X	X	X
Communities of 100 or more				X	X	X	X	X	X
Peace-keeping machinery					X	X	X	X	X
Social segments above family			X	X	X	X	X	X	X
Formal political leadership					X	X	X	X	X
Trade between communities				X			X	X	X
Special religious practitioners	X	X	X	X	X	X	X	X	X
Levels	Band	Band	Band	Band-Tribe	Tribe	Tribe	Tribe-Chiefdom	Tribe-Chiefdom	Chiefdom
Traits	1	1	2	4	6	8	9	13	17

These stages are not seen as stable entities, but only as arbitrary slices made on a continuum. Just as we make arbitrary criteria to define where one ecological zone ends and the next begins, we need conventional terms to talk about different degrees of evolutionary complexity. I find it occasionally useful to add the intermediate terms of band-tribe, tribe-chiefdom, and chiefdom-state for a total of seven evolutionary types. A scalogram of sequential traits is an even better description of our current systems model of evolutionary processes.

Carneiro (1968) developed a scale of fifty traits in a rough evolutionary sequence across one-hundred societies around the world. This yields a fairly discrete model of the systematic changes that occur with the expansion in energy available, population growth, political centralization, economic specialization and exchange, and so forth. In Table IV I have abstracted out the Canadian societies in the sample and made some corrections. The time level is the ethnographic present. There is an element of interpretation in determining the presence or absence of a trait, but we have some precision in our definitions. For example, gift exchange and some sporadic trade exist between individuals in different communities in all societies, but "trade between communities" means some form of regular trade network.

Kinship Systems

Kinship generally is more important in primitive societies than in modern societies, and the studies of kinship have been seen as important to understanding the structure of primitive society. It is a more personal kind of society in which kinfolk are more important in living groups, work groups, and marriage arrangements.

Native people were generally tolerant of diverse kinds of marriage arrangements. For example, *fraternal polyandry*, by which two or more brothers married the same woman, occurred on rare occasions in most societies. For example, if an older brother was hurt and unable to hunt, his younger brother might move in to do the hunting for the household and become a second husband. *Monogamy* was the most common form of marriage and the exclusive form in the Iroquoian societies. *Polygyny*, having more than one wife, occurred in more than 20 per cent of the marriages in ethnographic present times only in the tribal and chiefdom societies of the west. *Sororal polygyny*, by which a man marries two or more sisters, was by far the most common form of plural marriage.

Where a couple live after marriage would be usually determined by economic advantage. In band societies there is a need for flexibility to move where game herds shift, and postmarital residence is usually *bilocal* (in either the husband's or the wife's camp), or *neolocal* (a new camp).

In farming tribes, such as the Huron, the women produce the bulk of the food and men move into the wife's community, a *matrilocal* pattern. If physical strength or the cooperation of men is emphasized in tribal or chiefdom subsistence economics, then the postmarital residence pattern is usually *patrilocal*, moving into the husband's community.

Mode of postmarital residence seems to be the primary determinant of ideological concepts about descent. If people live with *either* of their parent's kinfolk, or set up a new household, they tend to develop a *bilateral* descent system, an ideology, common to both the Inuit and the modern Canadians, that they equally descended from both sides. If children routinely grow up in an environment dominated by the mother's relatives then a *matrilineal* descent system evolves. Following the ideology of descent, and coordinated with it, is the development of lineal social groups (*lineages*, and a collection of related lineages making a *clan*), lineal inheritance, lineal patterning of marriages, and lineal patterning of kinship terminology. Historical and other influences do sometimes mix up the patterns, so that for example one occasionally finds lineal groups in a society with an ideology of bilateral descent. The most common chain of events seems to be (1) sex roles in subsistence, (2) postmarital residence patterns, (3) ideology of descent, (4) a variety of coordinated kinship forms.

Kinship terminologies (the terms of reference one uses for one's relatives) are internally systematic. This is because there is a correlation between terms and behaviors. Terms are related to a society's social rules respecting incest prohibition, marriage eligibility and preferences, where a married couple will live, reckoning descent, inheritance, and succession to offices and titles. The distinctions between several systems show up in just the terms for what Canadians call aunts, uncles, and cousins. However, since these concepts are so foreign to Canadians, they are difficult for us to understand.

The first comparative study of kinship systems was that of Lewis Henry Morgan, published in 1870 as *Systems of Consanguinity and Affinity of the Human Family*. In the process of studying Iroquois customs he found that they classified kinship relations quite differently from Europeans. They had a *unilineal* system while the European systems are bilateral, tracing descent in both the mother's and father's line. The Iroquois system is female-oriented, while the Europeans are male-oriented; the Iroquois have a *matri*-lineal system while the Europeans tend toward the *patri*-lineal—for instance, they carry on the father's name rather than the mother's name. The centers of matrilineal organization in Canada were the Iroquoians in the east and the Tsimshian and certain neighboring western Dene, such as the Haida, Tlingit, and Kaska. Morgan was also impressed by the fact that the Ojibwa, who were just north of the Iroquoians, had a system that was unilineal like the Iroquois, but it was patrilineal. The rest of the Canadian societies tended to be loosely bilateral in descent.

The *Iroquois* system occurs in many places in the world where the mother is lumped together with her sister and the father with his brother. It bifurcates the parents into their different lineages and merges those of the siblings of the same sex within the two sides. Thus in a bifurcate merging system there is one term for both mother and mother's sister and one term for father and father's brother. The mother's sister behaves somewhat the same as the biological mother so they are covered by the same words. Parallel-cousins, mother's sister's children, are within one's own lineage so they are called brother and sister. Mother's brother's daughter and father's sister's daughter have special terms. They are cross-cousins, in that one crosses from one sex to another in the parental generation in order to trace the kinship connection. The category is important in strongly lineal societies because it is definitely in a different lineage, and is therefore a marriageable category, often a preferred one because it is otherwise socially close. Among the Haida and the Kaska the preferred marriage was between a man and his mother's brother's daughter—a cross-cousin marriage.

Crow is also a bifurcate merging system when the focus is on uncles and aunts, but it is more specific than Iroquois when the focus is on cousin terms. It makes fine distinctions between members of one's own descent group, and broad, lumping categories of the relatives of the parent who is not in one's own descent group. It equates the same-sex members of the in-marrying parent's descent group regardless of generation. Thus, there is lumping across the generations. Iroquois is simply unilineal and can go either way. Both the matrilineal Iroquoians (Huron, Petun, Neutral, and Iroquois) and the patrilineal Ojibwa (as well as the bilateral Cree) used Iroquois cousin terminology. The Ojibwa were only weakly patrilineal. Crow is used in *strongly matrilineal* descent groups.

For example, in the matrilineal Crow system a man's brother's children are referred to by the same terms as his own children: son and daughter. His maternal cross-cousins—mother's brother's children—are also called son and daughter though they are in his own generation. None of these "children" are in his lineage. His parallel cousins are called brother and sister. His paternal cross-cousins, father's sister's children, are called father and father's sister. The only Crow systems in Canada were in the matrilineal block in the northwest: Haida, Tlingit, Tahltan, and Kaska. All these are Dene-speaking peoples.

Another possible system is called Hawaiian. This is a generational, extremely lumping, system associated with bilateral descent. There were Hawaiian systems of cousin terminology in the western groups, such as Salish, Nootka, Kwakiutl, Carrier, Sekani, Slave, Beaver, and Gros Ventre. Blackfoot had a mixture of Iroquois and Hawaiian elements.

Most Canadians and people of European descent use a system that has such general terms as uncle and aunt that it does not tell whether one is referring to one's mother's or father's side; and terms such as cousin, which ignore both the lineal side and the sex. The technical term for this kind of bilateral terminology is *Eskimo*. This is a simple system in that the main distinction is between lineals (one's parents, grandparents, children, and grandparents) and collaterals (everyone else—aunts, uncles, brothers, sisters, nieces, and nephews). This type of system is found in societies that de-emphasize lineages and typically lack clans. These are societies that emphasize the nuclear family and have no strict rule about where a married couple will live. The simplest *and* the most complex tend to have Eskimo kinship terminology while the intermediate societies tend to have lineal systems.

In Canada such simple societies as the Inuit, Micmac, Malecite, and Kutenai used Eskimo terminology. However, there are exceptions. Simple societies such as the Ojibwa and Kaska developed lineal features, apparently more because of the diffusion of influences from adjacent societies than from internal structural evolution. We also find relatively complex societies such as the Salish with bilateral descent, Hawaiian cousin terminology; yet they have patrilineal clans. Lineal descent and the appropriate terminology seems to have evolved independently in many cultural traditions around the world, primarily because of patterns of unilocal post-marital residence, lineage work groups, lineage inheritance, and so forth. It did not evolve in all traditions and there were secondary borrowings of lineal ideas and practices between societies. Morgan's early problem of explaining the differences between European, Iroquois, and Ojibwa systems of kinship can only be resolved by a comparative analysis of cultural dynamics.

TABLE V
Kinship Traits by Case Studies

	Inuit	*Cree*	*Huron*	*Blackfoot*	*Kwakiutl*
Polygamy	rare	rare	none	common	common
Postmarital residence	bilocal	patrilocal	matrilocal	patrilocal	patrilocal
Descent	bilateral	bilateral	matrilineal	bilateral	patrilineal
Lineal groups	none	none	clans	none	clans
Cousin terms	Eskimo	Iroquois	Iroquois	Iroquois-Hawaiian	Hawaiian
Aunt terms	Eskimo	bifurcate-collateral	bifurcate-merging	bifurcate-merging	lineal

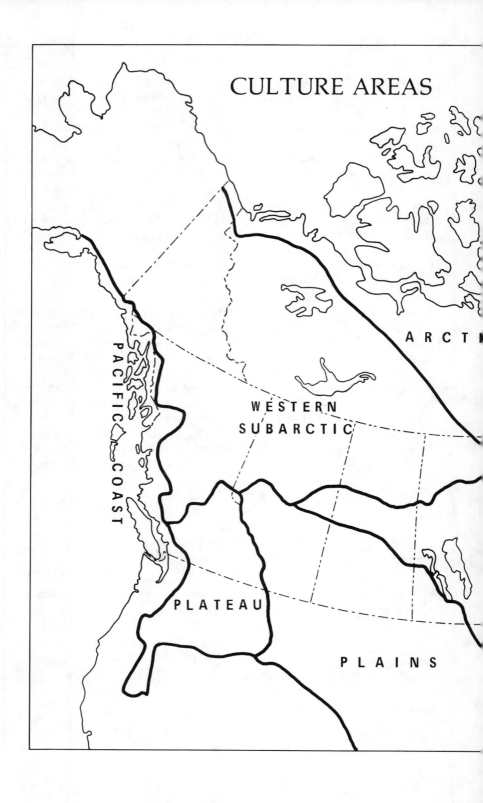

CULTURE AREAS

PACIFIC COAST

WESTERN
SUBARCTIC

ARCTI

PLATEAU

PLAINS

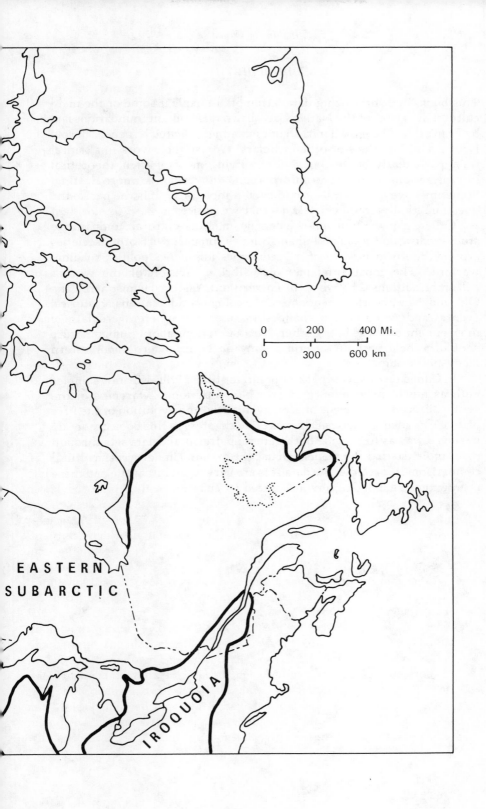

EASTERN
SUBARCTIC

IROQUOIA

0   200   400 Mi.
0   300   600 km

Commentary

This book, by synthesizing data, attempts to explain some of the main cultural dynamics of the Native Canadians. It is built on foundations laid by Franz Boas, Edward Sapir, Diamond Jenness, Alfred Kroeber, Harold Driver, and hundreds of other scholars. We use their work in a critical way, particularly by testing and modifying most of their theoretical interpretations. The raw information, however, is more lasting. Sometimes we question its accuracy, but most often it is the gaps—the questions that were never asked—that we notice.

Other gaps in our knowledge lie in cross-cultural comparative studies. How do Canadian Indian societies compare with other societies around the world in terms of art, economics, linguistics, politics, religion, warfare? The most fundamental historical division of the world's cultural traditions is between the Eastern and Western Hemispheres, the Old and New Worlds. Sequences of ecological adaptations, historical events, and evolutionary changes in one hemisphere were largely independent of those in the other. No assumptions about human nature should be held without careful testing on both Eastern and Western Hemisphere samples.

In Canada we expect that comparative studies will also draw samples with as much independence as possible, with some awareness of the subtle differences in terms of ecology, history, and evolution of the fifty Native Canadian societies. The next five chapters in this book are set up in such a way as to provide both general patterns and data sets through case studies so that the reader can use the material in new cross-cultural comparisons. Of course, the data sets are very brief, but at the end there is an extensive bibliography, organized by chapter.

CHAPTER 4

ARCTIC
Inuit:
Environmental
Adaptations

WHITE SCHOLARS HAVE written more about the adaptations of the Inuit than they have for any other primitive society (Balikci 1970, Birket-Smith 1959, Boas 1888, Briggs 1970, Brody 1975, Damas 1963, Rasmussen 1931, and Vallee 1962 are eight of the best Canadian Inuit ethnographies). Whites speak of the climate in negative terms, even though in living in the Arctic they have gone to extremes to duplicate a southern lifestyle in their housing, transportation, and work. They may become oppressed by the long and extremely cold winter nights and the isolation of small communities. Companies and government services have a high turnover in jobs; not only from people who quit to return south, but from people who move from job to job in the north because of local dissatisfaction.

The Inuit, by contrast, usually prefer to live and work in the Arctic, even when they have lived for years in the south. They have made successful cultural adaptations that are applicable to the lives of anyone in the Arctic. White residents have not assimilated enough of the philosophical, social, aesthetic, recreational, and other dimensions of Inuit life to really enjoy living in the Arctic. This chapter is primarily about traditional Inuit culture and its self-reliance, ingenuity, flexibility, and survival techniques.

The Arctic

The Arctic Circle runs at 66½° north latitude, the line around the earth where the sun never sets on the longest day of the summer and never rises at mid-winter solstice. The farther north of the Arctic Circle one goes the more extreme is the seasonal fluctuation in the available light, swinging between long nights in the winter and long days in the summer. One geographical definition of the Arctic is in terms of the land between the Arctic Circle and the North Pole. The more useful definitions of the Arctic are in terms of temperature and vegetation. Thus the Arctic is also defined by some as the area north of the line of 50°F. average temperature for the warmest month and by others as the area north of the tree line. The tree line zigzags across Canada from about the Mackenzie Delta to the northern border of Manitoba at Hudson Bay and then across the top of Arctic Quebec. Another significant ecological line is that of the southern limit of subsurface permafrost. That line is 400–500 miles south of the tree line through the center of the Subarctic, dipping southward from northern B.C. to the southern end of James Bay in Ontario and through the center of the Labrador Peninsula.

Technically most of the Arctic is desert since it receives only about eight inches of precipitation per year. However, when the tundra surface melts in the summer most of the land can be wet with mud flats and shallow lakes down to the permafrost layer. This wet desert is possible because the air is very cool and will not absorb more moisture. The Arctic vegetation is mostly primitive forms such as lichens, mosses, and grasses, which can stand the extremes of cold and dryness. More than 100 species of birds summer north of the Arctic Circle, feeding mostly on the great swarms of mosquitoes, black flies, and sand flies.

Knud Rasmussen (1931), an early anthropologist, traveled across the Arctic and found that his Greenland Inuit dialect was enough for "complete understanding" with most of the Inuit bands he met. Even place names were repeated. Essentially one Inuit language is spoken in Greenland and Canada. He had communication problems with a group in the Coronation Gulf area but farther west still he did well among the Mackenzie Inuit, and met increasing dialectal problems in Alaska, but he was still generally understood. In southern Alaska he needed an interpreter. These southern Alaskan Eskimos are considered to speak a different language, called Yuit or Yupik, instead of Inuktitut. Some of these Alaskan Natives prefer to be called Eskimos, rather than Inuit.

"Eskimo" is a Cree word meaning eater-of-raw-meat; the Eskimos had a higher proportion of meat and fish in their diet than any other known society, and it was mostly uncooked because they had little fuel for cooking though they occasionally used the small flame of a blubber lamp in winter or burned willow or vegetation in summer. "Eskimo" is not a derogatory term; however, these peoples usually prefer "Inuit," which in their language means "people." *Inuk* is their term for an individual.

An area as vast as the Arctic was bound to develop important cultural variations. Thus, for example, many of the Alaskan Inuit had wood to make tools with, while the rest were far above the tree line and had only driftwood, animal products, and stone for tools. Perhaps as important as environmental differences were communications. Though the Alaskan Inuit tended to be in better communication with each other and with Indian groups—a communication that stimulated their development—in Canada and northern Greenland there were pockets of isolation that contributed to regressive cultural variations.

The Polar Inuit of northern Greenland were so isolated when first contacted by European explorers that they believed they were the only people on the face of the earth. They had lost the knowledge of making canoes and sleds and did not hunt caribou or fish for salmon. The Netsilik, "people of the seal," of north central Canada, specialized in hunting caribou in summer and seals through the sea ice in winter, but apparently lost the common Inuit ability to hunt seals with harpoons by kayaks in the open water. Farther south, the Caribou Inuit of the Barren Grounds were more isolated than the Netsilik and regressed to the point of losing their marine skills and a lot of the usual Inuit technology. Apparently communication links were an important part of a group's long-term adaptability.

There were three Inuit cultural types in north central Canada: Copper to the west, Netsilik in the center, and Iglulik to the east. Damas (1973) compared these groups. In response to more open water conditions, the Iglulik emphasized the sea-mammal phase in their annual cycle. Their hunting of basking seals was more developed, more widespread, and done for a longer part of the cycle. They hunted large sea mammals from the edge of ice floes. They hunted seals, walruses, and even whales from kayaks. These are activities that one or two men can do; thus community groups tended to be smaller and more scattered than in the other areas and there were less formal arrangements for sharing meat. Iglulik economic sharing and political leadership tended to operate along kinship lines, with an older male acquiring influence within the community.

The Copper and Netsilik lived in a more severe environment and they developed some unique innovations to cope with these conditions. Their principal winter activity was hunting seals on the sea ice through their breathing holes, an activity that works best with large cooperative groups of about a dozen hunters. This seems to have led to larger social groups in winter than among the Iglulik and to the elaborate institutions of seal-sharing partnerships. They also had relatively large aggregations of people in summer for weir fishing and occasionally for hunting at caribou crossings.

Physical Adaptations

Racially the Inuit might be thought of as a subgroup of Indians, with only about 20,000 in Canada today. They are short and stocky in build and express some classic Mongoloid features such as high cheekbones, small and flat noses, and the Mongoloid eyefold (Hughes and Kallen 1974, Sheppard and Itoh 1976, Stewart 1973). The stocky build, flat noses, and eyefold are all thought to be racial adaptations that conserve body heat in the cold climate. The Inuit have a higher basal metabolism rate than Canadians generally, indicating some cold adaptation. They also have a greater tolerance to cold in the hands and fewer active sweat glands for cooling than non-Inuit. However, physically acquired adjustments to cold seem to be more important than racial adjustments. Regardless of race, people who live and work in cold environments acclimatize in a few years' time. Traditional Maritime fishermen seem to acquire as much cold acclimatization as the Inuit.

Initial research showed that the Inuit, who adapted to outdoor activities, had greater blood flow in their hands than Whites, who had not adapted to outdoor activities. That research still did not distinguish between genetic and acquired characteristics. It was necessary to add samples of Inuit who lived and worked indoors and Whites who lived and worked outdoors. That research showed a mild genetic base for cold adaptation. Living and working with chronic exposure to the cold, regardless of racial characteristics, leads to a major adaptation to the cold. Thus the temperature of the hand is higher and the blood flow is about double for both cold-adapted Inuit and cold-adapted White fishermen in the Maritimes.

Even more important than either race or acclimatization is the cultural adaptation. The most obvious dimensions of cultural adaptation to the cold are the technological, such as housing and clothing. Just as important, however, are the social, philosophical, and artistic dimensions of environmental adaptations. For example, the terrain, climatic changes, and animals are incorporated into a comprehensible and workable world view by which humans can survive. In fact, the pervasive characteristics of Inuit environmental adaptation are not specific culture traits, but the general cultural habits of flexibility and ingenuity, a readiness to find new solutions. "The flexibility may be seen in family organization, in the loose definition of the form of marriage, in the casualness of adoption . . .

in the various patterns of community organization and the ease with which one changes into another . . . in the recreation patterns that become destructured when practised by the Eskimos" (Willmott 1960). This flexibility and ingenuity seems to have made their adjustments to White society somewhat smoother than that of Indians in the north.

Clothing

Inuit clothing was cut and sewn to fit closely. This tailoring was a relatively recent invention in the north that diffused through both the Old and New World northern or Boreal zone before it spread southward into the temperate regions. Its recency is indicated by the fact that the Inuit were the only people in the Western Hemisphere to use the thimble regularly. People in ancient Egypt, Greece, and the Inca empire wore robes, skirts, and other non-tailored clothing. Inuit clothing had tightly sewn seams, no buttonholes, and large garments that controlled the flow of air around the body. A key feature in the design of the parka was that it went all the way from the hips over the shoulders and then over the head. The warm body heat was trapped with a tight fit at the shoulders and in the hood. The amount of opening allowed in the facial part of the hood controlled the amount of heat in the parka.

As caribou hair is hollow and thus traps air, the fur is ideal for insulation, softness, and lightness, especially for winter garments. Sealskin is waterproof, stronger, and more durable than caribou so it is preferred for wetter summer conditions, particularly for kayak travel. Waterproof summer boots, for example, were made from sealskins. The Inuit preferred the hair of the wolf, dog, or wolverine to surround the facial opening because it would not frost over from the moist breath. Bear fur will not absorb moisture and is thick, and therefore was used for bedding and occasionally as an emergency sledge that could be loaded with equipment and dragged through the snow without collecting a heavy layer of snow. Pants were made from long-wearing, warm pelts such as caribou or polar bear. Small containers were made from the whole skin of a duck or a fish.

A loose-fitting fur sock was usually worn, with the fur inside. A soft boot was sometimes worn over the sock. Then, over that, high *mukluk* boots were worn with a harder sole and the fur facing outside. The thick hide of the walrus was excellent for outer boots and for special outer winter pants, allowing the hunter to sit still on the ice for hours waiting to spear a seal as it came up to its breathing hole.

The inner parka was a tunic of soft fur or bird skins with the hair or feathers on the inside that provided space to collect the warm air circulating off the body. This had to be taken off and dried out each day so that the moisture from the body's sweat would not accumulate and decrease the insulation value of the parka. An outer parka was worn with the hair out. This was roomy enough for one to pull one's arms inside the parka and warm them up against the body. Women with infants made their parkas looser to provide room for the child, which was usually carried on the back with aid of an inside strap, wearing only a fur hood. Roomy mittens extended inside. The total weight of the clothing was about ten pounds. The cold weather clothing used by Europeans before they copied the parka was from twenty to thirty pounds in weight. To protect the eyes from snowblindness due to the glare of the sun on the snow, goggles made of ivory or wood with small horizontal slits were used.

Shelter

In the summer skin tents were used. In late fall people moved into permanent winter dwellings. Several of these together constituted a co-operating community. They were placed where the ice would be smooth in winter, near good hunting grounds, by a supply of fresh-water ice for drinking (sea ice loses its salt after about one year), and routes were available for overland travel to inland frozen food storage caches.

One form of winter house was a small, semi-subterranean earth lodge with earth-packed rock or sod walls, a driftwood or whalebone roof covered with sod, and a low tunnel entrance covered with a skin-flap door. It was lighted and heated only with a stone lamp that burned blubber oil from a moss wick. Body heat was also a heating factor in the small, well-insulated house. The tunnel entrance was usually slightly lower than the floor and there were raised sitting and sleeping benches around the sides. Since warm air rises, they did not lose their warm air out the doorway and they slept in the warmest part of the house.

The igloo or snow house was built in much of the Arctic while out from the base camp hunting and traveling in the wintertime. A new one could be built in 45 to 60 minutes, depending on size, at the end of every day. They would be left standing and used on a trip back along the same route. Again, the principles of a low tunnel entrance and a raised sleeping platform were used in the more elaborate igloos that were to be used for more than two or three days.

The igloo is a small dome-shaped house made of snow blocks. The blocks are cut with a long antler or bone snow knife (*pana*). They are about six inches thick and 18" by 30", laid out along a ramp. As the blocks spiral upward and lean increasingly inward they form the dome. The dome is finished off with a specially cut king block at the top. The entrance tunnel is built facing away from the prevailing winds. The overall design is very strong and stable. Once an igloo has melted and frozen a little from the inside heat, a person can crawl onto the top and sit there without breaking the house. It will easily withstand winds because of its round aerodynamic shape.

In the high Canadian Arctic (as opposed to Hudson Bay, Quebec, and Labrador) igloos were built for regular winter use; these were large ones. They were often combined or built with interconnecting tunnels. They were then often insulated on the inside to keep them from melting from internal heat. Skins were suspended across the inside to leave a cold air space between the insulating skin and the inner dome of snow blocks. A window was added by substituting a block of clear ice for one of the snow blocks.

Transportation

The *kayak* was made of sealskin tightly bound over a frame of wood or whalebone. The top was covered with a decking except for a round hole in which the hunter sat. It was very light, fast, and seaworthy; and was propelled by a double-bladed paddle. Some Inuit also made a skin-covered open boat, the *umiak*, which could carry several people, both for travel and whaling. In some areas a small temporary raft to cross a river was made by filling a deerskin with shrubs and sewing it up tight.

The Inuit sled was usually made of small pieces of bound driftwood or of whalebone, looking like a ladder with runners. The pieces were lashed together with hide thongs through holes made with a rotating stone-tipped bowdrill. The hide thongs could bend and give enough to prevent the sled from breaking as it went over rough ice. The runners, usually several feet long, were of wood with a whalebone undersurface for longer wear. In the powdery snow, the runner had to be very smooth and ice was the best surface. In order to have a layer of ice, the runners would be additionally covered with a layer of frozen mud, moss, or seal's blood to which water would stick and freeze.

The traces and harnesses by which the dogs were tied to the sled were made of hide. Generally a fan hitch was used in Canada, so that each dog pulled on a line directly attached to the sled. The fan hitch was best in open country. The in-line hitch, with dogs paired behind each other, was more for narrow trails, as in forested areas, and was widely used by the Inuit of Alaska.

Snowmobiles came into use in the Canadian Arctic in the mid-1960s. They have made it possible to travel farther to hunt, and to live in large settlements and still travel far enough on weekends and summer trips to supplement wages with trapped fur animals and hunted meat. A one-day trip by snowmobile takes three days with dogs. Snowmobiles are, of course, expensive to buy and operate. They increase dependency on southern supplies and on a money income to operate them. However, even full-time trappers have almost all turned to the snowmobile. The speed of traveling the trapline prevents loss of their catch to escapes and predation by foxes or wolves. The concentration is more on furs which can be sold, such as the Arctic fox, and less on meat animals such as caribou to feed the dogs.

There are a number of technical problems with snowmobiles. They are better on the hard-packed snow and in open country than in the deep drifts of a forest. They can break down and leave a hunter stranded; it is best to travel in pairs so that a broken vehicle can be hauled back to the village by the other vehicle. The snowmobiles make a lot of noise. The Inuit, however, have discovered that seals will not panic and dive into the water if you approach without changing the pitch of the engine. Then you can approach close enough to shoot it with a rifle. When you do get close enough one person jumps off the snowmobile, quickly sits in a stable position, and shoots.

The traditional technical skills of the Inuit have been applied to modern problems. A snowmobile broke down on an expedition on Ellesmere Island, and stranded the hunter far from home in sub-zero weather. The hunter built an igloo over the machine and completely dismantled the engine. After some 24 hours of work he was able to get it going again and return home.

Hunting

Boas (1888) found that the Central-Inuit had great knowledge of their terrain and the annual cycles of weather and animal habits in their local areas. Each local band followed its own annual pattern of hunting, fishing, and fowling to fit the local environment. They used magical chants, formulae, and rituals in hunting: to tell the distant caribou to come and feed in the hunter's area, to give the spirit of a dead seal a drink of water so the other seals would know of his good treatment, etc.

Balikci's study (1970) of a Netsilik subgroup showed an annual round in 1919 of six camps: three on the ice of Pelly Bay in winter and spring hunting of seals at their breathing holes; one in midsummer spearing fish at a stone weir; one in early fall hunting caribou inland; and one in late fall fishing through the thin river ice. They hunted other animals and had many other activities, but this shifting of camps for a particular resource is typical of band societies the world over. They had acquired a predictability about the seasons, the migration of animals, and the habits of each species to develop a productive annual round and to hunt animals well. The size of hunting groups was a part of this ecological adaptation, since the concentration or scatter of game caused people to concentrate or scatter accordingly, although people had their own social and recreational needs. There was some preference for large social groupings when this was permitted by a plentiful supply of food.

The Inuit were habitually inventive, seeking alternatives when one method failed. Even the usual annual round could vary widely according to circumstances, such as substituting musk ox hunting on land for sealing on the ice in winter. The collection and fissioning of hunting groups was flexibly related primarily to food resources, and secondarily to the fluctuation between devisive social conflicts and the positive aspects of social aggregation (feasts, games, dancing, etc.) Finally there were what might politely be called demographic adaptations, the capacity to keep the human population small enough and productive enough to survive. This meant infanticide, particularly of females since they did not hunt. Also suicide in crises conditions, invalidicide, and senilicide were adaptive in that unproductive people were eliminated.

Boas (1888:669) described a case of senilicide: "Another case was that of an old woman whose health had been failing for a number of years. She lived with her son, whose wife had died late in the autumn of 1886. According to the religious ideas of the Eskimo, the young man had to throw away his clothing. When, later on, his mother felt as though she could not live through the winter, she insisted upon being killed, as she did not want to compel her son to cast away a second set of clothing. At last her son complied with her request. She stripped off her outside jacket and breeches, and was conveyed on a sledge to a near island, where she was left alone to die from cold and hunger."

Starvation was usually not due to the general lack of game in the region, but something such as a shifting of a migration pattern. Bands regularly harvested only a minor proportion of the available food potential in their areas, usually less than 25 per cent. The land has a human carrying capacity—it can support only so many hunters at a given level of technology and hunters too can easily be over-populated so that they starve and turn to infanticide and senilicide. Hunters are not happy-go-lucky people, though they may seem to have a lack of concern for tomorrow and squander the windfalls of today in feasting and widespread sharing.

The seal and walrus were major animals hunted by the Inuit. Inuit had an elaborate knowledge about the behavior of these animals and used that knowledge in hunting them. In winter the mother seals may dig a hole in a snowdrift for their infant with a nearby passage through the ice into the water below. When the hunter discovered one of these he caved in the "seal igloo," killed the baby, and waited for the mother to return to harpoon it.

hunting methods

① *Utok* was the "sneaking up" method of hunting. The hunter moved upwind so the seal could not smell him. In this he approached a sunning seal by crawling on his stomach and imitating the movements of the seal by flapping his arms like flippers and moving his legs together like the tail of a seal. He might rhythmically scratch on the ice to imitate the sounds of another seal. When he was close enough he threw his harpoon. A hunter could also approach camouflaged behind a white screen.

The harpoon had a wood shaft about four feet long. A foreshaft was fixed to this with a ball-and-socket joint so that it would swing with the prey's movement without detaching. A detachable, barbed ivory head was rammed into the animal, fell free of the wood shaft, but was held by a long line and allowed the hunter to draw in a heavy thrashing animal.

② *Maupok* was the "waiting method." In this technique the hunter had to find one of a seal's several breathing holes, wait for the seal to come up to breathe, and then harpoon it. The hole, chewed out from below the ice by the seal, was indicated on the surface by a tiny rise of frost caused by the moist breath of the seal. Without disturbing the hole the hunter had to determine the shape of the hole so that he could tell the direction in which to plunge his harpoon. Then he placed a small thin stick in the hole that would move when the seal entered the hole. He then waited, sometimes for hours, for the seal to come to that particular hole for his one chance to harpoon it. Once it was harpooned, he had to cut a large hole in the ice and pull the seal to the surface of the ice.

The Inuit developed a technique by which a single hunter could haul a 2,000 pound bull walrus out of the water and up on the ice after he had killed it. He put a makeshift block and tackle together by first cutting two or three holes in the ice surface and an equal number in the tough skin of the walrus. Then he passed a line back and forth between the ice surface and the walrus to distribute weight and multiply the leverage. Then, pulling on the line, he slowly slid the walrus upon the ice surface where it could be butchered and hauled away by sled.

Birds could be taken in late spring when the ice became unsafe and the hunters had to stop hunting seals and walruses. Nets of sinew were attached to long poles enabling people to catch hundreds of little auks. Large auks were caught in stronger nets among the cliffs and ledges. Ducks could be snared in slip nooses. Other birds might be brought down by bolas, stones tied to each other with long lines that tangle up a flying bird. Bird's eggs could be eaten raw or made into sausages by pouring them into seal intestines and allowing them to ferment. Meat was usually eaten raw and people learned to like fermented meat (*issuangnerk*).

Women could hunt birds in the summer. They could also spear fish through holes in the ice of inland lakes. The fish were attracted by small ivory lures and then speared. Men hunted from their kayaks in the summer: seal, walrus, beluga whale, and narwhal. To haul the large sea mammals through the water they were floated by blowing air into their bodies through a pipe inserted in their bodies. A man in a kayak could tow as many as five belugas in this way. At the end of summer in some locations the families might journey inland to hunt caribou with bow and arrow. They might drive them through rows of rocks arranged to resemble men (*inukhuit*). They might ambush them one at a time, after they have tripped one with lines stretched across a runway. A shooting pit was sometimes made for the hunter to hide in. Or they could spear them when the caribou were trying to ford a stream. Musk ox or polar bears could be driven and surrounded by trained dogs and then speared. Foxes could be taken in a trap shaped like a large stone beehive with a hole in the top. The fox would jump in to get at bait inside and be unable to leap high enough to escape.

Philosophy and Personality

The technical knowledge of hunting would not mean much without the philosophy, personality, and skills of a hunter (Nelson 1976). The Inuit hunter had self-assurance from personal knowledge, observations of hunts, and listening to countless stories of the details of hunts. The Inuit were highly observant of their own surroundings and their own experiences. They related these experiences back to the social group in stories told during the long winter nights. Leading a physically active life, they were in excellent physical condition. They were not very concerned about physical comfort so they traveled lightly. They learned to ignore the discomforts of cold, wet, and physical exertion.

The hunter's life was in hunting. That was where his life's commitment dwelt. Success in hunting was a sign that a man was leading a proper life in religious ways, propitiating good spirits, observing religious taboos. He was alert for signs of game. He had foresight—where the animals would be, when the sea ice would be dangerous. He had great perseverance under difficult conditions—waiting many hours for a seal to come to a breathing hole, or trying to snag a floating seal from shore with a retrieval hook. He did not take unnecessary chances. He did not do dangerous things for excitement.

He had learned to be imaginative, to improvise. Trapped on an icefloe moving away from the mainland Inuit could use a makeshift raft of ice to carry a sled and dog team across open water. An emergency sled could be made from frozen meat. A boat was quickly repaired, a gaff hook was made by twisting a wire, a jammed gun was cleared. Pieces of twisted whalebone were covered in fat, frozen into balls, and left on the fringe of camp to be swallowed by pestering wolves. Inside a wolf's stomach the whalebone would unravel and kill the wolf.

Hunters were cooperative. They worked together without question, selfishness, complaints, or thanks. The people saw a need for assistance and came to help without comment or expectation of reward, and shared the proceeds of efforts; all received shares of the hunt. Distributions were still regulated. For example, an older woman in the house was usually a food boss and no one could take food without her permission. Even gifts of food to children by other households had to be approved by the food boss before being eaten by the children. However, on the trail it was not stealing to take the food one needed from another person's cache.

The Netsilik women cut a seal into fourteen named parts and ideally twelve of the parts were given to the twelve wives of the twelve men who had formal and long-lasting seal-meat sharing partnerships with the hunter who killed the seal (Balikci 1970). Men sometimes even addressed each other in terms of the part of the seal that they received or gave to each other. Thus one receiver would be addressed as "my hind quarters," another as "my shoulder," and so forth. This was a reciprocal system which contributed to strong ties between the families. The system in operation was flexible for smaller groups or to substitute new families if one family in a hunter's sharing system moved away.

It was important to keep social relations running smoothly. Do not disagree openly, except perhaps to mildly ridicule a lazy person. Keep a calm face. Suggest, rather than order. Let people learn things through their own errors. Be good natured and contented with your life. Find humor in your own errors and misfortunes. Respect the *ishumata*, "he who thinks," the person with wisdom.

Although the Inuit did in fact have a lot of control of their lives in the Arctic, they did not see themselves as manipulating the elements of their habitat. They had more individual autonomy than urban people, yet they were more fatalistic than urban people. They saw themselves as minor integral parts of the world of nature. They were capable of extremely decisive actions, such as killing and eating animals for their survival, but had a philosophy that was submissive to the forces of nature. Conceal unhappiness. Do not become overly concerned with other people's problems, out of tact. Be indirect and indefinite in criticism or placing blame on people. Say "if" not "when" in references to the future. Say "one" or "there are those who" not "you" in personal reference.

Social Survival

Inuit kinship structure was similar to the modern European and North American form. Like us, they recognized descent bilaterally or about equally on both the mother's and father's side and did not extend lineal organization into lineages or clans. We have an "Eskimoan" terminology because we use such general terms as "aunt," "uncle," and "cousin" that ignore lineage. This was a kinship system which emphasized families, was egalitarian, allowed for free mobility of the family from one group to another, and was generally very flexible. The Inuit were even flexible on kinship terms so that not all the groups used what kinship experts call Eskimoan terms. This family-oriented, egalitarian, flexible system was characteristic of band-organized hunting and gathering societies the world over, as well as modern industrial states.

It was in the middle evolutionary range of tribes, chiefdoms, and pre-industrial states in which there was a great rise of clans, ranked social classes, and a rigid social system. The common element in bands and industrial states was that independence, flexibility, and egalitarianism were the most efficient when people had to move freely in response to rapidly changing natural resources (in bands) or a labor market-administration (in industrial states). The relatively fixed and abundant resources of tribes, chiefdoms, and early states promoted a more static structure. Then, with industrial states the state itself redistributed resources and people had to move in response to changes in jobs. In addition to flexibility in the kinship system, the Inuit expressed flexibility in such things as easy adoption of children and the accepting philosophy of *arunamut*, "because nothing can be done."

A common North American Native practice was formal friendship between unrelated adults of the same sex, usually living in different communities. The friends visited each other, exchanged gifts, and stayed at each other's house when they visited. Among the Netsilik sharing partners were chosen by a boy's parents in early childhood and these became lifelong friendships. They shared food, hospitality, and sometimes their wives.

The Iglulik had "song cousins." Song cousins had a mild, fun-oriented competition in exchanging gifts and perhaps exchanging their wives when they visited each other. They also competed in singing their new songs to each other, judging them in terms of beauty, composition, and delivery. They sometimes castigated each other in a humorous way. This institution, through a network of friendships that paralleled kinship ties, served a broad social function of maintaining peace and some minor economic exchange between communities.

The Netsilik (Balikci 1970) recognized differences between (1) seal-meat sharing partners, (2) avoidance partners, (3) identical name partners, (4) joking partners, (5) song partners, and (6) wife-exchange partners, although there was, of course, much overlap of these in such a small society. Avoidance partners did not talk to each other, turned their backs to each other when they were in the same house, and would not mention each other's name. People with the same names joked and exchanged identical gifts, such as giving each other their harpoons.

Joking partners were usually friends of about the same age, often living in different communities, who might wrestle each other as well as belittle each other in minor teasing.

Sometimes joking partners became song partners. They would come together at drum dances in large igloos on the ice in the winter sealing time. Each partner would compose a song and teach it to his wife. Before the assembly in the igloo one man drummed and danced his song while facing his song partner and his wife sang his song. Then the drum was handed over to his partner, who drummed and danced while his wife sang. It was a teasing song, but it was still a friendly exchange rather than the *nith* song duel. Often, song partners exchanged wives (*kipuktu*) for brief periods. Wife-exchange partnerships seem to have been quite variable, initiated by either men or women, were short- or long-lasting, and sometimes led to a permanent exchange of mates with the children following their mothers into the new households.

When men had a lifelong training as hunters they could easily turn their killing philosophy and their weapons on each other. The traditional Inuit could kill much easier than we do in modern society. Old, blind, and crippled people were left behind to die when they became too much of a burden on the family. They practised female infanticide to control the population size and in preference to sons who could carry on the hunt. Men died of accidents more frequently than women because of the dangers of the hunt, and also died fighting each other. Thus the sex ratio was balanced, in a brutal way.

The Inuit also practised survival cannibalism. For example, Rasmussen's Netsilik informants told him of a severe winter with famine. The people moved to fish for Arctic cod, but that was not enough. "Some froze to death, others starved, and the bodies of the dead were eaten by the living—in fact were killed to provide food, for these poor people were driven almost mad by their suffering that winter" (1931:120).

The Inuit did not fight over property or material goods, but over social status and interpersonal relations. Most of the disputes were between males and most were over women, especially regarding adultery and wife stealing. There were other causes such as insults over skills in hunting and revenge for an earlier killing. Blood feuds could develop between kin groups. Thus formal friendships and other non-destructive mechanisms of dispute settlement were developed.

Social problems were usually solved by extensive discussion and the development of a working level of consensus. This does not mean that there was wholehearted agreement, but only that people had talked it out and that there was some concurrence on the action that people would take. For example, if a person became a threat to a community by getting into arguments and murdering his enemies, the community would collectively decide to execute the murderer. This decision would normally be discussed with the murderer's own relatives first so that there would be no revenge killings later on.

One important means of resolving conflicts was ostracism and withdrawal. Families were always free to leave one community and join another. When the Thule Inuit of Greenland had a dispute with the local U.S. Air Force base the Inuit community migrated to another site.

The Inuit also resolved disputes through various forms of regulated combat, such as wrestling and buffeting. In buffeting they took turns punching each other on the arm or the side of the head until one person was knocked down. These were simply extensions of the wide variety of physical competitions, recreations, sports, and magical performances of shamans that the Inuit developed. To keep in physical condition and to be entertained they had arm wrestling, foot wrestling, the mouth pull, high kicks, dancing, cat's cradle, single and group juggling, the cup and ball game, and others. In fact people spent a lot of time developing and playing new indoor games, an environmental adaptation to cold weather and long winter nights. This creativity with games is seen in their creation of many variations on western games, with the players agreeing on the rules at the time. Variations of checkers allow backwards movements or kings to move the entire diagonal of the board. Variations of card games allow each new dealer to determine how many cards will be dealt, the wild cards, the winning score, and so forth.

Polar night festivals might go on for weeks, often with a lot of gambling for stakes. There was a ring and pin game, with two people competing to be first to push a pin into a hole in a piece of bone or antler suspended by a thong from the ceiling. There was a roulette game by spinning a long tool. There was a hand game, to guess which hand holds a stone.

There would be tug-of-war contests. Men would compete at high jumping and man-to-man strength tests. In the Mackenzie area a man wearing a frightening "Indian" costume with long hair and a threatening dagger would dance and scare the children. When he was finally forced to leave there would be a shower of toys, beads, trinkets, and tidbits of caribou fat that the children would scramble for. Puppets made from the whole stuffed skins of fox, bear, birds, and so forth were made to behave like live animals by pulling on attached fiber strings. The festival would end with games of darts for prizes.

The Inuit word for shaman is *angakok.* This is one of their performances that Boas (1888:668) described: "An angakok began his incantations in a hut after the lamps were lowered. Suddenly he jumped up and rushed out of the hut to where a mounted harpoon was standing. He threw himself upon the harpoon, which penetrated his breast and came out at the back. Three men followed him and holding the harpoon line led the angakok, bleeding profusely, to all huts of the village. When they arrived again at the first hut he pulled out the harpoon, lay down on the bed, and was put to sleep by the songs of another angakok. When he awoke after awhile he showed to the people that he was not hurt, although his clothing was torn and they had seen him bleeding."

The most unique means of Inuit dispute settlement was the song duel, the *nith* songs. Inuit took pride in their ability to tell stories and make up songs. Narrative songs were a major form of education and entertainment during the long winter nights. The song duel took this medium and allowed an airing of personal hostilities in a socially controlled situation. Each party composed songs about their dispute and in ridicule of the adversary. Each person's version of the disputed events was put into the form of a comic, dramatic, and artistic presentation. The opponent's sexual and hunting inadequacies would be described. The opponent might be compared to animals. Through taunts, distortions, satires, and buffoonery they took turns singing insulting songs at each other while the audience joined in with chants, comments, and essentially cheering and booing.

Along with poetic repetitions and the recalling of specific persons, places, and events these are the kinds of things that were sung: "You were like a wolverine in the tall grass feeding on mice. I made a noise and you ran away. I threw a large arrow at your fat ass. It was annoying to you and you ran away fast." "You had immoral desires for your daughter-in-law. You had to have sexual help from a friend to take care of your wife. People say that you felt your own sister at night. You had no one to go with you, no kinsmen or pretty women."

A participant may drum, dance, or butt heads with an opponent in the performance. Among the Netsilik the wives of the protagonists also took their turns and sang their own songs while their husbands danced and drummed. In some communities these competitions were enjoyed so much that they were kept up year after year, with the families joining in to learn the songs and sing along in support of their favorite. Thus, while the philosophy of the society was highly cooperative and worked to diffuse expressions of anger, the song duel encouraged the expression and acceptable social resolution of anger. The winner was the person who could swing public opinion to his side, but even the loser was respected for his performance and the two sides might exchange gifts in final reconciliation.

The Survival Functions of Art

Inuit art is important to art theory because it came from a survival-oriented society in which art related to survival functions. Art alleviated boredom over the long winter nights and thus saved people from Arctic hysteria and suicide. It served as a carrier medium through which people expressed their emotions without excessively damaging the delicate social fabric of a small community that had to live together and cooperate for long periods in isolation. Art was also a medium for technological and ideological information that helped people know how and why to live in the Arctic.

The aboriginal Inuit were skilled carvers. Though they did not do a great amount of it, they made mostly small figurines of ivory. What they competed in, valued, and were particularly skilled at, was making up and presenting songs and stories. The institution of song cousins contributed to peaceful inter-community travel and exchange. The institution of song duels, the *nith* songs, helped to resolve social conflicts within a community. The people remembered their hunting trips in great detail because they knew that the social telling of them was a pleasurable activity that could go on for hours when there was nothing else to do. Children learned to be hunters by listening to these detailed stories of weather conditions, ice conditions, animal behaviors, and hunting techniques.

Boas (1888:648-9) wrote: "Among the arts of the Eskimo poetry and music are by far the most prominent. Some Eskimo are very good narrators and understand how to express the feelings of the different persons by modulations of the voice . . . Besides these tales, which might be called poetic prose, there are real poems of a very marked rhythm, which are not sung but recited . . . they treat of almost everything imaginable: of the beauty of summer; of thoughts and feelings of the composer on any occasion, for instance, when watching a seal, when angry with somebody . . . Satiric songs are great favorites."

For some songs there were accompanying dances. In the style called "throat singing" two singers placed their mouths together and alternately blew down each other's throat, producing a sound by vibrating their partner's vocal chords.

In modern times the Inuit built on their earlier carving skills to make soapstone sculptures and then later to carve blocks for printmaking. Whites probably bought these sculptures and prints because they recognized real carving skills and that this art was coming out of a primitive aesthetic tradition. Aboriginal Inuit aesthetics was perhaps advanced for a band level society. It is, however, difficult to appreciate the main stream of Inuit art—music, songs, and stories. This intangible oral art is difficult to understand and to appreciate from the outside of a culture, while something like sculpture can be quickly judged by existing Western criteria, and by its exotic source can have the added aura of meaning something outside of Western cultures.

Commentary (Summary)

The Inuit have some biologically inherited or racial adaptations to the cold: stocky build, flat noses, eyefold, higher basal metabolism rate, and fewer active sweat glands. And, like people generally who live and work in cold environments, they acquire a tolerance for the cold. However, their major adaptations are not biological at all, but part of their learned or "cultural" traditions.

The pervasive adaptive features in traditional Inuit cultures seem to have been self-reliance, ingenuity, flexibility, and development of survival techniques. Communications between groups, however brief and infrequent, seem to have been crucial to the maintenance of a full complement of survival techniques. Some techniques were lost in conditions of extreme isolation.

Different conditions in physical environments led to different patterns of exploitation, social groupings, political forms, and meat-sharing arrangements. Thus, the environmental severity and the cooperative sealing on the sea ice of the Copper and Netsilik seem to have led to the formation of larger social groups and to a unique form of seal-sharing.

Inuit clothing, shelter, transportation, and hunting techniques are widely known for their effective fit to Arctic conditions and have been widely imitated by Europeans in the Arctic. Less well known is the importance in Inuit adaptations of their philosophy, personality, social structure, and arts. Whites in the Arctic could learn from these, as well as the more obvious material and technical Inuit innovations.

CHAPTER 5

SUBARCTIC
Northern Algonquians: The Acculturation of Isolated Hunters

THIS CHAPTER FIRST describes the general features of the Subarctic. It then focuses on the northern Algonquians in terms of their personal traits and their experiences of historical acculturation to White society. The sharing and cooperation of hunters, the history of the fur trade, the organization and territories of trappers, and animal conservation are the major themes of research discussed here.

Subarctic

The Subarctic is a wide belt of boreal forests, taiga or stunted forests, tundra, rivers, and lakes that runs south of the Arctic for 4,500 miles from Alaska through Canada to Newfoundland. It is an area of extreme temperatures, with a long cold winter and a short warm summer; freeze-up and thaw are the major climatic changes in the year. The various aboriginal calendars of the north inevitably include a "moon of the freeze-up" in the fall and a "moon of the thaw" in the spring. The breakup of ice on the rivers is a spectacular event with a roaring sound and often great blocks of ice are pushed up onto the shores. When there is no ice one can travel the rivers and lakes by canoe, but much of the land is muskeg or swamp. Rivers and lakes abound in a low, sloping terrain. After freeze-up you can walk everywhere and travel with a sled or toboggan.

Tundra soil is relatively infertile because of its low nitrogen content. The soil is thin or even missing in large parts of the Canadian Shield—in the center of the Subarctic—because that area was scraped clean by the action of continental glaciers. Soil in the boreal forest is thin and too acidic in base materials for many plants. Even if the climate were warm enough, it would be poorly suited for agriculture. Some northern communities, however, do raise a few cold-adapted plants, such as potatoes, for their own use. Various kinds of berries are widely gathered for food in the Subarctic: blueberries, strawberries, salmonberries, rose hips, currents, and cranberries.

The trees of the boreal forest are those that were good "pioneers"; they were able to survive under marginal conditions. As the glaciers moved south over the thousands of years, the forests moved south as well and then when the glaciers retreated, the trees moved north again. These are the spruce and balsam fir, some tamarack and jack pine, and some deciduous birch, willow, alder, and poplar. The forests are carpeted with mosses in the south and with lichens toward the treeline. Because of its wet conditions the boreal forest has large populations of aquatic insects, such as biting black flies and mosquitoes.

The pulp and paper industry has been cutting very heavily in the boreal forests. Thousands of square miles of the slow-growing forest have been cut, thus reducing the animal populations on which the northern Natives depend for their livelihood. The appeal to the industry of those who wish to harvest the wild animals is to leave significant stands of mature trees to protect the moose and other animals in the winter and to leave strips of vegetation along the shoreline so that the beaver will survive.

In the summer of 1970 it was revealed that the mercury levels in fish caught in Lakes Matagami, Waswanipi, and Gull in Quebec were too high for safe human consumption. The chloralkali plant at the Domtar mill had been dumping mercury for four years into the water system. The Natives of those areas were asked to stop eating the fish and the fish plant at Matagami was closed down. A similar sequence of pollution and restriction on fishing occurred in the English and Wabagoon Rivers in Ontario because of mercury dumping by the Reed Paper Company. This mercury pollution was stopped, but it may take decades for the lakes and rivers to recover.

Caribou, Moose, and Beaver

Large caribou herds in a barren grounds area migrate because they use up the feed in wide areas, but small herds in the forested areas tend to move around the same area all year, onto the open ground in summer and back to the protection of the forests in winter. They feed off lichen, mosses, herbs, and grasses. Severe forest fires can burn through the ground-cover of lichens to the soil and it takes over twenty years for the lichen cover to return enough to be adequate for caribou to feed on. Thus fires, along with forest clearing for pulp and paper and the overkill, have contributed to the decline in the stock of caribou.

Moose tend to be solitary, but may congregate in groups of four or five in the winter breeding time. The Indians say that they are the easiest to hunt in the late winter on snowshoes when there is a hard crust on the surface of the deep snow so that the moose cut their legs when they try to run. They are easy to track in the snow and can best be stalked when there is a slight wind that covers the noises made by the hunter. They also travel a shorter distance when frightened than caribou. Moose hunting can be easily combined with beaver trapping because both animals live in aquatic areas.

Trappers today try to avoid shooting beaver because it damages the pelt. Since quotas are imposed the trapper is selective, taking only large animals in the winter, when the fur is in its best condition. Before trapping at a specific lodge the trapper often studies the fresh incisor marks on the "bones" of chewed wood around the lodge for large teeth marks, to ensure that there are large mature beavers in the lodge.

In 1634 the Jesuit priest Paul le Jeune described traditional beaver trapping by the Montagnais. In the spring deadfall traps were set with a wood bait. In the winter they would break open the lodge and then hunt them down their tunnels and where they swam up under the ice.

Three main trapping methods are used: (1) in the runways, snares are set that allow the small beavers to pass through but catch and drown the adults; (2) the beavers are driven out of the lodge and into a net that catches the entire family and then the young beavers are set free; (3) the beavers are trapped in their tunnels by driving stakes across the tunnels and then the tunnels are opened.

Cultural Variations

The western Subarctic had more caribou, buffalo, and musk oxen while the eastern Subarctic had more moose, deer, and waterfowl. In kinship orientation the western area was somewhat matrilineal and the eastern area patrilineal. The Kutchin, Han, Tutchone, and Kaska in the far west had matrilineal clans that one had to marry out of—that is, were exogamous. Those clans regulated marriage and were the focus of funeral feasts that have loosely been called "potlatches" after the west coast feasts. The Ojibwa and Ottawa in the east had patrilineal exogamous clans. The rest were bilateral. The west tended to have bilocal or neolocal post-marital residence and the east had more patrilocal post-marital residence.

From Alaska to the western shore of Hudson Bay the Indians spoke Dene languages. All the societies were different from each other, and were stereotyped by each other and by early writers. For instance,

Chipewyan literally means "pointed skins": their tunics had a dangling tail. They were the most numerous of the Dene, but still had an aboriginal population of only about 3,500. Early White writers stereotyped them for the harsh way the men treated the women.

No band-organized society in the world had an institution of slavery. However, the Cree and Chipewyan had guns earlier than the Slaves, became aggressive, and captured people and made them work on a temporary basis. The Yellowknife got their name for hammering out native copper nuggets into tools and weapons. After their population declined because of disease, they were absorbed by other societies, primarily by the Dogrib, whom they resembled. The Hare and Beaver were named for the animal that outsiders thought were eaten by these tribes, though the diets of the Subarctic hunters were quite similar. The Hare wrestled to settle some disputes, as did the Inuit, who lived immediately to the north of them. The Kutchin wrestled in games from the smallest boy to the largest man to establish a hierarchy in this sport. Sekani means "dwellers on the rocks," which in this case refers to the Rocky Mountains, as the Sekani lived in the upper Peace River country in northern Alberta.

The eastern or Algonquian Subarctic people are noted for their excellence in using bark, especially birch bark, to cover conical and dome-shaped houses, canoes, and containers. The women chewed artistic designs on birch bark. They boiled food in water-filled bark vessels by dropping heated stones into the water, taking the stones out to be re-heated, and so forth. They used a cone of bark as a moose caller, and bark was used to wrap and store food.

The Algonquian Subarctic people became noted in historic times for trapping beaver and fine furs. Thus, much of the story of their acculturation to European Canada is in relationship to the fur trapping and trading industry. However, the most prominent themes of social science research on these people has been on their practices related to land use, territories, and the social organization in hunting and trapping.

The Beothuk lived at the eastern extreme in Newfoundland and are extinct today, in part because of the destructiveness of the earliest contacts with Whites. The other major facts in their genocide were the great evolutionary difference between the simple Beothuk and the European settlers who destroyed them, and the geography of an island home that left them no place to retreat. Travelers in the early 1600s noted that they had stores of dried meat. The Beothuk made vessels of sewn bark in several sizes to cook and to store dried meat, fish, and seabird eggs. They were noted as seal hunters and had large, sea-going canoes. They were seen harvesting the eggs of seabirds on the Fink islands, 40 miles offshore. They also hunted the great auk, a bird that could not fly well and was clumsy, and that therefore became extinct in historic times.

The Beothuk decorated their bodies with red ochre and were given the name Red Indians. Reports of people with red skin coloring became twisted around in Europe so that the stereotype developed, spread, and persists today that the New World Natives have red pigment in their skin. In fact, the red-haired northern Europeans have the reddest complexions in the world. This development of a stereotype against the facts is surprising since Indians clearly have brown skin; and red ochre has been used the world over, including Europe, for body paints. The Anglo-Saxon warriors at the time of their conquest by the Romans preferred to use blue body paints. Because the Beothuk stole from the European fishing stations they were actively hunted down and killed. Shanadithit was the last Beothuk: she died in 1829.

The Micmac or Malecite were in Prince Edward Island, Nova Scotia, and New Brunswick. Living in a coastal area they too made great use of fish, shellfish, seabirds and their eggs, and seals, as well as the land mammals that are so important farther north. In historic times they were far enough south to grow some corn, beans, and squash. The Ojibwa and Ottawa of central Ontario were distinctive in their intensive use of fish, waterfowl, and the wild rice that grows in profusion in shallow water areas around the Great Lakes. The Algonkin live in Quebec and are culturally closer to the Montagnais than to the Ojibwa.

The Cree, Montagnais, and Naskapi spoke distant dialects of the same language in early European contact times and apparently were culturally quite similar to each other prior to the Europeans' influence on them. Their aboriginal heartland was a huge area across northern Ontario, central and northern Quebec, and Labrador. The first use of the term "Canadians" was in reference to a group of Montagnais who lived on the north shore of the Gulf of St. Lawrence. They were people who traded with the Iroquois at Stadacona, a walled town of several hundred people. In historic times the westernmost Cree spread to the north and west and increased greatly in population.

Aboriginally there were about 20,000 Cree, and, in spite of severe population declines due to epidemic diseases, they have more than tripled in population since then. The Cree cultural adaptibility and high rate of population growth have never been explained. The Cree were also the major source of the Metis, particularly through marriages with the French and Scottish. Another unexplained situation is that very few English married Indians.

The Cree today are the largest Native society in Canada, with a population of over 70,000 in six dialectal groups (Ellis 1973). This excludes perhaps an equal number of Metis of Cree heritage who do not usually speak Cree today as a first language. The dialectal groups with their approximate populations are as follows: (1) Plains—28,000, Alberta and western Saskatchewan; (2) Swampy—27,000, western James Bay, Hudson Bay, and westward along the Saskatchewan River; (3) Eastern—7,000, eastern James Bay; (4) Northern—3,000; (5) Moose—3,000, Moose River south of James Bay; (6) Woods—2,000, scattered in northern Manitoba and the Tete de Boule in southern Quebec.

There are now major linguistic differences between the Cree dialects and Montagnais and Naskapi. Since in historic times there developed considerable cultural divergence between these groups, these dialectal categories are also meaningful in terms of different cultures. Using their syllabic writing system most Cree, Montagnais, and Naskapi adults are literate today in their Native language as well as in English or, more rarely, French.

Technology

Pre-European hunting relied on stalking and ambush with spears or bow and arrow, and traps, snares, and drives. Even these techniques did not change very much until the late 1800s. A trap usually catches the animal when it releases a baited trigger. The log deadfall trap, for example, worked when an animal disturbed a baited trigger, causing a heavy log to fall on the animal. A snare is a noose which catches the animal by the neck or leg. With a spring pole snare the animal is pulled up and strangled. With a heavy balance pole snare one can take a bear: the bear reaches its head through a noose to get the bait and sets off a trigger which releases the light end of the pole. The pole sweeps upward, tightening the noose and choking the bear.

Snares are used more for small animals such as hares and are generally set by women or children. These are often set on an animal runway or at a gap between two fences. The snare was of sinew or *babiche*, a thong of rawhide, before metal wire was introduced in the early 1900s.

Fishing was often done with large traps called weirs that were built in a stream, often with wicker basketry to hold the fish. Natural basins in a rapids were sometimes improved by stone weirs to act as fish traps from which the fish could be netted with nets attached to long poles. Nets were also set under the ice after freeze-up by cutting special holes in the ice. In addition they fished with hooks, harpoons, and fish spears.

They made tailored tunics and leggings, often worn with moccasins. Men wore a breechcloth underneath and often a cap. Robes were woven from rabbit skins cut into long strips. The house was usually a small dome- or cone-shaped wigwam with a sapling frame and covered with mats or a layer of spruce boughs. Evergreen boughs could also be laid over the snow on trails between the several wigwams within a community. Lighting was available with bark torches and firelight.

Bags were made from animal stomachs; bladders; the skin, sewn shut at one end, of a caribou leg; and the skin of an entire fish. The Algonquians made wooden and bark spoons and bowls in several sizes. Influences from the outside were seen in some use of soapstone bowls in the north and pottery bowls in the south. A quick knife could be made from the thin rib of young caribou, which has a naturally sharp edge.

Spruce roots, *watap*, were widely used as twine for sewing bark bowls together or sewing the bark covering of a canoe to its frame. The canoe, caulked with spruce sap gum, was light for portages and could be easily repaired from local material in the forest. The dog-pulled sled, as used by the Inuit, was rare. Most people backpacked their goods with the aid of a tumpline strap from the pack to the forehead. For major moves and for hauling in game, the toboggan was used. Babies were wrapped in a bag made from moss, then wrapped in leather or fur, and then lashed to a cradleboard that could be laid on the ground or carried on the back.

Personality

In the 17th and 18th centuries the northern Algonquians were described as stoic, independent, and individualistic. They tried to remain amiable even in the face of personal provocations. The more isolated Algonquians are still introverted, guarding against upsetting emotional experiences. These characteristics seem to have been common among most band-organized hunting and gathering peoples, such as the Inuit and Subarctic Dene, as well as the northern Algonquians. However, there have also been contextual differences in the expression of their personality—in the colonial context and in the context of their own people.

When Indians related to Whites they were usually forced into a subordinate position. Elements of this subordination are related to the cultural gap between living as hunters in a band-organized society and the institutionalized world of an industrial-state society. Thus the Natives from band societies have tried to relate to the state institutions through persons rather than to the institutions—market system, legal system, education system, etc. They have a hard time working with impersonal institutions of all kinds. Social scientists have written about the injustices of placing a few paternalistic Whites in a position of great power in the towns that have developed to service Native needs. These towns, such as Fort Rupert, Eastmain, and Fort George on James Bay, have usually had a small White community connected with the Hudson Bay Company, the R.C.M.P., medical and educational service, and a Christian missionary. Tribal societies, such as the Iroquois, and especially chiefdom societies, such as the Kwakiutl, have been able to relate their own aboriginal institutions to those of the White state society or to rapidly create institutions that could effectively handle Whites. Trading posts were not as necessary among chiefdoms because the chief could assemble all the village furs and bargain directly with a ship captain.

Band societies were too simple, too personally run, and too egalitarian to work without intermediate White brokers through much of historic times. Only now are they in the process of creating effective society-wide institutions to relate to the White institutions. Traditionally they were extremely self-reliant, competent, and confident as hunters, but were forced to express a personality in the presence of Whites that fitted in with a colonial social structure of submission and subordination. Around Whites in town they were described as shy and superstitious by the missionary, sneaky by the trader, and unmotivated by the teacher. The few ethnographers who have followed them into the bush have described them as decisive, skilful, resourceful, and as having a very positive personality. Subarctic hunters learn personal restraint in interpersonal relations and control over the fear, pain, and hunger of a difficult life. They avoid boasting and are hesitant about intervening in the lives of others. However, they are shy only when powerless.

Windigo Psychosis

Mental diseases everywhere are expressed in the terms of the culture in which they occur. The Windigo psychosis was one of the culturally specific syndromes of mental illness that showed this to be true (Parker 1960). It occurred among the traditional Cree and Ojibwa, who believed that it came when people were possessed by the spirit of the Windigo monster. The Windigo has been described in many forms, but in essence it seems to be of giant size, superhuman in strength, filled with rage, and cannibalistic. Some say it is the ghost of a person who has eaten human flesh. It has jagged teeth and claw-like hands. It vomits ice and has a heart of ice, which must be destroyed to kill a Windigo. A person who becomes possessed by the spirit of a Windigo acquires obsessive thoughts of cannibalism and may even attempt to attack and eat others.

The initial stage usually includes such symptoms as depression, nausea, distaste for ordinary foods, and periods of staring and semi-stupor. The individual may become obsessed with bewitchment, homicide, or suicide. He may hallucinate in seeing others in the community as fat, delicious animals. Finally he may become homicidal. There are dozens of documented cases of Windigo psychosis cannibalism, usually involving the killing and eating of a relative. Some say that once a possessed person tastes human flesh he will never lose a craving for it, and he must be killed. Others say that a human Windigo can be cured by eating grease, which will melt the ice inside him. People should never eat ice because it could turn them into a Windigo.

The most common circumstances for the psychosis were among men who had come back from an unsuccessful hunt for food. As these societies had periodic food scarcities, starvation and survival cannibalism did exist. Child-raising was initially free and easy without deprivation, but as the children grew older they were toughened up. They were told that a Windigo would take them if they were bad. There were stories about starvation and cannibalism. Food was withheld to punish a child. The teenage boy's quest for a vision involved days of fasting in search of a guardian spirit; great self-reliance was required. Men were competitive over hunting abilities: Hunting was at the heart of a man's self-esteem and of his belief in supernatural support. A failed hunter could thus believe that someone was working magic against him or that he was worthless, failing in skill or supernatural power. Women too sometimes acquired the Windigo psychosis, usually in connection with interpersonal hostilities, insults, and gossip. The therapy for this illness was a shamanistic diagnosis and treatment to drive out the Windigo, and the revitalization of one's supernatural powers through drumming and singing.

Shamanism and Hunting Magic

In Ojibwa, the regular shaman was called a *Kusabindugeyu*. He received his power from Thunder, Owl, or Whip-poor-will. He treated illnesses by magically removing intrusive objects in the patient placed there by a spirit or by sorcery. He placed a tube on the patient's body and sucked out the disease-causing object, which was often a small feather. Through clairvoyance he might be able to find lost objects or know someone's thoughts. He might demonstrate great feats of strength, such as lifting a man with one hand. The historic Ojibwa developed a church, the Midewiwin Society, that had a healing ceremony with rites that symbolized stopping places on the Ojibwa migration route along the south shore of Lake Superior. The initiates received power from their medicine bags of charms.

Northern Algonquian religion was integrated with the hunting orientation of these societies. Bears, for example, were treated with special respect, apparently as part of an ancient boreal tradition that extended from Europe to northern Asia and North America. Like the bull in the Mediterranean and South Asia, the eagle in North America, and the jaguar in South America, the bear is formidable and dangerous, and is thus respected. The bear is human-like: it can stand on its hind legs, is intelligent, and has only one or two offspring at a time and cares very well for them. A hunter would talk or sing to a bear before killing it. A bear would be eaten with proper ceremony, and its skull would be put in a safe place where the dogs would not chew on it, high on a pole or in a tree.

There were numerous other elements of magic associated with hunting. For example: During menstruation, women were avoided by the hunters. The Naskapi believed that one should not look at the moon while shooting game. They had a special ritual communal feast, called *Mokoshan*, in which they ate the bone marrow fat of caribou. This reinforced the relationship of hunters with the caribou spirits. A hunter might carry a small bundle of charms to help in hunting: These were typically the inedible parts such as beaks, claws; or a weasel skull. In the worldwide practice of first fruits rites, the eastern Cree treated the first goose of the year in a ceremonial way. The head was cut off, dried, decorated, and kept as a hunting charm until the next year. The Mistassini marked the start of the winter hunting season by ceremonially feasting on the first beaver killed. People might decorate the hide of an animal with paint as a sign of respect. Hunters believed that the spirit of an animal could report to its living relatives the treatment given by a hunter. Hunters needed a guardian spirit and at 13 or 14 years of age would stay alone in the woods for several days to fast and to seek a vision, and to meet the spirit of an animal that would become their guardian for life and help in hunting and other activities.

Some men developed a relationship with spirits, a communion that helped to predict where game animals could be found or where to find lost people or objects, and other such things. This kind of shaman, a *djasakid*, would have a small circular lodge about twelve feet high that converged slightly near the top and left an open top. It was built with poles, and for siding had sheets of bark or mats. After dark the shaman was bound hand and foot and put inside. The shaman would sing. The lodge would sway, shake, and thump as the spirits came and went. The thongs that had tied the shaman would fly out the lodge or would be found much later twisted into the top of the lodge or in a distant place. The spirits might ask to smoke tobacco before they went to work and smoke would rise from inside the lodge. The spirits might be sent in search of caribou or moose and then report on what they had seen. The shaman in the lodge would answer questions, using the strange voice of a spirit. Some say that this "shaking tent" ceremony could be used to destroy a Windigo.

Scapulimancy was also used to locate game, particularly caribou, when concrete information about their whereabouts was missing. With this method—another ancient boreal trait—a caribou scapula was cracked over a fire and the pattern was interpreted in terms of geographical features such as rivers with spots of caribou herds. Sun illumination was a blessing given to the devout hunter. Sunbeams breaking through a heavy layer of clouds could be a supernatural sign that game could be found where the streams of sunlight struck the ground. A hunter might place beaver-chewed sticks near his head for good luck in beaver trapping. People learned from their dreams generally, but the dream of sunbeams that struck the ground was particularl auspicious. Other methods of divination were also used: gazing upon a decorated object, a pool of water, or a mirror until the information sought after was given; or noting the position of thrown fish bones. One's power (*manitu*, a pervasive power in man and nature) could be built up by drumming, singing, and smoking.

Sexual Division of Labor

The sexual division of labor is usually as follows (Landes [1971] describes the lives of northern Ojibwa women): The men hunt large game and geese, and trap beaver and fine furs while women snare rabbits and shoot land birds such as grouse and ptarmigan. The men make things of wood, such as toboggans, sleds, snowshoe frames, and spoons; women acquire skill in preparing and dressing the pelts and skins, making things of leather by knotting and braiding, such as the webbing of snowshoes, moccasins, mittens, rabbit skin blankets, and cloth clothing today on sewing machines. The men do the butchering and skinning while women scrape, soften, and smoke the hides. Men repair motors, guns, lanterns, and canoes, and make and repair fish nets and usually make sewing repairs on their own clothing. They cut and haul wood, while women chop and split it up into small pieces. Women cook, wash the clothing, and care for infants and small children. Both men and women work at setting up tents.

Seven Indian women from Fort George, Quebec (1971), produced a booklet as a record of their traditional cooking. The oldest recipes involve skinning and preparing animals for roasting by hanging them over a fire—geese, fish, beaver, haunch of bear, and porcupine. The more modern recipes involve boiling and baking with flour, lard, sugar, and baking powder. Bannock is a simple bread roasted over an open fire, fried, or baked.

"The best pemmican is made from the dried, powdered fish. It can be used with lard, bear fat, caribou fat or moose meat. Smoke the dried fish or meat. Pound it and make a nice powder. Melt the fat or lard. Put the powder in. Mix like a batter. Some people like to add berries and sugar. . . Pemmican is used, especially in the winter, by trappers—when they walk all day and want to travel light" (Fort George, Quebec 1971). Mashed brains or a thick soup of cooked fish eggs can be fed to babies. Teething children are given bones to suck or caribou hide to chew.

"A bride and groom may eat bear meat at their wedding feast, though goose is undoubtedly the most popular menu for such a day" (Fort George, Quebec 1971). The steam tent, *mitdutsan*, is used to cure people or to purify the body. It is made of willows and is covered with a blanket. Three or four hot stones are rolled inside and covered with wet moss to steam. Native women had a knowledge of the medicinal properties of plants, midwifery, and even some surgery. For example, a Naskapi hunter accidentally cut an artery in his arm and his wife sewed up the wound with a needle and thread.

Acculturation of the Northern Algonquians

The northern Algonquians have strong cultural continuity. They are closer to aboriginal life than most other societies in the U.S. or Canada. They usually still speak their aboriginal languages. Much of their food still comes from their own hunting and fishing. They often have a numerical majority in their own territory. Though they have had a large population increase in the twentieth century, young people still usually stay in the area, rather than migrate out to towns and cities. And today they are creating institutions that will ensure Native continuity in the future. Highways and a huge hydroelectric dam project are now being built in northern Quebec, under an agreement that on paper looks like the best treaty any state society has ever had with a band heritage society. The northern Algonquians thus serve as a favorable case in the worldwide history of the impact of state societies on band societies. What has their life been like? In the face of the general destructiveness of states on bands, how did they manage to survive so well? What can we project for their future now that White resource development projects are changing their world?

In the period of major European expansion in the sixteenth through nineteenth centuries people from band societies were usually perceived as hardly human by people from state societies. The cultural gap was so great that personal relationships between people from these two levels of evolution were rare. Band people were occasionally hunted like vermin in Newfoundland; Utah, Nevada, and California in the U.S.; Tasmania; Australia; and South Africa. People from band societies were generally peaceful and gave almost no military resistance to their conquest, but also did not make good servants or slaves. They despised servitude too much. They escaped at the first opportunity and had great self-reliance and capacity to survive on the wild foods of the land.

Canada has a good record of survival of its aboriginal societies, particularly when we consider that it had a high proportion of the world's few remaining hunting, fishing, and gathering societies. Only six of the fifty aboriginal societies of Canada have become extinct: Beothuk, Tobacco, Neutral, Yellowknife, Tsesaut, and Nicola. The Beothuk were exterminated by White settlers (Rowe 1977, Such 1978). The Tobacco and Neutral were reduced by disease, defeated in warfare by the Iroquois, and absorbed into other societies. The Yellowknife were reduced by disease and absorbed by the Dogrib and Chipewyan in the early 1900s.

Four Indian communities north of Great Slave Lake now call themselves Yellowknife; this seems to be only a revitalization of the term. Tsesaut and Nicola were small Athapascan-speaking groups in British Columbia that presumably were absorbed by surrounding Indian groups. As to the remaining 44 societies, there is the question of the history of their cultural change and adjustment to life as an ethnic group integrated within the larger state society of Canada.

Acculturation occurs when two societies are in relatively continuous contact. The most common sequence of acculturation conditions in the New World has been: (1) *trade and war*; (2) *colonialism*, when the Natives were in the majority and were distantly ruled by a foreign European minority; (3) *neocolonialism*, when the Natives became an ethnic minority in their own land. When Natives were being destroyed and removed from the Caribbean, most of South America, and the eastern half of the U.S., northern Canadian Natives moved slowly through these acculturation stages. This seems to be primarily because Europeans were slow to settle in the north. The north has been protected by its isolation. Much of the north is still more colonial than neocolonial, though Whites try to be economically, politically, and ideologically dominant everywhere over Natives. However, when Natives have a clear numerical majority as in the Northwest Territories, they can usually retain some self-pride, social status, and other defences against White domination and destruction of their culture.

The current nationalism of such previously band-organized societies as the Dene and Inuit makes sense because of their colonial, rather than neocolonial, relationships with the Canadians. They now have more political awareness, organization, and coordination than they have had in their entire history. The Dene Declaration, (which opposed the Mackenzie Valley Pipeline) and the Inuit call for a certain degree of sovereignty over their territory, Nunavut, rise out of a creative process of defences against deculturation and assimilation. This kind of ethnic nationalism is not as viable in southern Canada, where the Natives have been a numerical minority integrated into a subordinate position in Canadian society.

Naskapi: Hunters without the Fur Trade

Henrikson (1973) describes the Naskapi from fieldwork in 1966-68. They had little influence from the fur trade because their area was low on fur-bearing animals. Thus the Naskapi are perhaps closer to the aboriginal situation than the Natives in the fur industry. In March and April they hunt seals on the coastal ice, or fish for trout through the ice on the inland lakes; however, seal hunting is relatively new to them, as they were traditionally an inland people and preferred to hunt caribou. In May and June they hunt mainly geese and ducks. In July they fish for cod,

Arctic char, and salmon. A small fish called caplin that schools near the shore is gathered in great numbers on the shore and dried for dog food. In late summer a few hunters might try to go briefly inland to take some caribou for their skins, because the skins at that time of the year are preferred for fur coats. However, the main inland migration from Davis Inlet on the Labrador Sea to the Labrador Barrens is in the early winter. At the time of Henrikson's study 145 Naskapi were exploiting a territory of 15,000 square miles, a density of only one person per 103 square miles. The ecology of this vast territory would not support many more hunters.

No family has special rights to any area or its resources. Since the caribou are so nomadic it would be very difficult to hunt them by designated territories. It appears that aboriginally all the Subarctic hunters made an annual, semi-nomadic round through a given territory with common hunting rights for all. Only when trading posts provided a stable food supply in exchange for furs could a more static territorial system be established in the interest of conservation and the slow harvest of fur-bearing animals. The economic system shifted somewhat from cooperation to competition. This competition increased the necessity for the establishment and support of family territories by the traders in order to prevent over-exploitation and extinction of the fur-bearing animals.

Changes in weapons and in the ecology also undermined the aboriginal style of common rights in hunting. When only spears and bows and arrows were used, cooperation helped in driving and ambushing the animals. The introduction of muskets was a significant advantage over the aboriginal weapons, but it was particularly the efficiency of the modern repeating rifle that undermined the advantages of large hunting units. Once a herd of caribou had been located a single good hunter could kill dozens. A hunter might shoot fifty caribou in a camp with only three families, and other families would often hear of his good luck and move in to share in the meat and skins.

The Naskapi have little elaboration of economic or political power, no tribal politics of chiefs. It is an egalitarian society. Each household is self-sufficient and can make independent decisions about when and where to move, to hunt, or to fish. There is no significant accumulation of property or inheritance. Prestige and leadership flow from physical strength, endurance, skills, and a reputation for cooperation and sharing. Successful male hunters, usually in their 20s and 30s, are the most respected. They hold clear leadership roles within the family and the camp community. Among the Naskapi the position of camp leader is *watshimao*, the "first man" to take initiative (Henriksen 1973). This man's tent becomes the camp center where the day's hunting is described in detail and plans are sketched out for the next day.

The Naskapi do not give or take orders outside of the family, or tolerate meddling in their affairs. They are reluctant to give advice, and when asked for it will often say, "It is up to you." The decision of who will be the "first man" this time for a camp move to a better source of game or on a hunting party is a matter for sometimes rather delicate discussion and consensus. If things are going well and plenty of game is being killed, it does not matter. Two, three, or more hunters will go out, with the most experienced and skilled hunters leading the way. In the hunt they can send each other high-pitched vocal signals for over two miles in the quiet of winter. However, if a leader fails to find game time after time there will be pressure for the less experienced, less skilled hunters to lead the way and make more of the decisions. Leadership can flow back and forth, shifting day to day, adhering to the most successful hunt leader.

When drinking their beer of spruce sap, sugar, and yeast, the Naskapi have an interesting verbal fight called *aienomon*. A man who has a complaint against another will sit in his tent and shout his complaint out, over and over again. The person he complains against will hear the shouts and sit in his own tent and shout back his own answer. The people of the community listen to this shouting match and give appropriate sympathy. Conflicts are also settled by moving one's tent to another place.

Sharing is a pervasive feature of band society, though more for hunters than for fishing or plant gathering societies (Price 1975). This is because meat is more often taken cooperatively and comes in a large single piece. Fish and plants are more often taken by individuals working alone, and are small and scattered in the environment. The division of fish and plants the world over is less ritualistic and compulsive. Among the Naskapi the man who makes a single kill of the camp in one day always gives the entire animal to his hunting companion or to the oldest in a larger party. When they have the meat back at camp it is then shared between all families. If a single hunter kills several caribou he will skin the animals where they lie, return to camp, and allot a caribou to each of the hunters in camp; then each will pick up his allotted animal. It is not an amorphous distribution. People know precisely who is giving what to whom. Still, sharing meat, especially in communal feasts, ensures good luck while hunting. Sharing has a magical effect on hunting success, in that it is necessary to share in order to maintain a good relationship with the supernatural forces.

There is always a social distance element in intimate economics (Price 1975). Meat is the major shared good. Food is a general and frequently shared good. Manufactured objects are usually shared just within the household. Among the Naskapi, the owner of the hook owns the fish taken by the hook. Fish or small game is taken home, cooked, and others might come to share in the feast.

Material goods are circulated in loans and trade, more in reciprocity than in sharing. Store-bought goods and furs taken in a trap move through society as private property in a system of calculated reciprocities. The ethics of sharing are pervasive and still influence even the movement of store-bought goods. Thus, among the Naskapi, children are usually sent to ask someone else for store-bought goods. The goods are usually given, but it is embarrassing to have to ask for them, though it is not embarrassing to ask for meat.

The Fur Trade

Before the Europeans came to the New World they had trapped beaver to make felt hats. The beaver was severely depleted, if not extinct, in western Europe, and by the late 1500s the pelts were obtained at considerable expense, mainly in Scandanavia and Russia. In the eastern Subarctic the Indians sewed beaver pelts together to make a winter robe. Thus, the early European travelers in the New World recognized that the Indian robes were made with skins of value in Europe; they purchased robes and skins and sold them in Europe. A cargo of beaver furs sold very well in Paris in 1581. By 1600 a rush in trapping and trading almost exhausted the beaver along the Atlantic coast and in the Gulf of St. Lawrence. Then there was a slow, steady march of depletion up the St. Lawrence River Valley; radiating outward through New England and southern Canada; up the Mississippi River Valley and through the Great Lakes area; and through the western U.S. and northward through Canada. It was a slow, steady sweep of extinctions and depletions for nearly four hundred years. Only in the past 100 years have there been any significant efforts toward conservation by naturalists, fur trading companies, and Indians.

The trading companies initially exchanged mostly metal tools for furs: axes, knives, pots, and guns. Then the liquor trade became important. Native societies exhausted the furs in their own territories and then became the middlemen in trade for furs from deeper in the interior. The Huron were briefly the chief middlemen, but lost out in a trade-related war to the Iroquois. Then the Ojibwa and Cree became the middlemen and later the transporters for Metis and European middlemen as the trade reached around the Great Lakes and into northern Canada.

Bishop (1974:344) divided northern Ojibwa history into several periods:

1. In most of the 1600s the search for European trade goods concentrated the Ojibwa who were living along the north of Georgian Bay and Lake Superior in patrilineal clan villages. Social life intensified, new economic and social alliances were formed, and communal reburial ceremonies became more important.

2. Dispersal (1680–1730) set in when the fur trade expanded and some Ojibwa moved around the Lake Superior area as traders.

3. Permanent interior settlement (1730–1780) came about as the Ojibwa settled in the last of the good fur-bearing regions in northern Ontario and eastern Manitoba. Midewiwin rituals replaced reburial services as the primary ceremonial.

4. Large game hunting under conditions of competition among traders (1780–1821) ensued as the Northeast Company and Hudson's Bay Company set up trading posts. Hunting groups became smaller and more numerous. The human population in the area doubled in about seventy years and overhunting led to declines after 1810 in the supply of large game and beaver.

5. Dependency on the trading posts (1821–1890) occurred when the trade competition ended. There was a shift to smaller game. Small bilateral residential groups developed and the old patrilineal clans died out. The population continued to increase.

6. Early government influence (1890–1945) and missionaries brought in some integration with the developing Canadian culture, which underwent fundamental industrialization and urbanization changes in this period, while the Subarctic Indians remained relatively conservative.

7. The era of village Ojibwa, begun in 1945, set a pattern for semi-permanent settlement in lakeside villages. The current pattern involves living in government-built houses; a wide use of modern material goods; and a mixed economy of harvesting wild foods, trapping furs for sale, a little wage work when available in the northern bush country, and some welfare and other government-related sources of income.

It is possible to trace several similar changes in the Mistassini and Waswanipi areas in central Quebec. Trapping was unimportant and the fur trade was light in the 1600s and 1700s, but some beaver and marten furs were exchanged for tools and clothing. In 1800–1850 trapping increased, especially of beaver, and the hunting groups became somewhat smaller, just as they were in northern Ontario. In 1850–1900 strict hunting territories and conservation developed. The abstract systems of European measurements were gradually accepted: time, weights, money systems, etc. Chieftainship increased as a form of social organization, and disputes over property rights and trapping areas became common. Canvas replaced birchbark and caribou skins in tent covers. Western clothing replaced hide and rabbitskin clothing. Many European foods became significant. In the early 1900s several important technological changes occurred: Canoes were covered by canvas rather than birch bark, steel traps and snare wire replaced deadfalls and twine snares, and repeating rifles replaced muskets. Shotguns and outboard motors first came in in the 1920s. During 1900–1950 shamanism diminished, and winter trapping of furs became the basis of the economy.

A French trading post was established on Mistassini Lake in 1674. In 1802 it was leased to the Northwest Company of Montreal, which merged with the Hudson Bay Company in 1820. After that, Rupert House became the main post and route to the coast. Once the monopolies were established, the small interior posts were closed and the Indians were encouraged to go to the coastal towns to trade.

Rupert House became the first Hudson Bay Company post in 1668. HBC was the official European power in northern Canada and across the Prairies until those areas were ceded to the Confederation of Canada in 1869. Then federal control was nominally established, but HBC in effect continued to serve as the government of the north until the end of World War I. Revillion Freres, a competing trading company, helped to end both the economic and political power of HBC. For example, HBC was still supplying the outdated muskets, ball, and shot to the Natives in 1900; Revillion Freres competed by offering modern rifles in exchange for furs. In the 1930s the federal government began to make welfare payments and provide social services to the Natives.

Each family came one at a time and spent hours at the Hudson Bay Post in September for their winter outfitting. The trader would study the trapper's record of fur-dealings and grant him credit accordingly. The amount was laid out on the counter in rows of HBC beaver tokens. Food, clothing, ammunition, nets, tobacco, needles, thread, and so forth would then be purchased for use over the next several months on the traplines. This pattern of hunting for most food, and of trapping for furs for exchange with trade goods, maintained these northern Natives in a relatively traditional lifestyle for some three hundred years. However, the Native population growth overcame its earlier losses to disease and continued to expand until it was too large for self-sufficiency. The Metis left when the trapping got bad in the 1920s and 1930s.

Supplies of bush foods were often inadequate, which generated an increasing need to purchase food. That meant that it was necessary to trap more to raise money just for food. Some fur-bearing animals were being seriously depleted, almost to extinction by the 1920s. When the railroad extended to Moosonee in 1932, on the Ontario side of James Bay, White construction workers and professional trappers exhausted the area of beaver in just a few years. James and Maud Watt, the traders at Rupert House, got the Quebec government to establish beaver preserves where only Indians could take beaver—and even they would be given quotas. A preserve was set up in 1932, 7,200 square miles around Rupert House under the Watts' management. This preserve system was introduced in the 1930s and 1940s across most of the southern and central parts of the province. In 1937 the beaver was so close to extinction in Quebec that the government outlawed the killing of any beaver in the province in that year. To this day Indian trappers are assigned territories and quotas for their beaver kill each year.

The quota is normally based on the number of occupied beaver lodges counted by each trapper in his territory in the previous year. In effect, they arrive at their own quotas. They are paid to keep a record of the number of beaver lodges and they become something of forest rangers with responsibility for a certain territory. They get possessive and protective about their territories. Some do not trap the center, leaving it as a nursery area. Quotas range from 6 to 90 beavers per section. A tag is given for each beaver and only tagged pelts can be sold. In the Mistassini region there are normally 7,000–8,000 beaver lodges, and only one beaver per lodge may be killed.

Beaver trapping has shifted from a quantitative, competitive slaughter to a qualitative harvest. The trapper is paid much more for pelts that are large, mature, and undamaged. Trapping today requires several thousands of dollars in capital equipment: a modern canoe, boat motor, guns, nets, tents, a radio, a stove, three or four sizes of traps, snowshoes, and sled or toboggan. Further, one has to buy and transport enough supplies for several months in the forest.

The economic position of trappers has been improving in recent years. Since 1970 the value of furs has strongly increased because of European demand. In January 1977 the average pelt prices at the Ontario Trappers Association auction in North Bay, Ontario, were $30 for beaver (33,815 sold), $22 for racoon (40,469 sold), and $128 for fisher. The top price was $420 for a good lynx pelt.

Quebec Cree: Groups and Territories of Trappers

Hunting groups as local bands had traditional, large, hunting territories. There was consensus that knowledge of and traditional use of an area established a right to continue to hunt in that area. However, this was not an exclusive right. Territories were yielded to common use. It was only in historic times when population pressures built up that family-oriented trapping territories were established at such places as Lake Mistassini and Fort George in Quebec. These smaller, more static, more exclusive territories were possible in central Quebec because the major land animal sought for food was moose, not caribou. Caribou travel in herds and are nomadic, and they are usually sought by a large number of hunters who have to range over a wide territory after the caribou. Moose stay in one place, each feeding in an area of one to two square miles; and can be stalked and killed by a single hunter.

In 1850 there were about thirty bands in central and northern

Quebec and in Labrador. The people were called Naskapi in Labrador, Montagnais in southern Quebec, and Cree in the west. South of them there was a similar array of hunting bands speaking the Ojibwa, Ottawa, and Algonkin dialects. The Ojibwa had some regulation of social groupings and marriages from their clan organization. These were twenty associations, each with a sense of descent from a common ancestor in the patrilineal line and symbolized by a totemic animal such as Bear, Beaver, Deer, Loon, Sturgeon, Turtle, or Watersnake. In modern times the Ojibwa have shifted from the clan totem system to the more flexible bilateral system.

The largest bands—200–300 people—would usually spend at least a few weeks of their summer together, on a lake or river front since summer travel was by canoe. Thus the bands were usually named after the lake or river where their summer camp took place. Summer was the time of trading, marriage feasts, and dancing. Moving back to the bush for hunting, the bands divided into local bands and scattered in all directions. Each local band exploited smaller areas, such as the watershed of one or more of the rivers that fed into the large lake used as the summer camp site. The local band, with 100 or so members, would stay together if exploiting a large herd of caribou: The cooperation of dozens of hunters and the concentration of a food resource would support such a large group. However, ordinarily even the local band would split up and scatter until the actual cooperating hunting groups were only a few families, some 20–30 people.

Rogers (1963:57) compared the data on fourteen bands that were still hunting in modern times in the eastern Subarctic. The size of hunting groups ranged from one to five families—six to twenty-two people—on the average. One, two, or three families were the most common, but one ideal was four families so that there would be two pairs of hunters. Two men, often from different families, usually co-operated to secure a moose, bear, or a small herd of caribou. Two men would often set their traps together. They would either build a communal dwelling (usually a small, one-room log house today) or each family might build its own lodge. The hunting camps ranged from ten to fifty miles apart. Territories ranged from 300 to 2,000 square miles, and averaged 260 square miles per hunter. These were mostly the modern trapping territories with precise boundaries assigned by the government.

Camp locations shifted somewhat from year to year as the game depleted in some areas or the supply of firewood was used up. The Natives liked to have a supply of spruce boughs for flooring in the lodge and that resource became scarce. There were also constant features, and some sites were used intermittently for several hundred years. River and land transportation routes reinforced the repeated use of certain areas.

An ideal location was on the west side of a lake with a small hill in the back. In this way the camp could be set near the lakeshore to avoid black flies and mosquitoes, and be protected from the chill of the northwest wind.

Rolf Knight (1968) studied Rupert House during 1960–1961. He found that the cash income of the Indians derived 40 per cent from wages, 38 per cent from welfare and transfer payments, and 22 per cent from trapping. However, a high proportion of their foods came from hunting, fishing, and gathering.

During 1964–1968 a McGill University team studied the Cree of the Mistassini, Waswanipi, and Nemiscau Bands. Among the Waswanipi many of the men looked for jobs in lumber camps and mining. In all communities some Indians made some cash income by selling firewood, working as guides to White hunters, or doing various laboring and semi-skilled jobs for Whites, such as stock boy, janitor, and maid. Government transfer payments were also important: Family Allowance, Old Age Assistance, Widow's Allowance, etc. Fort George had a small canoe factory which employed Indians. Jobs were somewhat available, but there were language problems in the more developed parts of the province because the employers preferred people who speak French and most of these Indians speak English as a second language.

In 1964 the Waswanipi band moved off their reserve to work in lumber camps or with mining prospectors. Some lived in groups along a new road that was built to link the frontier towns. The Hudson Bay Post at Waswanipi Lake was closed in 1965. Others moved to White towns. In the mid-1960s Harvey Feit found that the Waswanipi were taking 82 per cent of their food from wild foods in the bush. Seventy-nine per cent of the family heads were engaged in some traditional pursuits and 53 per cent were setting a winter bush camp; but 74 per cent took summer jobs. In 1966 a pulp and paper mill was built near the Waswanipi reserve and Indians were recruited for woodcutters and millhands. New roads were cut through their old trapping territories and towns.

The population density in the southern part of the Labrador Peninsula was about one person per two-hundred square miles (1:200) in 1829. People were still self-sufficient by hunting with densities of up to 1:100. However, the Native population increased rapidly in the twentieth century because of an assured food supply provided by the government, increased efficiency in the exploitation of the natural resources, and higher prices for furs. By 1954 the density was 1:66 and the wild-food resources were not adequate to support the Native population. Since then modern medical services have figured in yet greater population growth.

In 1972 an applied anthropology team from McGill University

studied the James Bay Cree situation in light of the possibility of hydroelectric and other development projects in northern Quebec. They found that about 50 per cent of the adult males were full-time hunters and 30 per cent were part-time hunters. The team concluded that hunting had reached its population limits in the north. About 700 hunters and their families are the maximum that the area can support without further depletion of game. "The large increase in young people in the next decade means they will have to migrate out or that many new jobs will have to be created in the North. The hydro-electric project could help to solve the crisis if it is adapted to meet Indian needs and if Natives become an integral part of the planning" (Ornstein, 1973, Vol. III: 227–232).

Conservation

Paralleling the international rise of concern over ecological deteriorations, it has become a dogma among Indian political leaders in recent years that the aboriginal Natives were conservationists. This theme is repeated in poetry and in political speeches to promote Indian land claims. Though conservation must be taken seriously by society, it is a distortion of that cause to perpetuate the myth that conservation is certain if the environment is left to some kind of "natural man." The depletion of game in historical times has had a great impact on the quality of life for Native hunters, and they have every right to press the morality of conservation on society as a whole. Traditional Native ideology, in both its supernatural and rational dimensions, was conservationist in that humans were an intimate part of the ecological patterns of nature. They believed that their success at hunting was related to their individual supernatural power or *manitu* and that it was ensured by a special rapport with the spirits of animals. However, all this is quite different from the actual conservation of animals.

There is strong evidence that the Natives were a major cause in the extinction of over one hundred species of the large mammals they hunted before Whites came to the New World. Then they joined Whites—who brought their more destructive weapons—in the full-scale slaughter of many more species, including the smaller animals and birds, such as the great auk and the passenger pigeon. The caribou have been overkilled in most regions of Canada because of human overpopulation and the ease of hunting these herding animals with rifles. Also, logging and forest fires have shifted large parts of the Subarctic ecology from a moss or lichen cover that favors the caribou to the grasses, bushy fields, and shrubs that favor the moose. Therefore hunting in the James Bay area has shifted during historic times from the herding caribou to the moose. The moose survives better than the caribou because it is more solitary, more erratic, lives in bushy or swampy areas that are hard for men to travel through, and is more difficult to hunt than the caribou. The caribou was eliminated in historic times from the James Bay coasts and is now rare anywhere in the southern part of the Labrador Peninsula. The caribou population in Canada has fallen to some 20 per cent of its aboriginal numbers, from 2.5 million to 500,000.

When Indians in the Plains received horses and guns, they began a massive overkill of the buffalo. This was decades before the Whites entered the Plains in any significant numbers to take part in the slaughter. When the Whites came, their slaughter was so wanton that it shocked the Indians. Whites often killed just for sport, something unheard of among Indians. Whites often took just hides, and the tongues as a delicacy. The Indians usually used the whole animal though there were cases of Indians slaughtering game and taking only the choice parts. In one case in the mid-1700s, the Cree rationalized that the more animals they killed the more there would be, a form of magical thinking. Before the Whites entered the Plains in numbers, the Indians on their own were depleting the herds at a rate that would have destroyed the buffalo in a few more decades.

Trade in musk oxen robes, especially following the decline of the buffalo herds after 1880, brought them close to extinction. The musk oxen were finally protected in 1917, when there were only five tiny herds left in the Barren Grounds. Fox, muskrat, and mink have fairly well maintained their numbers, but beaver and marten declined disastrously. Beaver are easily located and caught; thus, beaver were actually exterminated throughout most of the U.S. and through southern Canada.

Edward Rogers researched the subject of conservation among the Mistassini Cree. He wrote, "There is no evidence to suggest that the Mistassini are or were interested in the conservation of resources. . . . The term 'conservation' is employed in this paper to mean a conscious effort by an individual or a group to refrain from indiscriminate slaughter of game. . . . In the early contact period . . . game of all kinds was slaughtered whenever the opportunity arose . . . data suggest that conservation was not practised until the latter part of the nineteenth century. The practice then lapsed during the second quarter of the twentieth century" (1963:72). The areas around Native reserves and towns today are typically over-hunted and Indians have not imposed hunting seasons or preserves on each other.

Conservation and game management seem to be modern inventions brought about by the extreme depletions and extinctions of one species after another. The only aboriginal exception I could find was the Nootka of Vancouver Island, who restocked overfished streams with salmon eggs. Conservation was forced on the trapping Indians by concerned naturalists, and by large fur-trading corporations who wanted a long-term, orderly harvest of a moderate amount of furs, rather than a sudden harvest that would clean out the fur-bearing animals entirely. It is a case in which the actions of capitalistic, multinational corporations turned out to have long-term social benefits and preserve not only the fur-bearing animals, but a relatively traditional way of life for the Indians. When Natives speak of conservation they are repeating a lesson they learned through the destruction of animal populations by themselves and Whites and through the fur market system.

Today there is a need to conserve not only animals, but plants as well. For example, in the James Bay area the Natives, by removing the bark, have seriously depleted the birch forests along the coasts near their major settlements. Spruce has been depleted around many settlements by its use as firewood, and cedar has often been over-exploited for such uses as canoe ribs. This is, of course, a minor issue today compared to the Whites' cutting thousands of square miles of forests for timber, and the pulp and paper industry; but it is something Native communities will have to face in the future.

James Bay Agreement

The large-scale development of hydroelectric dams, forestry, and mining in the northern 60 per cent of Quebec began in the 1970s and forced a long-term settlement between the Natives and the governments of Quebec and Canada. The publicity has emphasized both the mercury pollution caused by a pulp and paper mill and the massive hydroelectric project on the La Grande River, though there are also fifteen major mining areas in northern Quebec.

In 1898 Quebec's northern boundary was extended to the Eastmain River—without reference to Native rights. Then in 1912 the border was extended north to Hudson Strait, and the federal government explicitly assigned an obligation to the Quebec government to settle northern Native land claims. Thus, the province of Quebec had a legal mandate similar to the federal government's mandate to Indians in the rest of Canada. However, it almost never exercised that mandate, and it virtually ignored the Indians until the time of the Quebec separatist movement after the late 1960s. Then Quebec began to behave as a nation that had special obligations to its internal colony of Indians. On the federal level in the 1960s, such French Canadians as Prime Minister Pierre Trudeau and the then Minister of Indian and Northern Affairs, Jean Chretien, supported both the assimilation-oriented policy that had worked so well in southern Quebec, and the *provincial* control of services to Indians. These measures led to the White Paper on Indians in 1969; it was soundly rejected by the Indians, particularly those of the Prairie provinces where racism has historically been extreme and the Indians were particularly alienated from White society.

In 1969 the Indians of Quebec were first given the right to vote in provincial elections. In 1971 Quebec's Dorion Commission recommended that the province recognize the special rights of Native people and reach an agreement with them. In 1972 Indians living on reserves in Quebec were excluded from the 8 per cent provincial sales tax on moveable goods because their social services were still being paid by the federal, rather than the provincial, government.

In 1971 the province announced the James Bay hydroelectric project. Officials of the federal Department of Indian Affairs and Northern Development (DIAND), the provincial government, and Indian and Inuit organizations met and established a standing tripartite committee. Studies were done, discussions went on for three years, and the Cree and Inuit went to the courts and got a brief injunction to stop the James Bay project. With $5.5 million in federal grants and loans, the Native associations of Quebec took the initiative in research, in the courts, and in the negotiations. In 1974 an agreement in principle was reached and in 1975 the final agreement was signed.

The agreement supports the hunting way of life and the conservation of game. There is also compensation of $225 million, exempt from taxes, which will be paid over twenty years. Natives are employed to hunt for the widows, orphans, and other welfare-dependent people in each community; run a northern wildlife management service and a regional police force; and sit on boards that control the industrial development of northern Quebec. The Native languages are accepted as languages of administration, along with English and French. They have their own school boards.

Lands in and around the 22 main Cree and Inuit communities are reserved for their sole use and will be administered by their own regional and local councils. On these (Category I) lands the Natives have exclusive hunting, fishing, trapping, and forestry rights. Sub-surface developments on these lands must be approved by the Native communities. In Category II lands the Natives have exclusive hunting, fishing, and trapping rights, but do not have exclusive occupancy rights. In Category III lands only the species of animals important as Native food and as furs are exclusive to Natives.

Some Whites were upset over the James Bay agreement because the development of the north will lead to its environmental deterioration. Some Indian leaders were upset because the Quebec Cree and Inuit agreed to cede their sovereign rights to their ancient territory. Other Indian groups immediately began to ask for what the Quebec Cree and Inuit got. The Naskapi of Schefferville, for example, wanted in on the same benefits and rights. The Natives living on the islands in James Bay, Hudson Bay, and Hudson Strait, who had in the past been administered by the Northwest Territories, wanted a similar agreement. The honesty of the administration of the agreement will, of course, be crucial in the long run. However, in its present form, the agreement's support of a traditional way of life is better than the Alaskan land settlement of a few years earlier. (See McCullum and McCullum [1975] for a general review of Native land claims in northern Canada and Berger [1977], O'Malley [1976], and Watkins [1977] for discussions on modern development in the Northwest Territories.)

Commentary

Band-level societies the world over survived only on the environmental fringes of the world: in forests in Southeast Asia and the Congo; deserts in the western U.S., Mexico, Australia, and southern Africa; and in the Subarctic and Arctic of Asia and North America. The more viable areas were taken over by agricultural, pastoral, and intensive-fishing societies, thus absorbing, displacing, and acculturating the simpler hunters. In Canada this displacement occurred with the Iroquoian expansion into southern Ontario and Quebec, with the Blackfoot conversion to horse pastoralism, and with the spread of intensive fishing in British Columbia. This displacement process was accelerated with the European conquest and colonialization of the Western Hemisphere.

The Naskapi is a northern Algonquian group that has survived as somewhat traditional hunters with a very low population density in a poor and isolated environment. The Quebec Cree continued as hunters because their involvement in the fur trading system (1) gave them economic support, (2) was a factor in their seasonal scattering over the landscape in search of furs, and (3) introduced trapping territories and other conservation methods.

The fur-trade system had disadvantages. The monopolistic elements in the trading network reduced the Natives' potential income. To the extent that the Indian, Metis, and White societies of the north developed into a single class-structured society, the fur trade system re-enforced the subservient position of the Indians. Where fur trade monopolies did not develop, the overkill of game tended to eliminate the hunting way of life. Where fur trade systems did not develop because of the natural scarcity of fur bearing animals, as in the Naskapi case, the Indians were not better off than the Cree, who were involved with the fur trade system. In the sense of the value of cultural continuities, the fur trade monopolies were beneficial to the north. Now the James Bay agreement, which like the fur trade system has been widely criticized, is supportive of a continuing harvest of fish, fowl, furs, and food mammals in northern Quebec.

Canada is fortunate in having the survival of so many hunting societies. There is still an old current of "social Darwinist" thought around, by which it is morally right that these weaker societies with their "inefficient" uses of the environment should die out. However, modern evolutionary theory has taught us that there is great value in diversity. And new humanistic perspectives are helping us to understand values beyond materialistic efficiency. Canada should treasure these societies. Although they cannot be kept as museum pieces, Canadians should encourage their survival and learn from them.

East to West: A Pictorial Essay

Onondaga town. Attack by the Hurons and Algonquians and the French Auxiliaries, 1615. (Public Archives of Canada.)

THE ILLUSTRATIONS HERE are classics, derived principally from paintings by George Catlin and by Paul Kane, and photographs by Edward S. Curtis. Since these artists often posed their subjects, the results are usually formalistic. The artists produced their materials in a romantic tradition for Whites, but they also wrote realistic background materials on their pictures.

Catlin became sufficiently acquainted with Indian customs in the 1830s to see their practical and humorous sides. In one painting here he illustrates the bow-and-arrow method of hunting buffalo. In another, an Indian speaker has gone on so long that snow has covered the listeners—you see only their feathers sticking out of the snow. Catlin exhibited his paintings in a traveling "Indian Gallery" show that people paid to see.

Raised in Toronto, Paul Kane saw Catlin's Gallery in London, talked to Catlin, and was inspired to set off in 1845 on an Indian-sketching odyssey from Ontario to the Pacific Coast. At the end of the century Edward Curtis began systematically to record traditional Indian cultures in photographs. Most Catlin paintings went to the Smithsonian Institute and many Kane paintings ended up in the Royal Ontario Museum. The Curtis photographs were published in twenty volumes called *North American Indian*. Most of the Curtis photographs here are available in 35 mm transparencies from the National Film Board of Canada and in prints from the Public Archives of Canada.

By the time of Curtis the Indians were wearing European-style clothing and Curtis was trying to reconstruct images of an earlier way of life. For instance, he had the traditional style of cedar bark garments made for his Pacific photographs. Catlin, Kane, and Curtis all preferred subjects who were physically attractive and prominent, such as chiefs. If we understand these kinds of distortion, these illustrations are still the best visual descriptions we have of that early way of life.

Inside an Iroquois longhouse. From an early drawing by R.J. Tucker in the Parker Museum in Rochester, N.Y.

Micmac domestic scene, Nova Scotia, published in 1833 by Lt. Robert Petley in Sketches in Nova Scotia and New Brunswick. (P.A.C.)

Assiniboine mother and child with cradleboard. (P.A.C.)
Right: *Assiniboine hunter with pack dogs.* (P.A.C.)

Ojibwa camp on Manitoulin Island in Lake Huron, 1845, by Paul Kane (1859:5). Inside their birchbark tents, he said, it is warm, but "The filth, stench, and vermin make them almost intolerable to a white man." (Royal Ontario Museum.)

Assiniboine bowman. (P.A.C.)
Right: *Blackfoot religious society bundles.*
(National Film Board of Canada.)

Stampeding buffalo into a compound near Fort Carlton; by Kane. The dry grasslands were fired to drive game into a two-acre log enclosure. (R.O.M.)

Hunting buffalo with bow and arrow; by Catlin. (R.O.M.)

Listening to a very long speech while it is snowing; by Catlin. (R.O.M.)

Inside the Piegan tipi of Little Plume, on the right, with his family. On the floor between Little Plume and his son are a pipe and a tobacco cutting board. Hanging from the walls are such things as large decorated hides, a sacred medicine bundle, and an arrow case. His son, Yellow Kidney, is sitting in the rear of the tent, the position of honor. (P.A.C.)

Conclusion of the Blackfoot Sun Dance in which
the dancer tears his own flesh with thongs
skewered to his body. (P.A.C.)

Right: Blackfoot (Piegan) couple with horse
and loaded travois. (P.A.C.)

Salish interior with a dog in the foreground that has been shorn for its wool, woman with shaped head in the background spinning the wool, and woman in the foreground weaving on a continuous warp loom. The child in the cradleboard to the left has its head wrapped to flatten the forepart. (R.O.M.)

Inside a house in Nootka Sound, 1778, showing clothing, cooking, sitting benches and mats, interior designs, and drying fish; by John Webber. (P.A.C.)

A Nootka (Hesquiat) woman illustrates the traditional woven bark cape, the burden basket held by a tumpline to the forehead, and digging for roots. (P.A.C.)

Left: *A summer fishing lodge on the Skolomish River. Notice the use of mats to cover the lodge, the use of both woven bark and fur strip robes, and the carved animal head at the front of the closest dugout canoe. (N.F.B.)*

A Kwakiutl (Oagyuhl) wedding party arriving in large canoes. (P.A.C.)

The Kwakiutl bridal group in front of the house. In the center is the bride with the ring in her nose. On each side of her is a dancer hired for the celebration. Her father is on the left and the groom's father is on the right, behind the man with the box drum. (P.A.C.)

Kwakiutl masked dancers assembled in front of a chief's house for a portrait, around 1910; by Curtis. Their performances were held indoors by firelight with dramatic staging, actions, and sound effects. (N.F.B.)

Nootka attack on the Coast Salish village of Iehnus on Juan de Fuca Strait. (R.O.M.)

*Makah whaler from Cape Flattery, Washington,
shows his great harpoon and floats. These people
are related to the Nootka, who were also involved in
whaling.* (N.F.B.)

IROQUOIA
Huron and Iroquois:
Warfare among
Tribal Farmers

Agriculture

THE RICHNESS OF buffalo hunting on horseback in the Plains and the salmon fishing of the B.C. coast are unusual developments in the world. Most tribal societies in the past three thousand years have been simple slash-and-burn gardeners—horticulturalists—rather than hunters or fishermen. Agriculture tends to displace other forms of food production.

Agriculture is usually such an efficient form of food production that populations that used it expanded and thus migrated outward in all directions from the centers of domestication. Agriculture is also diffused by borrowing between societies. In the New World the major center of plant domestication was highland Mexico, where plant-gathering societies began domesticating and growing their own plants several thousand years ago. They started with avocados, then added gourds and squashes, then beans, and finally, corn. These cultigens and horticultural techniques first spread slowly through Mexico, but increased sharply once well developed.

After about 1500 B.C. agriculture swept south through Central and South America, east through the Caribbean Islands, and north through North America. By A.D. 1000 there were secondary centers of domestication in new ecological settings: Colombia and Venezuela (giving us the tropical plants such as peanuts, tomatoes, sweet potatoes, pineapples, chocolate, and manioc [tapioca]); highland Peru (white potatoes); the Southwest U.S. (the domestic turkey and varieties of corn with a deep root system for arid lands); and the Mississippi Valley (the sunflower, used for the oil from its seeds; and quick-maturing varieties of corn for the short growing season of the northern temperate climate). With few exceptions—e.g. California, which already had rich food resources in acorns, fish, and shellfish—agriculture spread to wherever it could be practised with the cultigens and techniques then available. Agriculture did not spread north into Canada much beyond southern Ontario because the growing season is not long enough for consistently good corn crops. If the northern Indians had used the white potato of the South American Indians in the Andean Mountains, they could have carried agriculture somewhat farther north, because it is a cold-adapted plant from a cold natural environment. Given enough time, domestication-oriented societies might also have domesticated the buffalo, caribou, and moose, just as wild cattle, reindeer, and horses were domesticated in Asia. In recent times moose have been tamed and used to pull sleighs, but true domestication requires selective breeding. The northern limit for good crops of tobacco aboriginally and still today is southern Ontario and Quebec.

This chapter describes the Iroquoian-speaking farming tribes of Ontario, New York, Pennsylvania, and Ohio.

The Iroquoians

The Iroquoian language family was divided into two branches: the Cherokee and Tuscarora in the south, around North Carolina and Virginia; and the rest in the north, around Ontario, New York, Pennsylvania, and Ohio. According to glottochronology estimates, Cherokee and northern Iroquois separated from each other about 1000 B.C. and the northern Iroquois diversified into several languages after about A.D. 700. These separations and diversifications were probably a direct product of population growth, and spread because of the greater productivity of agriculture. The Iroquoians split off from the western Siouans, who continued a hunting way of life. The population of the most northern Iroquoians in the 1630s was approximately 56,000: Huron-Petun 20,000; Neutral-Erie-Wenro 20,000; and five New York Iroquois 16,000 (Seneca 7,000, Cayuga 2,000, Onondaga 3,000, Oneida 1,000, and Mohawk 3,000). The Susquehanna (also called Conestoga) were Iroquoians who lived in Pennsylvania south of the New York Iroquois and were loosely allied with the Huron against the Iroquois.

The Erie were south of Lake Erie and the Neutral were around the eastern end of Lake Erie. The Neutrals had 40 villages and a population of 12,000 in 1640, after three years of population decline due to war, famine, and disease. The Wenro were probably a sub-tribe of the

Neutrals, with about 1,000 people. They were located between the Neutral and the Seneca. So many of their warriors were killed by the Seneca in the 1630s that in 1638 they abandoned their territory; and more than 600 people, mostly women and children, migrated 175 miles north and were assimilated into the Huron villages.

The Iroquois were five distinct tribes who lived in the lake country of northern New York. Their territories were long north–south strips from Lake Ontario to about the Pennsylvania border. The three western tribes spoke dialects of the same language—Seneca, Cayuga, and Onondaga. To their east were the distinct languages and societies of the Oneida and Mohawk that linguistically separated from the other Iroquois after about A.D. 800. The east–west spread of these societies was from about the Genessee River Valley to the Mohawk and Hudson River Valleys, with a concentration south of the Adirondack Mountains.

In the 1500s there were Iroquoians along the St. Lawrence River, apparently speaking dialects of Huron-Petun. Jacques Cartier found the village of Stadaconna in 1534, at what is now Quebec City. Some of the people there were Iroquoian-speaking and they lived in a large palisaded village with longhouses; there were about 1,000 inhabitants. They subsisted on fishing and hunting, presumably because corn farming is difficult that far north. The village of Hochelaga, where Montreal is today, had 1,500 people in about 50 longhouses. The village was circled by a triple palisade and was surrounded by large corn fields. When Samuel de Champlain landed there in 1603 these pioneering St. Lawrence villages at the fringes of the agricultural world had been abandoned.

The Huron lived in southern Ontario, concentrated by the time of European contact in villages between Lake Simcoe, Georgian Bay, and Lake Huron. The Petun villages were immediately southwest of the Huron. In the late 1630s the Huron-Petun had 20,000 people (2,000 warriors) but an epidemic reduced the population to 9,000 Huron and 3,000 Petun by the late 1640s. Huronia proper, the densely settled area, was 340 square miles and had a density of 60 persons per square mile. The true territory of the Huron comprised several times as much land, including their regular hunting and fishing areas and the buffer zone of southern Ontario used in Huron-Iroquois warfare.

Although the vocabulary list of the St. Lawrence Iroquois indicates a close linguistic affiliation with the Huron, it appears that they were at war with each other and that the Huron destroyed and absorbed the St. Lawrence Iroquois. The historical data show that the Iroquoians vanished from the St. Lawrence Valley in the 1500s. The archaeological data show that the St. Lawrence Iroquois styles of pottery at the same time entered the Huron tradition while the styles of pipes did not. This is what we would expect with conquest because women made pottery and were usually taken as captives, while men made pipes and were usually killed in warfare. Over the centuries, and during this supposed Huron-St. Lawrence war, the archaeological data show a withdrawal of the Iroquoian occupation north of Lake Ontario, presumably because of the need to create a defensive concentration. The oral history of Huronia collected by the French in the 1600s supports this view, indicating a slow defensive concentration of palisaded villages at great distance from their enemies, who were all Iroquoian-speaking peoples.

Other theories about this Huron migration and concentration, such as better soil for farming in Huronia or better trade connections, are simply not supported. The soil was as good as or better than the soil in the areas they came from. There was moderate trade prior to the White fur trade, but there is no evidence that primitive horticulturalists were dependent on it or that they relocated to take advantage of it. The Hurons received tobacco from the Petun and Neutral and wild forest products from the Ottawa. Several families of traders were enough to supply their needs.

By the 1600s the St. Lawrence Iroquois had been eliminated. The Huron and Petun had overcome a history of hostilities between each other and formed a confederation allied against the New York Iroquois. The Neutral-Erie were trying to remain neutral in that war, but would occasionally conflict with the westernmost of the Iroquois, the Seneca. The Neutral also had hostile relations with the tribes to the west in Michigan, Indiana, and Illinois, loosely called the Nation of Fire and probably including such people as the Miami, Saux and Fox, and Illinois. Since the ethnographic descriptions in the early 1600s are best for the Huron, we can begin with them as a generalization for the early northern Iroquoians (Heidenreich 1971, Sagard-Theodat 1939, Tait 1971, Tooker 1967, and Trigger 1969).

The descriptions are best for the Hurons because the French explorers and missionaries were trying to establish mission stations among the largest and most tractable Native populations. The French failed to rise above the petty warfare between the Indian tribes, particularly in the case of the conflict between the Five New York Iroquois tribes and the remaining tribes. Although the French sent many missions and peace embassies to the New York Iroquois, these usually were unsuccessful. Thus the French were allied mainly with other Indians against the Five.

The Huron

The Huron had eight cross-cutting, exogamous, matrilineal clans that were very important in terms of marriage patterns, personal identity, and ceremonial life. The village segments of these clans had their own chiefs, councils, and even treasuries to sponsor trading expeditions and to pay debts against the clan, such as the blood money paid for murders. The structure of these clans, the specific totemic animals identified with each clan, and probably even the emblems used to portray the clans, were almost the same as those of the Iroquois: Bear, Beaver, Deer, Hawk, Porcupine, Snake, Turtle, and Wolf. Pan-tribal sodalities, associations *not based on common residence*, provided important and permanent links *between* the scattered villages, links that helped integrate the society. This integration is the essence of their *tribal* level of cultural evolution.

The Huron were sufficiently integrated in linguistic, economic, and political ways (through their confederation called *Wendat*) in the 1630s to be referred to as a single tribe. The confederation was primarily of the major villages as represented by prominent chiefs, but there was also a recognition of historical, geographical, and political clusters that we might call sub-tribes. The west to east sequence of these sub-tribes was as follows (Heindenreich 1972):

1. *Attignawantan* (They-of-the-country-of-the-bear) in the Penetang Peninsula. 13–14 villages. They were one of the founders of the confederacy, some two hundred years before the French came. Since the Attignawantan were about as large as all the other sub-tribes combined, they sat on one side of the council meetings and the other sub-tribes were arrayed along the opposite side.

2. *Ataronchronon* (People-beyond-the-intervening-swamp) from the Wye River to the Sturgeon River. About 5 villages. This sub-tribe seems to have formed during the time of French contact from villages previously associated with other sub-tribes and by the Huron who settled for protection near the Jesuit fort of Sainte-Marie on the Wye River. (Today this fort has been reconstructed as a provincial park.)

3. *Tahontaenrat* (The-place-of-white-thorns) in the upper watershed of the Hog River north of Orr Lake. This was a small sub-tribe with only one large village who joined the confederacy only in about 1610 and probably did not have an official position on the confederacy council until somewhat later. This is the sub-tribe that joined the Seneca after the Iroquois-Huron war, indicating that they were the least integrated into the union of sub-tribes.

4. *Attingneenongnahac* (They-of-the-barking-dogs) in the higher land between the Sturgeon and the Coldwater River. Three or four villages. They claim to be one of the founders of the confederacy in the 1400s.

5. *Arendaronnon* (People-of-the-rock) between Coldwater River and Lake Couchiching. At least four villages. They are reported to have joined the confederacy in about 1590. One village of Huronized Algonquians lived in the northeastern part of their territory close to Lake Couchiching. These people had once lived on the St. Lawrence River and came to the Hurons as refugees from Iroquois warfare.

Their confederation—if that is the term for a true tribe created from a collection of bands who speak the same language—was similar to but stronger and more unified than the league of the Iroquois (*Hodenosaunee*, People-of-the-longhouse). The Huron confederation was extended in a strong alliance with the neighboring Petun (Tobacco), who spoke a dialect of the same language as the Huron. The Petun had nine villages. They also had mild alliances with the Neutral, Erie, and Susquehannah. The Huron and Neutral called each other The Stammerers because of linguistic differences. The Hurons also had peaceful and cooperative trading relations with the hunting and fishing Ottawa who lived in proximity to them around the shores of Georgian Bay and on Manitoulin Island.

Villages

The Iroquoian longhouse (*ganonchia*) had a half-barrel or quonset hut shape, like a long, bark-covered, circular archway. Doors were at each end; and also in the sides of the longer structures. The walls started with two parallel lines of vertical poles bent toward each other and combined with other poles to form the top of the arch. This frame of poles was covered with slabs of bark, except for a line of smoke holes about twenty feet from each other. The smoke holes could be widened in the summer and narrowed in the winter by shifting the bark on the roof. A town crier went through the village calling for assistance in building a new house, but it was mostly done by the lineage that used it.

Longhouses varied in size, according to the size of the lineage. The average dimensions were 25 feet wide, 25 feet high, and 80 feet long. They ranged in length from 40 to 220 feet and in width from 18 to 30 feet, with the height always about the same as the width. Hearths were set along a central passageway, seasonally changing in size from several feet long for heating in winter to small cooking fires in the warm months. The families were nuclear, and lived in bunks or sleeping platforms on each side of the longhouse and shared the fireplaces in the center. Each family used one side for 12 to 20 feet. The bunk beds were in a pole frame with a bark floor one to four feet above the ground to avoid the chill and dampness, but not so high as to catch the smoke from the fireplaces. In winter, the inhabitants would sleep in their fur robes.

Storage areas were provided in vestibules at the ends of the longhouse, special areas set aside occasionally along the length of the longhouse, and in upper side bunks and in the rafters. Storage barrels were made of bark, and baskets were often made from the splints of black ash wood. There were also bark-lined storage pits dug into the ground in some areas. It was necessary to keep a large quantity of dried corn, beans, and squash, and to protect such things as fish nets, snowshoes, clothing, and dry wood.

Each longhouse belonged to a matrilineage headed by an influential older woman. The longhouse ideally included her husband, unmarried sons, daughters, and their husbands and children. It might also include the matron's sisters and their families. Since the Iroquoians adopted people captured in warfare, there might be some of these as well incorporated into the matrilineage and the longhouse. The women of the longhouse, and their children, belonged to the same matrilineage which formed a matriclan with other lineages related through the female line. The longhouse had the name, and sometimes the clan totemic insignia, of the dominant matrilineal family painted in red outside (Bear, Beaver, Deer, Hawk, etc.). The men usually moved into the longhouse of their wives when they were married, though there are recorded cases of patrilocal residence. The men could be divorced and required to leave the longhouse, thus returning to the longhouse of their own matrilineage. On divorce a man had no claim to the children he fathered.

The Europeans who stayed in longhouses complained of the smoke of the fires, dust from an earth floor, fleas, mice, and the lack of privacy from children and dogs; and said that people wiped their dirty hands on their hair or on a nearby dog, and that small children were allowed to urinate on the longhouse floor. Lice got into the fur bedding. To remove lice from furs, the side without hair was placed close to the fire; the lice would then emerge. Some longhouses had features such as a small sweating room. The longhouses of major chiefs were larger than others and were used for council meetings, feasts, and dances in the winter. In the summer outdoor public assembly areas were often used.

The longhouses were five to twelve feet apart to prevent the spread of a fire, and were usually built parallel to each other to conserve space, often facing the prevailing wind (to clear out the smoke?); and were arranged in clusters of related lineages.

The large villages had palisades, particularly those around the frontier of Huron territory that faced the south and east, the direction of Iroquois attacks. The palisade was built of one, two, or three tight rows of upright posts with their bases buried in the ground. It varied in height from 15 to 35 feet. The poles often had an interlacing of branches and bark. Galleries were built inside the palisades from which the defenders could shoot at the enemy, drop rocks on those trying to climb the walls, and throw water to put out fires set on the walls. The entrance was a narrow passageway, so narrow that one had to squeeze through it sideways, and it closed with horizontal sliding bars.

Village sites were always chosen with several factors in mind. A good supply of drinking water from a spring or a stream was important. There had to be arable soils nearby, preferably well-drained, sandy loams which were easy to clear and work though not as fertile as the silt and clay loams. Firewood was necessary, as was a large supply of poles for construction: a village of 1,000 people in 36 longhouses with a palisade required about 20,000 large poles. These were best taken from a secondary forest with smaller trees rather than from a primary forest. The villagers preferred easily defended sites in local topography with steep slopes on one, two, or even three sides; and they took advantage of natural obstacles such as swamps. Several villages were located on short streams that flowed north into Lake Huron. These streams would not be used by the Iroquois who came from the south, but would allow the Huron to travel freely northward for fishing and trade.

Villages were usually 4–5 acres in size, 800 or less in population. Larger villages were seats of authority in the sub-tribes and the residences of important chiefs. All the villages were economically self-sufficient. None had markets or specialized manufacturing. The people communicated over a network of trails along the high ground. Runners carried messages from village to village to announce important council meetings or other news. This travel was not extensive; the people lived and worked most of the time near their village, except in the warm months, when the men traveled widely in their hunting, warfare, and trade. Fishing camps were established at a moderate distance from the villages along the major streams. Away from the village the people made small bark shelters on a framework of three main poles.

Courtship, Marriage, and Divorce

Courtship among the Iroquoians was, compared to other primitive societies, a surprisingly romantic relationship which included the use of music and love songs. This type of courtship probably emerged because of the strong sexual division of labor in society, the relative freedom of women, the practice of monogamy (the only exclusively monogamous Native societies in North America were the Iroquoians), and the strong economic value of women. The young men were apparently more concerned about their beauty than the women. Thus, the women let their hair fall down their backs often in a single braid, while the men used several fancy hairstyles. The girls were as active as the men in initiating sexual liaisons. The women produced and prepared most of the food. Thus the blood money paid to relatives for the murder of a woman was significantly more than for a man. Some said that it was 30 presents for a male and 40 presents for a female.

Premarital sex often led to loose, trial marriage relationships called *asqua* which could lead to formal marriage. In *asqua* the couple lived together and carried out the male-female roles, but without parental arrangements, approval, or gift exchange. If the girl became pregnant she could choose a husband from among her suitors. Even in formal marriage there was a trial period of spending several nights together, and the girl would receive gifts such as shell bead necklaces and bracelets. After that the girl had to decide whether to accept the man or not, but even if she rejected him she could keep the presents. If she accepted, her parents would hold a marriage feast for the relatives on both sides.

The Iroquoians also had sororate and levirate marriages: when a wife died the widower might marry his sister-in-law and when a husband died the widow might marry her brother-in-law.

It was desirable to have children but the average family had only three. This low number seems to have been due to both a high infant mortality rate and the fact that women might not have sexual intercourse while breastfeeding a child—which went on for two to three years per child. Women were expected to prove their courage in childbirth and not cry out. Divorce was easy and could be initiated by either party; the man might be told to leave the girl's longhouse, or he could return to his own matrilineal longhouse on his own initiative.

Religion

Huron religious life included the old band-level concerns of shamanistic curing, hunting taboos, and rituals related to nature. Thus, all things had spiritual power (*oki*) which men tried to use to their advantage. The *oki* of the sky was the most powerful because it controlled the seasons and other natural phenomena; feasts were given and tobacco was burned in honor of the sky. One avoided offending animal spirits: Animal bones were not burned or fed to the dogs. Fish nets were never displayed before the dead. Shamans were concerned about illnesses caused by unfulfilled desires or dreams. Thus, a desired object or action was identified and given to the person or the desired action was acted out.

The advanced tribal character of Huron religion was expressed in cyclical religious ceremonies and in the establishment of social associations with predominantly religious functions. For example, the Huron had a winter festival in which the people feigned madness and demanded objects they had claimed to have seen in their dreams. The objects would be given. Then the madness would be ritually cast out. The Huron and Iroquois had medicine societies organized to cure illnesses through propitiation of a specific class of supernatural beings. Each society had its own songs, dances, rituals, charms, masks, drums, and flutes. In one Huron society the people ritually killed each other with charms. Another society handled burning charcoal and hot stones. Another danced as hunchbacks carrying sticks and wearing wooden masks. The Iroquois medicine societies were False Face, Bear, Three Sisters, Pygmy, Otter, Chanters for the Dead, and Eagle. Each society had its own techniques. Otter sprinkled water on a patient with corn husks. Bear blew on a body. False Face sprinkled hot ashes on a patient's head.

Four kinds of large feasts were regularly held, with food, smoking, songs, and dancing, for (1) thanksgiving—to celebrate, for instance, a good season of fishing or an escape from danger, (2) curing someone, (3) a dying man to say goodbye to his friends, and (4) the "singing feasts"— for the more egotistical reasons of announcing that one is going to war, to announce receiving the name of a deceased chief, or just for renown as a giver of feasts. Sometimes even the war captive that was being tortured to death was allowed to give a farewell feast.

The most famous Huron feast was the Feast of the Dead, held during a mass reburial ceremony. When deaths occurred there was a local funeral and a temporary burial or placement of the body in a bark casket on a raised platform. The death was publicly announced throughout the village and the people refrained from using the name of the deceased unless they added an honorific term to it. At a Feast of the Dead the bodies were dug up, the bones of old burials were stripped of their flesh (but the bodies of recently deceased people were kept intact), and all were wrapped in beaver robe bundles and carried to a tribal-wide burial place. In a huge mass grave the hundreds of bone bundles and bodies were taken out of their robes, thrown in a pit lined with beaver robes, somewhat arranged with poles in rows and layers, and covered with beaver robes, sand, a wooden shrine, and a ring of wooden poles. The largest ossuary excavated, at the village of Ossossane, had some 1,500 skeletons. A Feast of the Dead was usually held every time a village moved and the old village was used as the site for the cemetery. For any particular village a move was only every eight to twelve years; one or two Huron villages would probably move each year, each offering itself as a site for a Feast of the Dead.

Economy

The average Huron diet was 65 per cent corn (about 1.3 pounds per day); 15 per cent in the other domesticates of beans, squash, and sunflower seeds; 10 per cent fish; 5 per cent meat, such as deer, rabbit, bird, turtle, and clam; and 5 per cent wild forest products, such as wild rice, berries, nuts, roots, maple sugar, and leafy vegetables. Dogs were raised to be eaten at feasts and ceremonies. Dry corn was usually pounded into a flour in a log mortar. This flour was then boiled in water in a pottery vessel to make a corn gruel (*sagamite*), fried on a hot stone griddle or baked under ashes to make small loaves of unleavened corn bread, or baked in a wrapping of fresh corn leaves to make a deep-dish corn pudding with bits of fruit or fat like Mexican tamale. It was made into a succotash stew by adding beans and usually some meat or fish. The special sweet varieties of corn were raised and eaten, sometimes without cooking and sometimes by burying in mud to make a fermented food called *liendohy* or "stinking corn." A variety of popcorn was raised and popped. Corn was also roasted and eaten on the cob. Squashes were either boiled or baked.

There was only one family meal, usually late in the morning. Then people might also gather for a more informal meal in the evening, but usually they would take snacks of sagamite, corn bread, cold hominy, or whatever had been prepared in the family pot. The men ate first and by themselves. Everyone ate squatting on the ground, sitting on their bunk bed, or standing up; and used their fingers. The food came in bark dishes, carved wooden bowls, and woven cornhusk trays.

The annual cycle started with the winter season of manufacturing (mats, nets, snowshoes, clothing, pottery, woven bands of shell beads or *wampum*) and feasts, gift exchanges, dances, gambling, story telling, political council meetings, religious and curing society meetings, warrior team meetings. Winter was a period of intense socializing. In the warm months the people scattered out: the women and children worked in the fields and the men fished or traveled long distances for hunting, warfare, or trade.

The women gathered and stored great quantities of firewood. They prepared skins and made clothing; pottery; basketry; wove mats of reeds, bark, or corn husks; and made leather bags, tobacco pouches, and hemp fiber cordage. The men made wooden bowls and ladles, fishnets, clay and stone tobacco pipes, bows, arrows, blowguns, shields, armor, axes, and adzes.

The men, wearing snowshoes, hunted deer in late winter when the deer, having difficulty traveling through the ice-encrusted snow, yarded together. In April the men would help the women cut and burn the forest cover for new fields. The women and children would then plant in May; hoe the weeds and protect the fields from birds, insects, and rodents through June, July, and August; and harvest and dry the plants for storage in September. Thus for six months of the year the women and children usually lived and worked in and around their fields. They might set up whistles that could be blown by the wind to scare the birds; and set traps and snares to catch the scavenging birds and rodents. They would also range into the forests to gather wild plants, particularly in the late summer, but would still usually have someone behind to protect the fields. A few men were selected each year to stay around the village to defend the women and children from the Iroquois warriors, but even they usually ended up fishing in the local streams. For example, the narrows between Lake Couchiching and Lake Simcoe were blocked off each year by a huge weir made with rows of stakes except where the fish traps were set. The villages were almost empty in summertime.

The Ottawa bands also ranged out for hunting, fishing, and fur trapping in the warm months; came back to settle near the Petun in the cold months; and traded their forest products for corn and beans. Other Algonquian bands regularly met Huron traders in the late summer. This pattern of peaceful symbiosis between a hunting band and a farming tribe has occurred all over the world: Semang-Sekai in Malaya, Pygmy-Bantu in Congo Africa, and Southern Paiute-Hopi in the southwest U.S.

Huronia has an average growing season of about 140 days, but frosts in some years reduce that close to the limit of some varieties of corn. One of the two main varieties planted by the Hurons ensured against a loss of the crop due to frost. A less preferred but safe variety (flint) matures in only 90 days and the preferred one (flour) matures in 120 days. The Huron raised 15 varieties of corn, 60 varieties of beans, and 8 varieties of squashes, though an individual matrilineage farming together would actually plant only a few varieties of each. Corn came in many colors: white, red, blue, brown, yellow, black, and speckled. Corn, beans, and squash were called The Three Sisters. A woman's religious association society was responsible for performing rites, involving costumed dancers characterizing these three plants, to ensure the fertility and productivity of the crops. Tobacco growing, pipe making, and smoking were male activities among the Iroquoians. The Huron imported most of their tobacco from the Petun and Neutral.

Seeds were selected by such factors as size, taste, color, and rapid maturation of the plant. Corn kernels were usually germinated in a bed of moist bark in the longhouse. The women used small seed baskets divided into three or more compartments for different varieties of corn or for beans and squash seeds.

The fields were prepared by girdling the trees to kill and dry them and by cutting the brush. When the field was dry the loose plant material was piled against the trees and the whole field was burned. The burning returns some nutrients to the soil, reduces acidity, and stimulates bacterial activity; but burning is detrimental in the long run because it decreases the organic matter available to the soil. The charred tree stumps were left in the field. Using moose antler or deer scapula hoes the women hoed the earth into mounds one pace apart between the stumps. Holes were made a few inches deep in the mound with a digging stick. Several kernels of corn and a few seed beans were placed in the holes. Sometimes the corn was allowed to grow a little and the beans were added later around the corn sprouts. The corn stalks supported the climbing beans while the beans added nitrogen to the soil. Over one hundred acres were planted in crops around all the large villages.

After only three or four years of use the fertility of a particular field would decline. New fields farther away would be opened up, but they too would lose their fertility in a few more years. The firewood in the surrounding forests would be gradually cleared out, and the women would complain about the distance they had to walk for firewood. The poles for house and palisade construction would be used up. After eight to twelve years at one site, a village would be moved. Usually it was moved only a few miles, though the long-distance moves discussed earlier that resulted in the concentration of villages in Huronia probably occurred at these times. Once abandoned, it took about thirty years for the fields to recover their fertility enough to be cleared and used again.

The economic distribution involved (1) extensive *sharing* within the lineages; (2) some calculated *reciprocity* in ceremonial exchanges, payments, gambling, and inter-societal trade; (3) public *redistribution* through feasts. Within the lineage the prepared agricultural land and the stored food was drawn on as a collective pool of resources, but manufactured goods were essentially owned and used by nuclear family households. However, special pools of manufactured goods such as belts of wampum, clothing, and nets were built up by lineages and clans as a kind of public treasury administered by the chiefs for long-distance trade, blood money payments, prisoner exchanges, and to negotiate peace settlements. Sharing is characteristic of the *intimate* economy of band-level societies and continues in all later cultures. At the tribal level reciprocity begins to flourish in the *private* sector beyond the household. Finally, chiefdoms see the expansion of a *public* sector in which there is political control and redistribution of economic goods for the general welfare. Thus, we see elements of chiefdom economics emerging in the chief's treasury fund.

Traders were part-time specialists even before White contact and the European fur trade. It seems that they acquired and defended their trading routes and contacts as a lineage-owned and -operated feudalistic enterprise. Apparently some fishing sites were also owned; it was considered theft to take fish from a privately owned fishing site. Rights to trade routes were acquired in the process of their discovery and pioneer use. The pioneer trader's lineage and clan then sponsored and shared in the trade route. Permission to use a lineage's trade route could be granted in exchange for presents. Aboriginally the Huron trade was probably for such lineage and clan needs as tobacco from the south and furs and birchbark canoes from the north, without much wealth or power to the traders. The trader gave corn meal, wampum, and fish nets and acquired goods to gamble with at dice or on sports such as lacrosse and to give away on ceremonial occasions. Some of these "masters of the trade routes" became important chiefs through their manipulations of wealth. This was because of the extreme utility of the iron tools of the Europeans, particularly guns for warfare and hunting.

Politics

The daily longhouse affairs were run under the longhouse matron, who had authority over her daughters and their children. The matron's husband, even though an outsider, had a voice in certain *longhouse* matters; and the matron's brothers, being in the same lineage, had a say in *lineage* matters. Only men were chiefs. Local clan segments within a village had their own civil and war chiefs who represented them in their respective civil and war council meetings.

The office of civil chief was usually held for life, but a civil chief could be deposed for gross incompetence. Though the society was generally egalitarian, the chiefs and their families constituted a slightly wealthier, privileged, and powerful social class. Succession of civil chieftainship was partly inherited because the selection was usually made from the maternal nephews of an existing chief. His own sons were ineligible because they were in a different lineage, but his sister's children were in the same lineage. Wisdom and ability at oratory were essential for the office. The people cultivated their ability to remember speeches. There was an age-grade element in which men usually gave up warfare as they grew older, about in their 30s, and took up the duties of politics, religion, and curing societies. The ceremony of succession usually took place in spring at the grave of the previous chief and involved a reiteration of the titles and duties of the office.

War chiefs arose by demonstrations of the charismatic leadership of raiding parties, bravery, and ability as warriors. The councils of war chiefs had separate memberships and duties, occasionally at odds with the decisions of the civil councils. One routine problem of the civil councils was to keep down the level of warfare, and for that reason they are sometimes called peace chiefs. The civil councils were concerned with keeping enough young men around in the summer to defend the villages from the enemy. This conflict of interest was recognized to the extent that civil chiefs temporarily withdrew from their civil offices when they went to war. Also, war chiefs could and often did become civil chiefs, but had to give up the war chief position. Councils of war chiefs met in the house of the most prominent war chief or that of the initiator of a campaign.

Some lineages within each clan and village were more important than the other lineages of the same clan. Chiefs from these primary lineages represented the clan in the village and at tribal civil councils. They were concerned with new construction and such things as feasts, dances, lacrosse matches, and funerals. Civil councils acted as courts for theft, witchcraft, murder, and treason, as well as routine matters such as agriculture and trade. The civil council usually met in the longhouse of the most prominent chief, who also acted as the head of the council and as something close to a village chief. At this and higher levels of government there was some transfer of political representation from a kinship to a territorial basis.

In warm weather the councils were usually held in the open and could be attended by all the older men, those over about thirty. Women had no formal part in the councils. The participants were all allowed to speak at length, often first summarizing the way they saw what had been said before and then giving their own opinion. Each speaker ended with the formal phrase that translates as "That is my thought on the subject," and the assembly responded with a strong *haau* or *hohoho*, a sound of approval. Finally, the council chief would summarize the consensus and announce the decision to the village. The decisions were not binding on individuals.

The Huron had councils of the sub-tribes, each village represented by at least the principal village chief or his deputy. The head chief of the principal village of a sub-tribe had some broad powers of representation and administration. He could grant or deny the passage of foreign groups across his territory. One was entrusted with all matters pertaining to the tribes the Huron visited along the shores of Lake Huron. Another was considered by the Huron to be somewhat in charge of the alliance with the French. The recognition of the head chief and the principal village could shift over the years. Seating at sub-tribal councils was in groupings by village. If a major chief and his deputy were absent a council meeting could be dissolved. The most important chiefs might be given presents prior to the meeting to influence their opinions, though this bribery seems to have been controversial. There would be an exchange of greetings. The convening chief would outline the issues and ask advice. Then in a ritual language of metaphors and speaking in a high-pitched and quavering voice the speakers would summarize other points of view and present their own view. Finally, the convening chief would summarize by giving the majority point of view.

At an even higher level a tribal confederacy council would be held at least once a year to discuss the defensive alliance. This council could prepare treaties, symbolized in the exchange of the woven bands of shell beads called *wampum*. The Huron sent a black wampum belt as a declaration of war.

League of the Iroquois

The Huron confederation was apparently similar to that of the Iroquois in the 1640s but, because of the Huron destruction, their league never developed the ceremony and elaborate procedures that flourished in the League of the Iroquois in the late seventeenth and through the eighteenth centuries. These confederations are one of the major routes of developing the political integration characteristic of chiefdoms. These societies were involved in an evolution from a tribal to a chiefdom level of cultural evolution and the confederation was a military, political, and economic institution created to centralize decision-making. The presence of the White trade in guns and steel tools for furs at first stimulated that confederation process in the seventeenth century, but the dominance of the White state institutions effectively ended Iroquoian sovereignty and redirected the evolutionary processes to that of an ethnic group within a state society.

The expansion of the principles of local government into a confederation never works very well. It is one thing to project the longhouse as a symbol of the whole society, but a society cannot operate as a longhouse. Genuinely new, broadly integrating institutions needed to be created; and that creative process was disrupted by the interference of White state institutions. As the Iroquois declined in power the League changed accordingly into a sub-cultural, ethnic revitalization institution.

In time the League of the Iroquois developed elaborate myths, symbols, and rituals about their *Hodenosaunee* or People-of-the-Long-house. The League had 50 titled positions: 9 Mohawk, 8 Seneca, 14 Onondaga, 10 Cayuga, and 9 Oneida. Each tribe had one vote and unanimity was the rule: each tribe had veto power. The origin story was that Deganawida, the Master of Life, assisted by his disciple Hiawatha, an Onondaga chief, founded the League. Hiawatha lived at a time of devastating blood feuds among the Iroquois tribes. His wife and children were killed in one raid and he took refuge in the forest, where he became a cannibalistic hunter, preying on travelers. Then the deity Deganawida made him his spokesman. (Anthony Wallace suggested that Deganawida and Hiawatha may have historically been the same person, with a split personality.) Hiawatha traveled from village to village to establish inter-tribal peace.

The conventional date for the founding of the League of the Iroquois is 1570. For the first hundred years or so it seems to have been essentially a reciprocal, non-aggression agreement without an elaborate institutional structure. The older Iroquois civil chiefs managed to channel the raids of the young men to tribes outside the confederacy, principally to other Iroquoian tribes such as the Huron and Erie. In 1614 the Dutch at Fort Orange began to provide steel tools and, reluctantly but increasingly after 1641, guns to the Iroquois. Slowly the gun supply of the Iroquois increased until they were the best-equipped in the northeast, while the French missionaries refused to arm the Hurons.

The League was never a static government, but a loose and continually changing confederation with the rule that no tribe could attack another tribe in the League. League officers were drawn from tribal officers. It was symbolized as a longhouse with the Mohawk guarding the east door, the Onondaga tending the central council fire, and the Seneca guarding the west door. The Onondaga were flanked by the Cayuga on the south wall and the Oneida on the north wall.

The early military success of the Iroquois did not come from the superior organization of the League of the Iroquois. It did not function well as a unified government until about 1690, though it was somewhat unified in wars after 1660. By 1660 the Iroquois were universally hated by all other tribes in the region, and coalitions of tribes formed to attack the Iroquois war parties. Hunt (1940: 7–8) wrote, "Despite the bluster of

Mohawk orators, there is not a single recorded instance of unanimous or anywhere near unanimous action by the League prior to 1653, and none save in peace treaties thereafter . . . The Hurons . . . kept peace with their Algonquin neighbors with no organization whatsoever, no ties of consanguinity, no common tongue or social institutions . . . Rarely did two of the cantons combine in an attack, and then only because their commercial interests were for the time identical. Never did two cantons combine for defense. Mohawk and Onondaga both cheered the French attack upon the Seneca, and Seneca and Onondaga were steadily antipathetic to the Mohawks, who . . . held the Hudson River country and the Dutch trade."

Warfare

The major studies about Iroquoian societies have tried to explain the ferocity of their warfare, torture, and cannibalism (Hunt 1940, Otterbein 1964, Trigger 1976). The specific question often focuses on the five tribes of the Iroquois proper. How were the Iroquois able to kill off the Petun, Neutral, and Erie; contribute significantly to the destruction and dispersion of the Mahican, Huron, Susquehannah, Mascouten, Miami, and Illinois; contribute to a long-term military harassment of the French; and fight against the Americans in the American Revolution? Warfare was important to all the Eastern Woodland tribes, but the Iroquois were the most successful at it for three hundred years. The Iroquois are therefore the only large group of Indians remaining in the northeastern U.S. and the major proportion of the southeastern Canadian Indians today.

Early Iroquois warfare was first explained largely in terms of innate Iroquois ferocity. Then the explanations shifted to the sophistication of political confederation. In recent years, especially since George Hunt's *The Wars of the Iroquois* (1940), the explanation has been that they carried out warfare as an extension of an economic, materialistic, competition to control the fur trade. Hunt saw them as capitalist entrepreneurs exploiting a hinterland of resources. Killing tens of thousands of their Indian neighbors in the 1640s was only incidental to business as usual. In this section I suggest several causes.

According to a variety of behavioral studies, mammals do not have a significant instinct for aggression against their own species. Of the aggressive instincts they have, most are mild, expressed in such things as the romping play of young animals that vie for position in a group. Humans have evolved toward mild emotional reactions, and have much less physical strength than other primates. Probably as co-operation and communication in human social communities increased, violent or strong individuals were eliminated by each other because they did fight.

Intelligence was selected over strength or rage reactions. Postures, gestures, vocal calls, and threatening positions, rather than simple physical force, are used by both humans and other primates to establish their social orders.

Band societies, as one type of social order, are generally peaceful and passive in social relations. They have elaborate peacemaking mechanisms within their social groups to soften, deflect, and control anger. Among band societies, those whose subsistence is based primarily on plant gathering (Washo, Paiute, Western Shoshoni) tend to be more peaceful than those which depend primarily on killing animals for a living (Inuit, Subarctic Indians). Thus the band heritage of tribal societies is important in patterning their participation in warfare. Tribal societies with a plant gathering heritage, such as the Pueblos of the U.S. Southwest, have much less warfare than tribal societies with a hunting heritage, such as the Iroquoians. Given a secure food supply with agriculture the Pueblos turned to elaborate religious, aesthetic, and social activities, while their warfare was largely defensive.

The Iroquoians had had agriculture for only about 800 years when they were contacted by Whites, and farming had been their predominant form of subsistence only for the last part of that. Thus they were still close to their hunting heritage and continued it in occasional hunts, with the character of sport hunting. The Iroquoians never developed elaborate religious ceremonies such as the Pueblo calendar of Kachina rituals. Their handicrafts were crude whereas the Pueblos expressed a rich and creative artistry in pottery, sandpainting, costumes, songs, dances, cotton cloth robes, and in other media. Iroquoian pottery was almost standardized in form, utilitarian in use, not very waterproof, unpolished, and unpainted. Pueblo pottery was produced in a wide variety of forms, both utilitarian and ceremonial, waterproof, polished, and painted. Although they lived in a forest, the Iroquoians did not develop much in the way of wood carving; the bowls and masks they did carve were rare enough to be considered valuable. When metal kettles were introduced the Iroquois stopped making pottery and carved bowls; the Pueblos continued their crafts.

What the Iroquois men did develop, however, was warfare, and had probably been doing so for several hundred years by the time of the first French descriptions. Related signs such as cannibalism began appearing around A.D. 1300 and proliferated around 1450–1500. After the Iroquoian shift to agriculture the women alone could produce enough food to sustain the entire society. Since the men were only marginal in the production of subsistence foods, they turned their energies to what might be called the masculine games of life—war, politics, religion, and long distance trade. Pueblo men played a key role in their agriculture and elaborated religion and art.

Two other background features in the warfare of tribal societies are their poor development of institutions to resolve intersocietal conflicts and the diffusion of warfare patterns from one society to the next. The increase in food production by tribal societies leads to increased population densities and more inter-societal contacts and potential conflicts. Tribes then develop such inter-societal institutions as trading partnerships, reciprocal feasting, territorial agreements, and political confederations. Warfare is also a new institutional means to define inter-societal relationships.

Finally, warfare spreads because avoiding it is structurally difficult: under offensive attack, a settled society must defend itself to survive. One militant society can force the militarization of its neighbors. There is evidence that some patterns of warfare spread all the way from Mexico to the eastern U.S. and southern Canada, soon after the spread of the domestication of plants. There are some strong similarities in war-related practices among Iroquoians, in the southeast U.S., and in parts of Mexico: "The sacrifice of prisoners, the removal of the heart, the killing of the victim on an elevated platform and in view of the sun, and the cooking and eating of all or part of the body" (Trigger 1969:53).

These are ideas about why tribes often go to war: (1) economic surplus, (2) continuity in masculine roles, (3) the transfer of skills and habits from hunting (and eating) animals to hunting (and eating) men, (4) the resolution of inter-societal conflicts, and (5) the diffusion of warfare throughout a region. The early northern Iroquoians (Huron, Petun, Neutral, Erie, Susquehannah, and Iroquois) were all involved in warfare. The central problems here are to explore what that warfare was like and the Iroquois role in the destruction of the other Iroquoian societies.

Huron-Iroquois Warfare

Traditional warfare was more an athletic event than a military event. It was usually fought without central control of the forces—in fact with little discipline or command at all. When enemy raiding parties met there was usually a shouting match that ended when a few people on each side had been hit by an arrow or clubbed on the head (the greatest danger was the later infection of superficial wounds).

In most raids, warring parties would kill and capture women and children without encountering significant opposition by warriors. The rationale of revenge-killing was to avenge lives from similar social groups. The killing of a child was seen as a positive act if done to avenge the killing of an adult. Other, less common raids, were on little, undefended, outlying hamlets. A further type of battle, seldom seen, occurred when enemy warriors who met by surprise lined up on opposing sides in a field, fired arrows at each other, and retreated when a few men were hit, or rushed in and clubbed the enemy.

There were occasionally well-organized and prearranged battles in the field, almost like a sporting competition. For example, in 1609,

Samuel de Champlain, two other Frenchmen, and 60 Montagnais met some 200 Mohawks in a historically important battle. The chiefs of the opposing sides met and arranged for the combat on the next day. The Algonquian chiefs assigned each man his place and part by carefully arranging as many sticks as men and drilling the men. On the day of battle the Mohawks advanced in an orderly way, led by three chiefs with large plumed headdresses. The Montagnais landed their canoes on shore, formed an advancing rank, and then Champlain was let through an opening in the ranks. Champlain fired his weapon and killed two of the leading chiefs and wounded the third, though they were wearing their arrow-proof armor. Many Mohawks were killed and prisoners taken. This battle impressed on the Iroquois the need for their own guns, the futility of armor against guns, the need for more mobility, and the need for surprise attacks.

Raiding parties were usually composed of units of only several men under an experienced war chief. One custom was for a war chief to invite· young men to a dog feast as an invitation to join his war party; the dog would be symbolic of a human being. Specific attack plans were made in secret, because the captives who had been taken in earlier raids and incorporated into Huron life were not always loyal and might get word back to the enemy. Also there was some spying, by persons who dressed as the enemy and entered enemy villages. The warriors shaved their heads for battle except for a central lock of hair left in defiance, to say in effect to the enemy warrior, "Take it if you can." The war party would leave the village marching off in silence, in a single-file procession, wearing their best clothes. They might wear a headdress made with a cap of fur or woven splints and a cluster of feathers. Chiefs sometimes wore horns in their headdress. At some distance from the village they stopped and changed into their old clothes, which their women would bring and exchange for their best clothes. On return they would stop at the same place and send messengers into the village to tell of their return and prepare for their reception. War feasts were given for the 500–600 Hurons who would take part in the annual summer raids.

Weapons were principally the bow and arrow for fighting at a distance and ball-headed clubs for close combat. Some wore armor made from rows of sticks bound together or sheets of wickerwork covered with rawhide. Shields were often made from wood. Each warrior carried a bag of dried food, principally roasted corn meal that, with some hunting, fishing, and gathering en route, would last for several weeks. In travel the warriors carried a cooking pot, wooden food bowls, spoons, pipes, pouches of tobacco, and reed mats to sleep on. They often made quick shelters by laying pieces of birchbark against small poles put in the ground. They cached corn along the trail in small birchbark bags every second day. These caches would be used on the return trip. Sometimes they put up a painted bark emblem symbolizing the village they came from on a tree along a major trail.

Once the raiders arrived in enemy territory they would usually scatter into small raiding parties and try to kill the small groups of women and children working in the fields. They might try to rush in and start fires in a village. Successful warriors would try to bring back the head or at least the scalp of those they had killed as a trophy of their success. These would be dried and hung from poles or from the palisade walls during warfare.

Prisoners

Prisoners were tied with a woven cord and brought to the captor's village; the males were usually taken to be tortured and killed. The captors would usually begin the torture right away by pulling out the prisoner's fingernails and cutting off the fingers he used to draw a bow. He would also be forced to sing his personal war song. Only one warrior could be credited with the capture of a specific prisoner; if there was a dispute, the prisoner was allowed to designate his captor. Prisoners were divided among the war party members and allocated to villages or clan segments by the decision of a sub-tribal council. Finally, each prisoner would be placed under the control of a single prominent family, who had an important part in the decision about whether he would be killed or adopted.

In preparation to be a warrior, young men would toughen themselves, prove their bravery, and make a kind of religious vow by making small cuts or burns on their arms and legs. There was a religious element in blood sacrifice. Thus, for example, one thing a hunter might do to invoke aid from his guardian spirit was cut himself and offer some of his own blood in sacrifice. Warriors learned to put up a brave front when captured and tortured. A warrior was supposed to ignore torture and sing insulting and scorning songs at his tormentors.

When a war party arrived with a prisoner back in their home village, the prisoner would often be run through a gauntlet of people who hit him with thorny branches or burned him with firebrands. Women were encouraged to join the tortures. After the prisoner was tied to a stake the villagers would do such things as hack off pieces of his body and burn him with firebrands or hot steel tomahawks. They might tear out the nerve strands from his arms, and make him run through the fires built down the central aisle of a longhouse. They began the tortures by attacking his extremities so that he would live longer, sometimes for several days. When he was too weak to walk they might carry him through the longhouse so that people could torture him. When he passed out they would stop, revive him, feed him, let him rest at least until sunrise so that the sun could witness his death, and then start over again. The leader of the torture would call on everyone to do their duty of torturing because it would be viewed by the Sun and the God of War. He would call on people to refrain from sexual intercourse during the night of torture, because this would distract them from their sacred commitments.

Torturing was also a grand entertainment with cheering and mocking commentary by all while the prisoner was being tortured. For example, as if using the torch in applying pitch to a canoe, one would say, "Come, let me calk and pitch my canoe," and then burn the prisoner. Or they might say to an older prisoner, "It is not right that my uncle [a term of respect for an older male] should be cold. I must warm you" (Tooker 1967:37). Just before his death an Iroquois prisoner said, "Sun, who are witness of my torments, listen to my words. I am at the point of death, but after this death, Heaven shall be my dwelling" (Tooker 1967:157). Finally they would roast the prisoner alive, often on a scaffold in the center of the village, and eat parts of his body, particularly the heart. After sunset on the day of his death the villagers would expel his soul from the longhouse and village by making loud and horrible noises.

An alternative to death by torture was adoption. Even during torture there was usually a testing period or mock adoption until the time of the prisoner's death. If his appearance, potential for assimilation as a Huron, and ability pleased his adoptive family they could decide to spare his life and keep him. Since women had a prominent place in longhouse and family decisions, their feelings toward the prisoner were crucial. In one case of an Iroquois prisoner about fifty years old, the initial decision had been that a family would keep and adopt him. However, preliminary tortures made while bringing him from his village had destroyed his hands; thus the family decided he would be useless and they tortured him to death instead. Apparently this was a fairly typical rationalization given by a mock adoptive family to a prisoner, and actual adoptions of adult males were rare. In the case of a true adoption, the prisoner would be adopted by a family who had lost a warrior in battle. After a ceremony that purged him of being an enemy, the adopted person took on the dead warrior's social roles as son, nephew, husband, and father.

Changes in the 1600s

In historic times the defence of trade routes against outsiders became quite ruthless, and warfare was brought to bear on the defence, expansion, and control of trading areas. Throughout the region the custom was established that traders, but not warriors, needed permission to cross the territory of foreign allies. Gifts were often given in exchange for this permission. As the Hurons, for example, wanted to serve as middlemen in the French–Indian trade, they tried to keep the French apart from other Indians. They attempted to prevent the French from contacting the Petun and Neutral and they kept the Petun and Neutral from crossing Huron territory for trade. Iroquois traders tried several times to negotiate trade routes through Huron territory to the northern Algonquians, but the Hurons refused to let them through. In the same way, the Mohawks controlled travel through their territory with the Dutch at Fort Orange (Albany, New York).

Warfare was an adventure in which young men could prove their manhood and gain prestige. It was to avenge earlier killings, to acquire booty and captives, and after about 1640 to dominate territories for trapping and trade. When the fur resources were becoming depleted in the Iroquois territory after 1640, the Mohawks went north and attacked the Huron fur brigades of canoes that came down the Ottawa River en route to Montreal. The Mohawks then traded the stolen furs south to the Dutch at Fort Orange. Meanwhile, the westernmost Iroquois, the Seneca, began attacking the frontier villages in the Huron homeland. There was political disunity among the Hurons because smallpox epidemics during 1637–1641 had killed about half the Huron population, and young and inexperienced men had assumed the political leadership. In 1642 the Seneca traveled along the route of the present Trent Canal system, crossed into Huronia at the narrows between Lakes Simcoe and Couchiching, and attacked the village of Contarea, south of Bass Lake on the southeast frontier of Huronia. Though the Hurons remained divided in their response, the Iroquois became bolder. In 1644 three of the four Huron flotillas of canoes carrying furs to the French were captured by the Iroquois. In 1648 the Seneca destroyed the large Huron village of St. Joseph, killing several hundred people. Finally, in the spring of 1649 about 1,000 Iroquois warriors destroyed two major Huron villages, killing all the men, women, and children except a few captives.

The Huron lost about 300 warriors; the Iroquois, 200. The Huron lost two battles that spring, but there were heavy losses on both sides. While the Iroquois themselves were fleeing back to New York, pursued halfheartedly by several hundred Petun, the Huron went into full-scale panic and flight. Their security and confidence vanished. The Iroquois had successfully invaded their country in large numbers in the spring, a time when war had never before been carried out. The Iroquois had marched through the snow with determination, and made organized attacks to destroy whole villages, tying the captives to their own longhouses and burning the whole village down. This was a new kind of genocide war. By May of 1649 fifteen Huron villages had been abandoned and burned by the Hurons themselves and several thousand fugitives crowded on Christian Island. Thousands of people starved to death, at least ten times more than had been killed by the Iroquois.

About 300 Hurons migrated to Quebec with the surviving French missionaries. Segments of two Huron sub-tribes were brought into Seneca territory, where they built their own village; but they were eventually assimilated into the Seneca. Today the Huron language is no longer spoken, but a community of Hurons (1,041 in 1970) still lives in Loretteville, a suburb of Quebec City. There is another community descendant from the refugee Huron and Petun, called Wyandot (a variation of the confederation name Wendat), in Oklahoma.

In December 1649 one Petun village was destroyed; the rest of the Petun dispersed, joining the Ottawa on Manitoulin Island, the Huron on Christian Island, and others migrated all the way to a migrant community of Potawatomi in Green Bay, Wisconsin. In 1650 some 1,500 Iroquois destroyed a Neutral village. A Neutral counter-attack killed or captured over 200 Iroquois, but in the winter of 1650–1651 some 1,000 Iroquois destroyed the major Neutral villages—one with a population of 1,600. After that the Neutrals fled in panic, dispersing to other tribes. Waves of war refugees streamed away from the Iroquois or assimilated into Iroquois societies. In 1653 the Erie managed to burn a Seneca village. However, by 1656 the Erie had been destroyed, scattered, and ceased to exist as an independent people. A Susquehannah village to the south was destroyed in 1675 and there were battles in this period with such societies as Shawnee, Nanticoke, and Delaware. The Iroquois pushed westward until they came into conflict with the Algonquian-speaking Miami and Illinois. Between 1679 and 1683 Robert de LaSalle and Henri de Tonty brought together a league on the Illinois River in opposition to the Iroquois. After devastating battles on both sides, the Iroquois were finally defeated and their western drive was ended.

In the east the Iroquois regularly blockaded the Ottawa River in the 1650s, but after the destruction of the Hurons there was very little traffic. In 1653 the Iroquois attacked Montreal. The French fur trade was down for decades after the Huron destruction, and it shifted farther north to the Ojibwa and Cree. There was a long series of French-Iroquois battles that ended in a massive French attack with 2,200 men in 1696, and a treaty in 1701. French-Iroquois relations improved so much in the eighteenth century that large numbers of Mohawks moved into their Christian mission communities, starting with Ogdensburg in 1749 and later moving to Caughnawaga and St. Regis.

Reasons for Iroquois Military Successes

The military successes of the Iroquois must be related to (1) their greater use of guns, (2) their particularly strong determination and persistence in warfare, motivated by a desire to dominate the regional trade (Hunt 1940), (3) the development of new and effective tactics of mass attacks on distant villages at any time of the year (Otterbein 1964), and (4) the panic that often spread among their enemies after the successful campaigns against the Hurons in 1642–1649. Once the Hurons were defeated, there was a domino effect of falling societies, with greater strength on the part of the Iroquois and panic on the part of the other tribes of the region.

The above are largely external factors. There may have been an internal factor as well, in Iroquois disunity. There was a continuing struggle within Iroquoian societies with the young and the war chiefs on one side and the old and the civil chiefs on the other. We know from the Huron data that a disease epidemic killed many of the older civil leaders. The same kind of thing could have happened among the Iroquois because they too had a severe disease epidemic. It appears that among the New York Iroquois in most of the seventeenth century (specifically from the start of the gun trade in 1641 to their defeat by the French in 1696) the young war chiefs were dominant. For example, the civil chiefs frequently arranged peace settlements with the French, but they were apparently unable to maintain restraints on the attacks on the French and their allies by the Iroquois warriors. The civil chiefs had no effective disciplinary control over the war chiefs, and a pattern of warfare was established to solve problems with other societies. The Iroquois did not particularly exploit the trade advantages they were supposed to be fighting for as civil chiefs would have encouraged. They did not politically organize other Indians, as the civil chiefs might have done. Instead, the society became oriented toward warfare.

By 1641 the Iroquois began to acquire muskets from the Dutch. In 1642 they attacked a French fort and fired through the loopholes. They attacked the Huron lines at close range, firing their guns and bows and arrows, then attacked with clubs. By 1647 the Hurons had learned to counter the Iroquois gun attack by forming a crescent line, dropping to the ground before the Iroquois fired their weapons, rising to fire their bows and arrows, and counter-charging. Then the Iroquois learned to use their guns in ambushes from the banks of rivers, by shooting to sink the canoes. The furs loaded on the canoes would float and be taken as they washed ashore, and a few of the voyageurs would be shot or captured.

The Iroquois did not entirely abandon armor and shields until the 1660s, because their enemies were usually still using bows and arrows against which the armor was a protection. Through the 1600s the Iroquois progressively increased their firepower. They increasingly relied on scattered warriors who fired from hidden positions of cover in the forest. Through their consistent successes the Iroquois were able to put increasingly large armies into the field, until the average was about 2,000 warriors in the later 1600s. Devastating losses in the late 1600s against the French encouraged them to use more winter attacks and night attacks. By the end of the 1600s they had abandoned clubs and tomahawks.

The Iroquois developed and used what military tacticians consider to be the basic principles of modern warfare: (1) an offensive is planned, (2) a concerted effort is used and the force is concentrated at a critical point, (3) the tactical units are integrated and work as a team, (4) the force has a mobility such that long distances can be covered and travel plans can be changed, (5) the strategic plan is simple and thus understood by all units, (6) surprise is used, (7) correct formations are used, (8) there is knowledge about the terrain and the enemy's defences, (9) a battle victory is fully exploited. When facing an enemy force the Iroquois fought in one line in forested areas and in two lines in open country. They learned to use the tactical line which coordinated fire and movements. The archers and gunners first fired their weapons, the second line rushed in with clubs and tomahawks, and the first line joined the second in the attack.

Though the Iroquois lost a great many warriors in their battles, they also took many captives and assimilated them into Iroquois society, including some Whites who refused to go back to White society. Also, in the same pattern as the earlier Huron, the Iroquois accepted foreigners who volunteered to join their society. Families and whole villages became Iroquois. In 1722 some displaced members of the Tuscarora tribe were formally adopted by the Oneida. Though they were never given a vote, they joined what was now called the "League of Six Nations." It was these somewhat alienated Oneida and Tuscarora who sided with the Americans in the Revolutionary War.

Modern Transition

William Johnson was appointed by the British as Superintendent of Indian Affairs for the northern tribes. He settled among the Mohawk, learned their language, and married a Mohawk girl. He sent his wife's brother (Thayendanegea, He-holds-the-bets, or Joseph Brant) to a mission school and later appointed him as his assistant. Under British sponsorship, the Iroquois became a powerful and acculturated society regularly used by the British as a military force against the French, other Indians, and later against the American colonists.

Joseph Brant became a colonel in the British army and drew the Mohawk, Seneca, Cayuga, and Onondaga into the British cause. The Oneida and Tuscarora joined the American side. The Americans sent an army under General John Sullivan against the Iroquois, who were allied with the British. He followed the program of scorched earth warfare that had been used by the Iroquois on other Indians, and that the French and Iroquois had used on each other. However, by this time the Iroquois had become rather rich. They had something significant to scorch. After the war White settlers squatted on Indian lands. Brant and many of the Indians who allied with the British migrated to Canada as a part of the United Empire Loyalist migration.

By the end of the 1700s the Iroquois were seeing their past greatness collapse. They were devastated by the American Revolutionary War, and lost most of their territory. Many had migrated in desperation into Canada. They needed a new ideology to explain what was happening to them in a new and wider world and to revitalize their lives.

Handsome Lake was a chief among the New York Seneca. He had been an alcoholic, but he began to have visionary dreams in the Iroquoian tradition. He related his visions to his friends and relatives and slowly became a widely accepted prophet. The spirits told him that the Iroquois would be destroyed unless they changed their ways. They laid out a "code" for adjusting to the moral and social order of the new society. Witchcraft, quarreling, and drinking were forbidden. The Iroquois were to follow the White farming techniques. They were to abandon communal longhouses and matrilineal groups in favor of individual family households. These features had been undergoing evolutionary changes that needed to be ideologically clarified. By 1800 the longhouse had been abandoned as a type of residence for smaller log houses. These teachings formed the basis of a church that spread through the Iroquoian communities in New York, Ontario, and Quebec, and still survives today. The longhouse was used as a place of worship; and elements of the League of the Iroquois ceremonies and the curing societies, such as the False Face, were woven into the Handsome Lake religion.

In the early 1800s, after the White encroachments and displacements of the Revolutionary War, the Iroquois took up the White style of agriculture: sedentary rather than slash and burn; animal-drawn plows; primarily male farmers; and new crops such as wheat, oats, hay, and fruit trees. Women did the kitchen gardening and took care of the small animals. While the importance of women in economics was falling, they became a conservative influence in Iroquois life and "tended to idealize and exaggerate the role they had played in traditional Iroquoian society. In this fashion, the vision of the aboriginal Iroquoians as a 'matriarchal' people was created" (Trigger 1969: 125). The Canadian Iroquois were forced by law to use patrilineal principles in establishing legal band membership, though there was some continuation of matrilineal principles in determining hereditary chiefs. Clan descent lost its function in inheritance and marriage, but there was still some retention of an ideology about matriclan memberships.

The Caughnawaga Mohawks retained much of the traditional male role because the men became fur traders, lumberjacks, and bargemen in the nineteenth century. In 1886 men were employed in the construction of a steel bridge near their reserve. Out of this they developed a tradition of working in high steel construction. Men moved to jobs in the big cities and lived in "Little Caughnawagas" in Buffalo, Detroit, and Brooklyn. The Mohawk male role thus continued to have excitement, extensive geographical mobility, absence from the community for long periods of time, work in all-male groups, and most of the responsibility for the home and family left to the women.

In 1784 a large number of Iroquois joined the migration to Canada of the United Empire Loyalists, particularly under Joseph Brant, to the Grand River community in Ontario. The original settlement was six miles on each side of the Grand River from Lake Erie to its source north of Guelph, a distance of about 60 miles. Most of this was sold piece by piece to buy food, supplies, and housing. Thus the present reserve is only some 72 square miles east of Brantford.

On the Grand River reserve the League of Six Nations was fused into a form of local government. There was some separation of the original tribes in their movement onto the reserve: Mohawks in the west; then one Cayuga group; Oneida, Seneca, Tuscarora, and even a Delaware community in a series of north-to-south settlements; Onondaga in the northeast; and a second Cayuga group in the far east. The Mississaugas of the Credit were moved into their own adjacent, separately administered, reserve in the southeast. Refugee elements of several Indian societies were drawn together for their own survival.

The ancient League was transformed into a mechanism of local government. The important relations were then with the governments of Ontario and Canada. The issues were boundaries, inheritance, taxes,

TABLE I
Iroquoian Reserves in Canada

Reserve	Population	Predominant Language
Lorette, Quebec	1,041	Huron
Caughnawaga, Quebec	4,515	Mohawk
Oka, Quebec	777	Mohawk
St. Regis, Ontario & Quebec	2,963	Mohawk
Bay of Quinte, Ontario	2,111	Mohawk
Gibson, Ontario	206	Mohawk
Thames, Ontario	1,011	Oneida
Six Nations	8,680	All Iroquois, Tuscarora

schools, roads, and other domestic issues. Then in 1924 a federal act abolished the hereditary council and instituted an elected council. The hereditary council refused to recognize the government's decision and continued a parallel government, but it had little economic or political power. Since then the League has lost its political and legal functions and become only a religious and ceremonial institution, bolstered by the teachings of Handsome Lake and some survival of False Face curing societies. "Longhouse Societies" perpetuated traditional clan ceremonies, elected *sachems* or high chiefs, and bestowed ceremonial names.

In 1970 the official Iroquoian bands in Canada and their populations and predominant languages were as follows (see Table I). (There is also a small community of Iroquois in Alberta, but they are not in the official list of reserves.)

In the nineteenth and early twentieth centuries, in both the U.S. and Canada, the Iroquois were always at the forefront of the national Native movements. A large number of the nationally famous politicians, military leaders, and sports figures were Iroquoian. Then the Iroquois became too assimilated into White society to struggle with Native causes. Now, in the last third of the twentieth century, the mantle of leadership has shifted primarily to people from the aboriginally band-organized societies, such as the Ojibwa, Cree, and Inuit.

Commentary

Band societies are small, flexible, and adaptive; tribal societies acquire a more fixed and socially held cultural orientation. Tribal societies get involved in activities significantly beyond biologically patterned needs and the common learned patterns of a residential community. Tribal people begin doing things *not* necessary for survival; participation in those things helps to integrate and organize a larger number of scattered people not bound together by intimate relationships. These tribal institutions and elaborations of culture take on systematic patterns that we can roughly characterize.

The traditional Huron-Iroquois pattern was focused on the *horticulture of the women and the warfare of the men.* In the next two chapters we will see cultural patterns that are *more economically oriented,* patterns in which the acquisition and manipulation of wealth become the major route to high social status. All three cultural areas had elaborate institutions of politics, religion, and voluntary associations that are missing in the Arctic and Subarctic.

CHAPTER 7

PLAINS
Blackfoot:
Influence of the Horse
on a Hunting Society

Origin of the Classic Plains Culture

THE FIRST MAJOR WAVE of White migration and settlement in the western Plains did not arrive until the mid-1800s. The settlement was that late because the original European settlement was somewhat confined in the eastern woodlands for cultural-ecological reasons. Having come from the woodlands of western Europe, the Whites felt more at home in the woodlands of North America than in the Plains. The Plains was conceived and described at the time as "The Great American Desert" and the myth persisted that the land could not be farmed. When the western migration finally began in the U.S. because of eastern population pressure, the people usually planned to skip over the "American Desert" to the woodlands of the west coast in California, Oregon, and Washington. Canadian settlement of the Prairies and Plains was slightly later than in the U.S. and was aided by *eastern* European migrants, who had already farmed a similar kind of steppe country in Europe.

The Indians that the Whites described between 1830 and 1880 had the most highly developed hunting culture in the world. It was a materially rich situation for hunters. A Native population of only 150,000 people was harvesting the herds of millions of buffalo. They were extremely diverse in languages, speaking some 25 languages related to each other in six families and four phyla. Still, there was a generally uniform culture, as though a few patterns for the region had developed over thousands of years. In the tall-grass Prairies to the east were

163

agriculturalists living most of the year in sedentary, earth lodge villages, who seasonally ranged into the buffalo country for hunting. In the western steppes to the Rocky Mountains were the nomads, who followed an annual round of hunting in a wide territory.

All the societies had the hide tipi; bows and arrows; leather containers, breechcloths, leggings, shirts, and moccasins; and buffalo robes. Things were light and portable, adapted to a nomadic hunting way of life. There were widespread practices of (1) shamanism, (2) a vision quest for young men, (3) a special relationship with guardian spirits, (4) keeping sacred bundles of charms for rituals, and (5) religious vows to the guardian spirit for power carried out in the self-torture of the Sun Dance. Warfare was prevalent and expressed in three inter-related orientations: (1) small raids to steal horses, (2) small raids to score strokes of bravery in a ranked, game-like system of "coups" against the enemy, without necessarily killing or stealing, and (3) revenge and territorial protection attacks to kill the enemy and take back their scalps and other war trophies. While they did only rudimentary work in art and were quite simple in religious practices, the Plains Indians, as hunters, seemed extremely advanced in such respects as politics, men's associations, warfare, and in the care, breeding, and riding of horses.

They were excellent horsemen, often owning large herds of specially bred and trained horses. As children they learned to ride, and became skilled in racing and trick riding. They could distinguish their own horses on sight. They had technical terms for several different kinds of horses: fast horses for hunting buffalo or for military attacks, horses to hunt in deep snow, general riding stock, horses to pull the travois, and others. Many societies had stories of the origin of horses that related back to the time of creation. The horse was intimately woven into the fabric of Plains culture in buffalo hunting, in warfare, and in travel and the transportation of goods.

There are, however, new facts that show that the spectacular qualities of the Plains culture recorded in the 1850s and 1860s were really a brief florescence that was only about 100 years old. For example, it came out that Spanish explorers in the 1500s met only people who were hunting on foot in the southern Plains. These hunters lived in portable skin huts which were much smaller than those of the 1800s. Dogs were used as pack animals and to pull the travois. Buffalo were usually killed by bow and arrow or lance after being driven into large compounds. The apparent evolutionary discrepancies could be accounted for by (1) the ancient ecological adaptations of simple pedestrian buffalo hunters, (2) the relatively sophisticated political and sodality organizations of tribal farmers along the rivers that stretched out into the Plains, and especially (3) a new evolutionary level of development stimulated by the Spaniards' introduction of horses. The breed of horse introduced had been genetically selected to work with men for over 3,000 years in the Old World, and were not just any wild stock. The grassy Plains was a natural ecological niche for horses.

There is also evidence that the Indians were killing off the buffalo at an accelerating pace: the ease of the kill on horseback encouraged an excessive slaughter; and more important, the Native population feeding off the buffalo was rapidly increasing. In 1700 there were an estimated sixty million buffalo in North America. When the Whites arrived in numbers in 1850 the buffalo had already been reduced to about twenty million animals. By 1885 the buffalo was close to extinction. Though the Whites were the major contributors to the final overkill, an ecological equilibrium that existed for pedestrian hunters had not been established for horseback hunters between the Indian population and the buffalo. The Indian population was increasing. The new capacity to exploit the buffalo on horseback had attracted a migration of most of the societies in the Plains. The buffalo population was rapidly declining, indicating that the Indians were quite capable of exterminating the buffalo. The Plains culture then would have again been radically altered because it was extremely dependent on that one source of food.

The main "plains" is a strip of land about three hundred miles wide along the eastern slope of the Rocky Mountains. This is a grassy steppe land where the buffalo were most abundant. Farther east to the Great Lakes on the north and to the Mississippi Valley is the "prairies," another connected parallel zone with more precipitation, taller grasses, and other vegetation. The prairies gradually became occupied through the western branches of the Mississippi River system by the eastern agricultural peoples after about 1,000 B.C. People were farming, for example, in Kansas in 1,000 B.C., and they had such traits as pottery, burial mounds, and settled villages. After A.D. 1 the Plains village people expanded west far enough to add a significant amount of buffalo hunting, but the population of solely hunting nomads in the western Plains must have remained very small. By the time the horse was introduced in the 1600s the Plains was occupied primarily by tribally organized agriculturalists, people who made an ecological shift to become the classical tribally organized Plains hunters.

The Blackfoot, however, were pedestrian buffalo hunters whose lives were radically changed, not only by the greater efficacy of hunting buffalo on horseback, but by adopting cultural practices from the Plains tribes to their south: men's age-grade societies, sacred bundle ceremonies, the Sun Dance, several features of the warrior's coup complex, horse pastoralism, and putting tipis in a circle for the summer camp.

The Blackfoot case is important in unraveling the complex history of the Plains Indians for three reasons: (1) they had only a hunting heritage,

(2) as they were about the last in the Plains to receive horses, some of their memories of the pedestrian period were recorded, (3) they became extreme in the classical features of the culture, such as horsemanship and warfare. First of all, there are only three surviving large societies in the Plains that had strictly a large game hunting heritage: Kiowa, Apache, and Blackfoot. The Kiowa's closest linguistic relatives are the Rio Grande Pueblos of New Mexico; thus they probably came from the west into the southern Plains in an early time period. The Apache-Navajo migrated southward through the Plains several centuries ago and then split into the Apache as southern Plains hunters and the Navajo as Southwestern hunters and farmers. The Apache were then largely driven out of the Plains by the Comanche in early historic times. The Ute, Shoshoni, and Comanche came eastward over the Rocky Mountains into the Plains from a plant-gathering heritage in the Great Basin.

Everyone else came from the east, drawing from other traditions. In the north the Cree, Salteaux, and Assiniboine had some fishing and plant gathering, as well as hunting, in their heritages. The Dakota Sioux were probably much like the Ojibwa before they took up the horse-buffalo complex and moved to the Plains. The Assiniboine (an Ojibwa word meaning people who cook with stones, "Stonies") are a branch of the Dakota Sioux. They originally lived in Manitoba and northern Minnesota, and were pushed west into Saskatchewan by the Salteaux and Plains Cree. With the introduction of the horse such settled societies as the Cheyenne, Crow, and Arapahoe abandoned their settled life to become nomadic hunters. The tribes that mixed agriculture and buffalo hunting were societies such as Mandan in the north, Pawnee in the center, and Wichita in the south.

Horses

Horses were brought into the southern Plains around 1650. It seems that Santa Fe, Mexico was the major early dispersal point. Apaches, who had been trained by the Spaniards in the care, breeding, and riding of horses, were the first Indians to spread the horse culture to other Native societies. People in the Comanche branch of the Shoshoni-Comanche language seem to have migrated previously into the Plains from the Great Basin. They apparently acquired horses from the Apache to their south and passed them northward to their Shoshoni and Ute relatives. A northern band of Shoshoni called Snakes, who had recently been made very nomadic by their use of horses, first traded horses to the Blackfoot in Canada around 1730. Thus the apparent horse diffusion sequence of Spanish–Apache–Comanche–Shoshoni–Blackfoot from New Mexico to Canada took about 80 years. Meanwhile the horse culture also rapidly diffused eastward into the mixed hunting and farming societies of the Prairies and still farther north in Canada. The Blackfoot probably contributed to the spread of horses to their Athapascan speaking allies, the Sarsi, and to at least one of their several perennial enemies, the Cree.

The recency of horses and the general transference of dog-related traits, particularly the pulling of the travois, is reflected in words used for horses. The Blackfoot called the horse the elk-dog for its great size. The Sarsi called the horse seven-dogs for its ability to carry or pull several times as much weight as a dog. Large dogs can carry up to a fifty pound pack and drag a load of about 75 pounds on a travois. A family could have several dogs, but there was a limit according to the need to kill enough game to feed the dogs and the need to control their movements, their fights, their chasing rabbits, and so forth. A horse feeds on grass which it can gather itself. A horse can carry about 200 pounds and pull about 300 pounds on a travois. A train of loaded dogs can travel only 5–6 miles a day while a horse-travois train can travel twice that. For transportation, a horse is more efficient than a dog. The horse permitted the transportation of large tipis, bulky articles, and great quantities of meat. Aged or disabled people could be carried on a travois, rather than being abandoned as in pre-horse times.

The Blackfoot

The Blackfoot were in the northern Plains and in the center of the ancient migrational corridor through North America. The Blackfoot and the rest of the Canadian Algonquians continued a hunting way of life into historic times, but other Macro-Algonquian relatives in the U.S., such as the Natchez and Creek-Seminole, became the most advanced agricultural chiefdoms north of central Mexico. The Yurok and Wiyot, their relatives on the coast of northern California, became fishing-oriented tribes influenced by the chiefdoms of the British Columbia coast. The Macro-Algonquians were one of the oldest and most culturally diverse peoples in North America. It may be that the Blackfoot stayed approximately in place for ten thousand years while their linguistic relatives migrated away from the Plains and abandoned big-game hunting. The major ethnographic sources on the Blackfoot are by Ewers (1958), Hanks and Hanks (1950), Lewis (1942), McFee (1972), and Wissler (1910–13).

From archaeological and early historical evidence we can reconstruct some features of the pre-horse life of the Blackfoot. They were in the northern Plains for a long time. They used the four-pole tipi foundation of the Plateau and western Plains rather than the three-pole foundation of the east. They had the ancient western tradition of abandoning a dwelling a person had died in. Their handgames were of the western style. They generally did not make canoes or eat fish, traits that were common almost everywhere except in the Plains. They had the ancient hunting practice of making rabbit-skin robes, they made basketry, tended plots of wild tobacco, and made some crude pottery in the style of the Prairie farmers. Many of these features rapidly vanished with the affluence that came with horseback hunting. Rabbit-skin robes were replaced with buffalo robes, basketry with hide containers, wild tobacco with trade tobacco, and pottery with iron kettles.

The Blackfoot tribe was composed of three large bands: Piegan (Poorly-Dressed-Skins), the largest band that was generally located in the southern part of Blackfoot territory; Blood (also called Kainah, Many-Chiefs); and Siksika (Blackfoot). The bands were allied with each other and the Athapascan-speaking Sarsi (Not-Good in Blackfoot) and usually allied with the Algonquian-speaking Gros Ventres (Big-Bellies in French, also called Atsina, Beggars in Blackfoot).

Men were the hunters and warriors. They did some heavy butchering of the meat. They made weapons, shields, drums, pipes, and often their own leggings and coats. Men dressed in finer clothing than women. They painted their faces more. They feasted each other, gambled, and planned raids, dances, and ceremonies. Women did most of the butchering, drying, and preparing of meat. They processed skins, and made most of the clothing, the leather bags, and the tipis. They gathered plant foods, carried wood and water, prepared foods, and reared the children.

A single household occupied a single tipi. This was usually just a husband, wife, and children. A prosperous hunter might have a second or perhaps even a third wife. These wives often were sisters, and would usually live in the same tipi. The first wife was the owner and manager of the tipi and would control the later wives that were brought in. The kinship structure was bilateral with some reckoning of lineal descent, reflected in a bifurcate merging kinship terminology. Post-marital residence was usually patrilocal to the husband's band. A dozen or so loosely related households formed a micro-band that stayed together in winter camp and occupied a segment of the great summer camp. The micro-band had names such as Small-Robes, Solid-Topknot, Short-Necks, Lone-Fighter, and They-Don't-Laugh. Households shifted membership in the bands according to their kinship alliances, friendships, agreement or disagreement with the band leadership, and wealth of the band.

Chieftainship was usually quite a limited power, given and taken from people by consensus. It was given to people who had a history of listening to others, sharing with others, and of showing restraint in exercising arbitrary power. Households, bands, and men's societies ran the society as a whole. A man was a chief because he was a responsible household head, a micro-band leader, and prominent in the men's societies.

The Blackfoot annual round was a pattern of small scattered camps most of the year and a gathering together into macro-bands of 100–200 households for the communal summer hunts, communal warfare, and dances. In a 1754 report the tipis (about 200) of the summer camp were organized into two long parallel lines with an avenue between them. The development of mounted attacks and the need to corral horses led to the use of a great circle of tipis at the summer camp, each band having a traditional place within the circle. After the spread of the horse, large segments of the macro-bands got together in some years for a few weeks of tribal-wide gatherings with thousands of people. Now assured of plenty of dried meat for the year, the horse bands still had to scatter back into small bands to locate grazing lands for their horses.

Hunting

The pedestrian Blackfoot usually built a buffalo pound at the foot of a steep cliff or slope, often at the bank of a stream. The walls were made preferably of logs or dog-travois poles, or else rocks, brush, and earth were used. The walls had to be fairly high but not necessarily strong because the buffalo would not try to push free if they could not see beyond the wall. On the top of the plains above the pound two lines of brush or rock piles were constructed to converge at the cliff jumping-point over the pound. The lines were built back a long distance, usually about one fourth of a mile, and runs up to two miles long have been reported. The piles were put closer together to form an increasingly solid appearance as the jump was approached.

The hunters attempted to drive the herd in the direction of the V-line of brush and stampede them over the cliff. A hunting camp might have several old jumps and pounds, and would select one and repair it according to the location of the buffalo migration that year. When a herd was sighted within range of a pound the hunters would often try to lead the herd in front as well as drive it from behind. A man would cover himself in a whole buffalo skin, attract the herd by his movements, and move in the direction of the pound. Meanwhile, men would approach the herd from behind. Sometimes they would start a fire in the dry grassy plains to help drive the buffalo. Whether following the decoy or being driven they could sometimes get the herd to move into the converging lines of brush. Everyone available from the camp was concealed along the V-line. When the buffalo veered from a straight-line run down the trap the concealed people in that part of the runway would jump up, shout, and wave buffalo robes to frighten them to keep moving in the right direction. If all went well the entire herd of perhaps as many as one hundred animals would fall over the cliff. Those who were not killed by the fall or by thrashing around in the pound were killed with lances and bows and arrows.

Pounds were also built in the form of a circular corral of logs and brush, several feet high. The best entrance to this type was a row of inclined logs, creating an artificial jump; and an entrance that could be easily closed when enough buffalo were inside. Antelope can be more easily lured into a V-line of brush than buffalo because they are more curious; hunters can attract them by hiding in deep grass and waving something the antelope can see. However, antelope are capable of extremely high jumps, and are almost impossible to pen in. The Blackfoot solved this problem by forcing the antelope to jump over a brush wall at the end of the V-line. On the other side of the brush wall they dug a concealed pit in the ground into which the antelope would fall.

When the summer migration routes shifted so much that the Blackfoot camp missed the herds or the hunters were not able to drive them into a pound, other techniques had to be used. Small hunting parties went out after game. Once a herd was spotted they would try to pick off animals one by one without driving the whole herd away. An individual could put on a wolf or buffalo disguise and approach the herd close enough to kill one with a bow and arrow without disturbing the entire herd. A wolf disguise works because buffalo are accustomed to their habit of waiting around for an opportunity to attack an infant or a sick animal; but the buffalo are not afraid of wolves, and can fairly easily trample or horn them if they harass too much. If the stalking method failed or the herd did begin to run then the hunters would try to run down and shoot an animal. Their chances of catching an animal on foot was only good in the first brief dash because the buffalo is fast and has the stamina to run for miles.

When horses first became available they were used to help drive the herd into a pound or over a cliff. Later the hunters would try to pick out a herd, ride around it to keep the buffalo running in a circle, and each hunter would fire his arrows into an animal he selected until it dropped. Hunting on horseback with the bow and arrow was considered more effective than with the flintlock gun. Distance was not a factor because the hunter could ride alongside the animal and shoot arrows at it. The greater range of the flintlock was of no advantage and it took too long to reload on horseback to get repeated shots.

The flintlock had the same disadvantage in horseback warfare. The flintlock was used largely for standing defence because of its greater overall distance and accuracy at a distance than the bow and arrow. It was like a hand-held cannon. To reload it one poured a measured amount of powder down the barrel, put in a wadding, tamped it down tightly, and then put a ball down the barrel. A fighter could cut the time down by not using a wadding or tamping it, but this resulted in a weak shot. This was so time-consuming and difficult to do on horseback that horseback warriors with flintlocks would usually take their first shot from the horse, stop and dismount, reload, and commence firing from the ground. With the use of the horse it became easier for lone hunters to contact and frighten the herds away. Stampeding the herd had been a problem in pre-horse days, but the new increase in mobility made it more serious. Men's associations were used to police the summer hunts and to keep lone hunters away from the herds.

A buffalo provides a great amount of meat; the bulls average 1,400 pounds; and the cows, 900 pounds. The meat was roasted on a spit over the fire or boiled in a skin bag with heated stones. A common technique was to dig a small pit in the ground, line it with a skin, and use that as a pot to boil foods in. The Blackfoot made ceramic pottery, but it was so heavy and breakable that it apparently never competed well with hide containers. When the iron pot was introduced through trade it quickly replaced both pottery and stone boiling in hide containers.

Jerky was made by slicing the meat into thin strips, slitting these with further holes, and hanging them on racks to dry in the sun or over a fire. When the jerky was quite dry it was stored in large, folded, rawhide bags that we call *parfleches*. Jerky can be eaten dry, mixed into a stew, or pounded into a powder for pemmican. In making pemmican the pow-dered meat is thoroughly mixed with hot melted fat. Sewn up tightly in skin bags the pemmican remains edible for years though it soon takes on a rancid smell and taste.

The Blackfoot hunted some deer, moose, bear, and beaver, particu-larly in the foothills of the Rockies to the west. They gathered wild plums, cherries, berries, wild turnip, and the roots of a wild lily called camas. They trapped eagles for their feathers. In historic times they trapped wolves and sold their skins to the White traders. The wolf trap was a large, pyramidal, log cage about 8' by 16' at the base and 8' high, baited with a large amount of meat. The wolves could climb the slope of logs and jump through the opening at the top. The meat would attract a whole pack, but the animals could not get out so ten or more were often taken in a single night. The Blackfoot thus could sell several hundred wolf pelts each year to the traders.

In personality the Blackfoot tended toward industriousness; aggres-siveness; egotism, in being easily moved to jealousy, envy, and shame; yet were "talkative, merry, and lighthearted," according to George Grinnell in 1892. They had a process of formal ridicule for social control that was similar to that of the Naskapi (McFee 1972:43). "When the people were quietly settled in of an evening a headman would call out to a neighbor asking him if he had heard about that silly fellow two tepees down who had been mistreating his wife? . . . Sarcasm, ridicule, and the accompany-ing laughter, added up to an evening of entertainment for all but the victim, who was highly motivated to mend his ways."

All Comrades Societies

The All Comrades Societies (*aiinikiks*) were age-graded: people passed from one to the next as they grew older. About every four years a man, after selling his membership to a younger man, could, if he was moderately wealthy, purchase a membership from an older man in the next appropriate society. According to similarities in the region it appears that the Blackfoot acquired this kind of society from the Mandan through the Gros Ventres. It originally had seven grades: Mosquitoes, Dogs, Prairie Dogs, Ravens, Buffalo With Thin Horns, Soldiers, and Buffalo Bulls. Sometimes people started new ones; thus the number increased to nine among the Blood, ten among the Piegan, and fourteen among the Siksika. The oldest group, the Buffalo Bulls, were usually in their middle 40s and included the wealthiest and most powerful men of the tribe.

The societies provided much of the political order of the tribe, particularly in organizing defences, moving camp to buffalo grounds, preventing lone hunters from stampeding the herds, ensuring that people shared their buffalo kills, and running the large summer camps. They sponsored mock war games, races, and dances. They would discipline a man by taking his property, including all his clothing. They disciplined a woman for marital infidelity by raping her, cutting off her nose, or ostrasizing her. There is no mention of men being disciplined for marital infidelity. In fact, it was considered a coup to seduce a married woman.

Among the Blackfoot a woman's society, Matoki, built the ceremonial lodge for the Sun Dance. The Sun Dance sponsor was a woman who, during a personal crisis, made a vow to purchase the Natoas Bundle in return for supernatural help in solving her personal crisis. At one time there seems to have been a re-enactment of driving buffalo into a pound in association with this important bundle. However, it became historically associated with sponsoring a Sun Dance. She had to be faithful in marriage, an ideal woman. She sponsored the building of the medicine lodge. She provided buffalo tongues which were sliced by certain women and distributed. At that point the women could make accusations of improper sexual advances and name the men involved.

Religion

Blackfoot religious practices primarily involved supernatural powers given by spirits. Individuals acquired a special relationship with a particular spirit, identified with an animal, or occasionally a personified feature of nature such as thunder. It was common to establish a lifelong loyalty and reciprocity with a guardian spirit, initially by going out alone to fast and pray on a vision quest. Individuals would make offerings of food, tobacco, and smoke to their guardian spirits. The guardian spirit might teach a war song and dance to a young man. It might teach a person how to cure a certain kind of disease. One man was told to carve an image of the spirit to cure internal bleeding. Another was told to have people with bowel disorders wear a squirrel skin on their belt for four nights. A third man was told the people would have power if he painted the faces of women with black circles and a dot on the nose at a Sun Dance.

A cluster of these related religious traits were institutionalized in medicine bundles or *saam*. A bundle is a collection of charms used as the focus of religious rituals. Each bundle has its own name and its own ceremony. Thus a beaver spirit had taught the rites of purification, smoking, and songs that belong to the Beaver Bundle, which contains the skins of birds and animals. In band-level societies individual shamans used a kit of sacred objects in their curing practices. The same kind of kit of objects—feathers, claws, beaks, animal teeth, crystals, strangely shaped stones, etc.—became the focal point among the tribal-level Blackfoot of a periodic social gathering for the presentation of a bundle ceremony. Objects were taken out and used in a mnemonic way to tell the story or sing the song associated with that object. Each ceremony had its own reputation for the ailments it was particularly good at curing or for its efficacy at other things.

In 1787 only the long-stem medicine pipes were present. In 1833 the Blackfoot had added otterskin medicine bags. Later on they added other large medicine bundles. In the late 1800s the Blackfoot had about fifty rituals for bundles and about twenty more for large stone tobacco pipes. When the society became quite commercial in the 1800s, these bundles and pipes, along with their associated rituals, were widely bought and sold. A rich man could buy a sacred bundle and acquire the power associated with the bundle. There was an inflation in the value of bundles from 9 horses in 1833 to 30–40 horses late in the century.

Shaking-tent shamanism in a variety of forms extended in an east-west band from eastern Washington to Labrador (Schaeffer 1969). As in shamanism generally, the practitioner used a spiritual helper to find out something. In curing, the shaman needed to know the cause of a disease (usually breaking a tabu, witchcraft, or some malicious action of a supernatural being) and the method to cure it (usually shaking a rattle, chanting, blowing smoke on the patient, and sucking the patient's body to draw out the disease-causing object). In shaking-tent shamanism the shaman's spirit helps the shaman to act as a seer or clairvoyant. The spirit enters the body of the shaman and people can ask the spirit questions or the shaman is given a vision which he later relates to the audience.

In 1793 a young Piegan had not returned from a trip to the Snakes. A famous Blood shaman was employed to determine the warrior's fate. The shaman was laid on his back in a tent and then all his fingers and toes were tied with strong sinew. He was sewed into a buffalo robe which was then wrapped with a strong line. Then a small, square house just large enough to stand in was built up around him with poles and a skin cover. This was hung with rattles. In twenty minutes the sound of a rattle was heard and he began to sing. In another fifteen minutes the little house began to shake. The strange voice of a spirit was heard, answering questions put to it. It said the warrior was returning with sore legs and would be back in two days. The spirit was off by one day. The warrior came back in three days with his companions. They apparently had set off on foot to steal horses, were unsuccessful, and had to walk back.

The escape of the shaman from his bindings is a magical performance that demonstrates the presence of the spirit. Magical performances of one kind or another are associated with shamanism throughout its great arc of distribution in Asia and the New World. The secret of this particular magic is to spit on the sinew to make it soft, slippery, and slightly expanded. Other shamans used magical sound effects, such as the sound of a spirit approaching the tent on horseback, dismounting, and coming into the tent.

Dances

Dances reflected the warfare orientations of the society. One, with five in a line, was for brave warriors who had never run from an enemy. Another was for warriors who had escaped when surrounded. In the scalp dance men who had killed enemies in battle mounted horses and were led around the camp by old men who sang songs of praise to them. One dance was for generous men noted for sharing their meat after a hunt. Grass Dances were held in the summer at the same time as the Sun Dance. At the Grass Dances the drummers were in the center and the dancers circled around, usually each with his own dances. Each drummer had a hand-held drum which he beat with a drumstick; they drummed and chanted in unison. Dancers often carried shields and weapons in their hands as they danced. Some wore only loincloths and moccasins. Others had fringed leggings and shirts of deerskin. A rich man might have white weasel pelts hanging from his clothes. In the reservation period people began to use the feathered headdresses and dance costumes.

A man who had lost his arm in battle carried a decorated bone from that missing arm as he danced. Another carried a small, carved wooden horse to remind people of his exploits in stealing horses. A third aimed his weapon at people in the surrounding crowd, in a pantomimic dance that reminded everyone of the time he killed a man with one shot in the head. Dancers who moved too slowly might be ritually "whipped" with a feathered wand by the leader of the Grass Dance. Between dances prominent chiefs gave speeches, telling of their brave deeds and exhorting people to be generous to the visitors. As gifts were given, war deeds were related.

Then there would be war dances on horseback in which battles would be re-enacted. A line of men on horseback would attack, circle the camp, yell their war cries, fire their guns, and form a marching line around the camp and sing their songs of victory. Old warriors would have sham battles on foot, making jokes of each other as they fought.

The Sun Dance lodge was built with a center post, a circle of ten poles around that, rafters from the circle wall to the center pole, an eastern door that faced the rising sun, and a cover of leafy branches on the top and sides. The classic Sun Dance itself was only for a few men who fasted, smoked, prayed, and danced from the wall to the center pole and back. At the end of their dance, usually a four-day ceremony throughout the Plains, their final torture was some form of tearing of their flesh, usually with leather thongs tied to skewers in the breast.

Warfare

In 1787 an old Piegan chief told of a battle that occurred before they had more than a few horses or guns. Since he was about sixteen at the time of the battle, it was probably in the 1730s. There were a war assembly, a feast, dances, and then some 350 Piegan warriors marched off. They sent out scouts who found the Shoshoni Snakes. Then they crossed a river on canoes and rafts. On the field of battle they lined up on two sides, made a great show of numbers to each other, shouted insults, and fired their arrows at each other; but their large shields were generally effective. Several were wounded on both sides but no scalps were taken.

In a later battle, with the help of ten guns, they beat a larger force of Snakes. After a few hours of shooting at each other there were advances and then the whole line charged. "'The greater part of the enemy took to flight, but some fought bravely and we lost more than ten killed and many wounded. Part of us pursued and killed a few, but the chase had soon to be given over, for at the body of every Snake Indian killed, there were five to six of us trying to get his scalp, or part of his clothing, his weapons, or something as a trophy of the battle'" (Lewis 1942:48). There was some survival of the old style of battle as late as an`1810 battle between the Piegan and Kutenai. They shouted insults, calling each other old women, and danced around in view to tease them but make difficult targets. However, the horse and gun led to the use of small raiding parties and mobile attacks.

After the spread of the horse, the Blackfoot usually rode in, fired their arrows, then engaged in hand-to-hand combat with lance, war club, and knife. Bows were made shorter for use on horseback. They were made more powerful per length with sinew along the back of the bow.

Shields got smaller, changing from about four feet to two feet, and were finally abandoned altogether except as ceremonial objects. After warfare on horseback became common there were many more casualties than before; and there was an elaboration of concepts about individual coups and war honors.

Although the Blackfoot were relatively late in acquiring the horse and many of the classical features of Plains culture, by the middle of the 1800s they had become extreme in horse stealing and warfare. In the 1700s there was considerable trade in horses, but by the 1800s the acquisition of horses was somewhat tied in with the warfare complex, and horse stealing became a much more important means of distribution than trade. The Blackfoot stole horses that had Spanish brands on them, indicating a chain of fairly quick turnovers over a period of a few years that moved horses over 1,000 miles. According to scattered reports, the Blackfoot were generally traveling mounted on horses after about 1750, twenty years after their first acquisitions. Descriptions in 1787 and 1800 indicate they had small groups of extra horses. By 1808 some Blackfoot had herds of 40 to 50 horses and one rich man had about 300. In 1833 Prince Maximilian reported that one wealthy Piegan chief owned as many as 5,000 horses.

In the 1800s horses were being bred for racing and buffalo hunting and then traded for European goods. A good buffalo horse was worth several times as much as an ordinary saddle horse. Horses were then at the center of a new wealth-based social ranking system. A man's importance depended largely on the number of horses he owned. Horses were necessary for the bride price in marriages. Women owned their own saddle horses and pack horses. Horses were used to pay admission to men's societies, to buy medicine bundles, and to purchase the right to perform the related ceremonies.

Horse Raids

Horse raids were usually planned and led by an experienced warrior in his thirties. He would select several young men in their late teens and twenties to go along on the raid, usually in the spring. One or two young boys might be taken along as apprentices to do the camp work and to learn how to steal horses, but they were kept in the background if fighting began. There are some reports of women going along on the raids. A young boy on his first war party was given a derogatory name until he had stolen a horse or committed a war coup. Then he was given a name that symbolized his act of bravery. Sometimes two young men consistently teamed up together to look after each other. It was a situation of high uncertainty, like gambling, and people used charms and personal rituals to ensure luck.

Before going the raiders would perhaps sit in a sweat lodge, pray, sing a war song, put on face paints, take a sacred object to be worn in battle, wear one or more feathers in the hair, and wear a magical war shirt. In pre-horse days they had used an armor of quilted leather that was somewhat effective against arrows shot from a distance; there may have been some transference of that idea to the concept of a magical, bullet-proof shirt. Some men attached weasel tails to their clothing. The Sioux type of feather war bonnet was not used until the modern reservation period. A warrior might have a special ritual like sprinkling water on his necklace.

The raiders usually told the band chief and others where they were going. On the night before leaving, they would walk around the camp, drum, and sing their war songs. Friends might give them food or extra moccasins for the journey. Others might ask to join the raid, but the leader had to be strict and keep the raiding party small to avoid detection by the enemy. The raiding groups ranged from two to about fifty men. They often left camp in secret in order to avoid being accompanied by hangers-on, meeting at night in a predesignated place outside the village.

The raid was a quick strike, usually at night or early dawn, to steal horses and to escape without detection. It was not to prove bravery or to kill anyone. The raiders often set out on foot, planning to ride the stolen horses back. By going in on foot, they could be much quieter and less visible than on horseback. Each man carried a pack in a blanket roll on his back held down by a strap across his chest, with one or more extra pairs of moccasins, an awl and sinew to repair clothing, rawhide ropes for catching and riding horses, a pipe and tobacco, and personal war medicine. Every man carried jerky or pemmican in a rawhide case tied on the blanket roll pack or slung on a shoulder strap, and carried a knife in a sheath at the belt. A bow and arrow or flintlock with shot and powder was also carried. This equipment weighed less than twenty pounds.

The expedition might be up to 300 miles one way on foot; hopefully the return trip would be on horseback. They might stop to kill game along the way. On the fringe of the enemy territory they would stop to build a war lodge of fallen trees covered with bark or brush. This served as a small fortress base where supplies could be left and from which they would send scouts into enemy territory. The scouts examined a valley for movement before they entered it, watched the movements and calls of birds and other animals, and examined old campfires and trails for tracks of horses or travois to determine the time and direction of their movement. When the scouts found the enemy camp they would try to estimate the number of people and determine the location, number, and quality of horses. With the raiding party at the enemy camp usually only one or two men would go in at a time to quietly steal the horses.

Ewers (1967:335-6) wrote "The attack usually was scheduled for daybreak. Then the leader and a few of his bravest and most experienced men walked noiselessly into the enemy camp. If dogs barked, they threw bits of meat to them, waited, circled the camp, and approached it from another direction ... Quickly they approached the best horses, which were picketed in front of the lodges of their sleeping enemies, cut the picket lines with their sharp knives, and led the prized animals away ... Sometimes the other members of the raiding party drove off some of the range herds ... it was important to make a quick getaway ... forty to sixty horses was considered a very good haul ... When near their camp, they stopped to paint their faces and decorate their horses. They then rode triumphantly toward the camp, firing their guns in the air to signal their return."

If caught by the enemy they would try to make it to a wooded area to defend themselves. Otherwise in the open they might try to dig fox holes with their knives for a defensive shooting position. In defence against horse raids the horses might be corralled. If people suspected a raid they would guard the horses overnight. In some cases in the 1820s and 1830s defensive fox holes or even trenches were dug around the tipis.

Scalp Raids

Occasionally large-scale scalp raids were organized to avenge the killing of a prominent leader or to prevent encroachments by other tribes on what the Blackfoot began to consider to be their buffalo-hunting territory—essentially southern Alberta, southwestern Saskatchewan, and northern Montana. Compared to their pre-horse territory west of Saskatoon, Saskatchewan, the Blackfoot had aggressively expanded their territory to many times its original size. They pushed the Kutenai out of the foothills and fairly well kept them in the Rocky Mountains. After a series of early wars they drove the Snake branch of the Shoshoni out of Canada and then out of Northern Montana. They became rather consistent in keeping the Plateau tribes out of the northern Plains: Flathead, Nez Perce, and Pend D'Oreille. Only the Plains Cree coming in from the northeast and the Crow from the southeast gave the Blackfoot effective military resistance until the arrival of the U.S. Cavalry.

The large scalp raid was an attack on an enemy camp by hundreds of warriors to keep other tribes out of their territory, to loot trapping parties or a trading post, and to avenge the deaths of a prominent warrior or chief. For example, in 1849 a Blackfoot attack force of hundreds of men found and killed a party of 52 Assiniboine horse raiders. When bands assembled for the Sun Dance a large war party might be organized. In preparation, the warriors first did a horse dance, circling the camp on horseback in their war paint and wearing fancy war clothes, carrying their weapons, and shouting. The riders then dismounted and danced next to their horses with a prancing dance that imitated a lively horse.

After changing back to their ordinary clothes, they rode off to battle.

Scouts were sent out. At first men often rode a plain saddle horse and left their fast buffalo horses for the battle itself. When the scouts found an enemy camp or war party, the warriors changed back into war clothes, mounted their fast horses, and attacked. The warriors were weak in planning or in chain-of-command organization—independent, self-seeking gladiators rather than an organized army. However, they were disciplined enough to form an initial charging line or to circle a camp. After that were random charging, firing bows and arrows, and clubbing from horseback. The good rider could bend behind his horse away from the enemy fire to protect his body.

There was little torture of prisoners in the Plains. There are reports of tortures by the Cree but this custom seems to have been recently carried in from the Iroquoian east. There was, however, a similarity with the east in taking body parts as war trophies, and an even greater elaboration of the individualistic game-like qualities of warfare. Hands, feet, and heads were sometimes taken as trophies, but the standard trophy was the scalp. The scalp was taken by cutting a circle of the skin around the crown of the head and stripping it away with the hair attached. People were usually scalped after they had been killed, but the scalping itself does not kill a person; there were people who survived a scalping. Back in the home camp the scalps and other body parts were carried through the camp in a circle dance on poles or slender, decorated wands carried by the wives and by other female relatives of those who had taken the trophies. Men sang their songs of victory. A warrior who had killed an enemy in battle could give the soul of the enemy to a deceased person to be his servant in the other world.

Coup Raids

Another kind of war raid was by young men who sought war honors. In this raid the plan was to acquire the highest possible war honors—coups—through the demonstration of extreme bravery. Since the gun was the best defensive weapon, taking it away from an enemy was the highest war honor. Below that was taking a bow, shield, bonnet, shirt or ceremonial pipe. A scalp was only about third in rank, because the enemy was usually killed first; stealing a horse was last because it was so common and did not necessarily involve combat.

Trade

Alexander Henry, an early trader, described the care that people took to respect social rank. When the Piegans came in to trade, some young men were sent in first to inform the trader that the band was coming in. They asked for a twist of tobacco for each family head coming in and a glass of liquor for themselves. On arrival the men assembled in sight of the trading post, sent their women to set up camp at the post, and approached ceremoniously in single file with the chief in the lead and the rest according to rank by their war honors and scalps. The head trader was expected to greet them, conduct them into the fort, seat the chief in a place of honor, and seat others on benches according to rank. Pipe ceremonies were conducted, starting with the trader and the chief exchanging the first pipe. The trader would fill his own pipe, light it, and offer it to the chief. The chief would give a smoke-offering to the earth, sky, sunrise, and sunset. Then the pipe was passed around the circle of visitors, who added other lighted pipes to the circle of smokers. A ceremonial round of liquor was given, and the traders were given their own keg. The fur exchange might not start until the next day.

The Canadians were unable to turn Plains buffalo hunters into Woodland-style trappers, but succeeded in bringing Cree and Ojibwa trappers westward into the Plains and the Rocky Mountains. The Blackfoot however, supplied some wolf and fox skins. The Blackfoot also sold pack horses and large quantities of dried meat for the Hudson Bay Company system. In periods of HBC monopoly the fur trade increased the prestige and authority of the chiefs because the HBC dealt only with chiefs. It purposely reinforced social order and social ranking. To enhance the authority of chiefs, it conferred honors in the form of medals and coats. When competitive companies came in they undermined the authority of chiefs by trading with junior men.

The Americans had less demand than the Canadians for horses since they shipped down the Missouri River. They shot their own buffalo meat and took the robes. American trappers came and cleaned out the beaver in about 30 years. Thus, for example, in 1805 the Northwest Fur Company took 77,500 beaver pelts and 1,135 buffalo robes. The steamboat began coming up the Missouri in 1833. During 1833–1843 the American Fur Company was taking about 70,000 buffalo robes per year out of the northern Plains.

The early effects of the buffalo-robe trade were a stimulus for development and a shift toward market production. The buffalo corrals were enlarged by additional corrals in a chain. There was greater wealth in horses, guns, and liquor. Polygyny was increased. The Plains Indians became a more affluent and commercial society. Tipis were originally 6–8 buffalo skins in size for a family of several people in the pre-horse days. In 1754, about the time when the horse was diffused throughout the society, the average tipi was about 12 skins and the largest tipi could hold 50 people. Then there was a further expansion related to the polygynous families of wealthy men. These were tipis of 18–20 skins and some were as large as 40 skins, which would have three or four fireplaces and would hold up to 100 people.

Polygyny grew in relationship to the trade in buffalo robes because women became commercially important as processors of hides. Prior to 1810 most men had one wife, but later two or even three were not uncommon. Young girl captives were occasionally sold, notably to the Cree who worked for the Hudson's Bay Company. After 1830 they were too valuable as hide processors to sell. By the 1830s wealthy men often had several wives. In 1840 even some poor men had three wives; having several wives was common, and one man was known to have sixteen wives. There was extensive warfare at this time and in 1847 a missionary estimated that between two thirds and three fourths of the adult population were women. In 1874 some men had twenty to thirty wives.

The fur trade competition among the Blackfoot intensified the social gradations. Men with large herds of horses could pay the bride price for more wives who in turn could work as hide processors. Girls were traditionally married at a younger age (16–18) than men (about 22). The age of marriage for women dropped drastically in the nineteenth century, and men were marrying off their daughters early—between ages 10 and 16—to take the bride price. Young men could not afford to marry until they were about 25. In 1885 girls were normally marrying at 12 years of age.

Within families a strong ranking system developed among the wives by sequence of their marriage. In fact, the term for wives lower than third or fourth wife means something like "slave wife." Lower wives performed the menial tasks, were sometimes beaten, and were most often suspected of adultery. In 1887 the Mormons migrated from Utah into southern Alberta and settled next to the Blood and Piegan reserves. They were escaping government harassment over their polygynous practices, and they were well received in a community with the greatest amount of polygyny in Canada.

Blackfoot relations with Whites were peaceful in the 1700s. In Canada the trading companies first tried to get the Blackfoot to come to their eastern posts, but the Blackfoot refused because they were unaccustomed to travelling by canoes, did not eat fish which would be the source of food on the long trip, and they had heard that many people died on the trip. Near the end of the 1700s the fur companies built forts in Alberta and Saskatchewan on the fringes of Blackfoot territory, and the Blackfoot traveled there for a relatively small amount of trade.

By 1830 the Canadian fur trade in the region was largely over. The supply of beaver was almost exhausted east of the Rockies and HBC was forced to introduce conservation methods. There were few travelers or traders in the HBC monopoly period from 1830 to 1870. However, the American trade in buffalo robes greatly expanded in this period. The Blackfoot probably killed about one hundred White American fur trappers and traders, notably between 1810 and 1844. The Blackfoot did relatively little trapping of small fur animals on their own, but raiding trapping parties fitted in well with their warfare patterns. They would kill the trappers, take their clothing and equipment, and sell the furs and horses at the Canadian posts. Later they became deeply involved in killing buffalo, having their women process the hides, and selling them to the American traders.

Relations on the U.S. side of the border were more violent because (1) the Whites worked for brash young companies bent simply on exploitation that did not have the experience, restraint, and long-term commitment that HBC had; (2) White trappers and traders came deeply into Blackfoot territory; (3) they set up trading forts; (4) they allied themselves in warfare with the Nez Perce, Flathead, and Crow; (5) they took out a massive trade in buffalo robes because they could cheaply transport the heavy robes by boat down the Missouri River; (6) there was a gold rush in Montana in the 1860s. The U.S. Cavalry massacred a Blackfoot band in 1873 and the Northwest Mounted Police moved in to control the liquor trade on the Canadian side in 1874. The Blackfoot were greatly reduced in population by smallpox epidemics. Within the next decade the buffalo were eliminated in their territory. In the winter of 1883–1884 nearly 600 Blackfoot starved to death in Montana. The surviving Blackfoot were then settled into reservations.

Winter Counts

Much of the history of the nineteenth century is included in the year-by-year oral histories called winter counts, kept by the Blackfoot. Just a word or phrase is the kernel of the remembered event. Then stories were told about that event and other things that happened that year were elaborated around the word or phrase. Most of the events are war raids, often symbolized by mentioning the death of a particular chief. Individual historians had different accounts, though they would coincide on major events such as epidemics and treaties. In at least one Blackfoot case a series of paintings was made on a skin as a memory aid in telling the stories of the winter count. The following is an abstract from Dempsey's synthesis of counts (1965).

1810—The Astoria Expedition passed in the summer of 1811 with the tails of their horses cut to distinguish them from Indian horses.

1811—Crying Bear was killed by Crees.

1812—The Gambler was killed by Flatheads.

1813—Bloods raided the Crow on the Big Horn River.

1819—Measles epidemic that killed about one third of the Blackfoot and Gros Ventres.

1831—James Kipp and 75 men established Fort Piegan at the confluence of the Missouri and Marias Rivers.

1833—"Stars, when they fell." This was a widely recorded meteoric shower.

1837-1838—An estimated 6,000 of the 9,000 Blackfoot died in a smallpox epidemic. It is difficult to conceive what it means to have two thirds of a society eliminated in two years.

1842—Many buffalo were killed at Women's Buffalo Jump near the Porcupine Hills in southwestern Alberta.

1845—A Blood named Going to the Sun escaped from Cree warriors by hiding in a hole.

1854—A time of starvation when they ate their dogs.

1855—The Americans made a treaty and paid the Blackfoot.

1864-1865—Scarlet fever killed about 1,100 Blackfoot.

1867—Blackfoot began to receive repeating rifles and were able to kill a large number of buffalo.

1869-1870—Smallpox epidemic killed some 1,080 Piegans, 630 Bloods, and 676 Siksika.

1870—Hundreds died on both sides when several hundred Assiniboine and Cree attacked a Blood-Piegan camp, not knowing that many of the Blackfoot had repeating rifles.

1874—The Northwest Mounted Police came and established Fort Macleod. The next year is called "When the whiskey trade ended."

1879—Most of the buffalo in Blood territory had been killed or driven south so the Bloods hunted in Montana.

1880—The Montana herd was largely finished off so the Bloods moved back to Canada.

1883—The Canadian Pacific Railway ("fire wagon") was built through Blackfoot Territory. The Whites supported Crowfoot as head chief of the Blackfoot and then the CPR got his cooperation by giving him a secret, personal payment of $700 annually. It was only discovered after he died, when the railroad asked whom it should be paid to.

Modern Period

In 1877 the Canadian Blackfoot and the Assiniboine signed a treaty ceding their land. They were soon settled on reserves and bureaucratically administered like a small internal colony by the White government and missionaries. In 1890 the White Indian agent and the local Anglican missionaries forced the Canadian Blackfoot to stop the Sun Dance. They pressured them to substitute tree platform burial with underground burial, though the people were afraid that the spirits would be eternally trapped below the ground. Plural marriages were dissolved and the extra wives sent away. Sacred bundles and the regalia of traditional societies were destroyed. In both the U.S. and Canada the Catholic missionaries were more tolerant of Indian customs, slower in their assimilation programs, and more complete in their assimilation of Indian children. The Catholics set up a school system on the reserves.

Many horse-related traits died out soon after the extermination of the buffalo. Camps became permanent, obviating the use of the horse for moving camp. Inter-tribal peace was forced on the Indians; thus the horse was not used in warfare. The Indian breeds of horses were replaced by larger and stronger workhorse breeds. Indians adopted the White saddle and bridle, methods of mounting, wagon harness, and horse commands. They shifted to cattle and sheep raising on horses, using horses to plow fields and to pull wagons, and they enthusiastically accepted the whole rodeo complex. Today Plains Indians have their own rodeos. There has been a creative revival of Plains dances in pan-Indian powwow dancing. And there is still some survival of such religious customs as pipe ceremonies, sacred bundle ceremonies, and the Sun Dance.

Today the Blackfoot are rural Canadians and Americans with a distinct ethnic heritage. There is a population of 10,000 Blackfoot in both countries. They raise cattle, sheep, and horses; some farm wheat, barley, and hay. The Montana tribe owns a lumber mill and is involved in producing and refining oil and natural gas (McFee 1972). The Montana reservation is run somewhat in the style of a large county government, except that it has some autonomy from state jurisdictions and relates directly to the federal government through a variety of agencies, particularly the Bureau of Indian Affairs. They sponsor the nationally famous North American Indian Days in Browning, Montana. The Alberta Blackfoot split into three separate reserves for the Siksika or northern Blackfoot near Gleichen (2,355 people in 1970), Blood (4,262), and Piegan (1,413) west of Lethbridge. The Canadian Blackfoot are involved in ranching. Many work in the petroleum industry in Alberta, and the Siksika own their coal mine (Hanks and Hanks 1950).

Commentary

The Plains represents a rare case in which a singular change precipitated other changes. Among the Blackfoot the introduction of the horse became the single essential change in the evolution of the cultural system from a band to a tribal level. Because it happened so quickly we could call it a *revolution*. It was a Neolithic revolution in microcosm, brought about by the introduction of a well-domesticated animal and the advanced complex of Eastern Hemisphere horse-related traits: saddles with stirrups, bridles, breeding, and so forth. Some 3,000 years of developments of horse-related culture were in effect handed as a package to the Indians.

The cultural traits were, of course, essential. For example, those societies, such as the early Western Shoshone and Washo of Utah and Nevada, who came across horses and did not have the equestrian cultural traits simply hunted and ate the horses.

One element in this American horse Neolithic was that the domestication and use of the dog was a preadaptation for the use of the horse: the dog was used to pull a *small* travois whereas the horse was used to pull a *large* travois.

Another element is that the agricultural and tribal-level societies of the pre-horse Plains had cultural systems that could easily elaborate cultural changes brought on by shifting from farming and occasional pedestrian hunting to the richness of horseback hunting. Thus the major zone of creation within the Plains was among the eastern tribes, whereas peoples with a simpler heritage, such as the Apache, Ute, and Blackfoot were on the receiving end of the innovations. The Sun Dance, for example, was invented by the Plains Algonquians such as the Cheyenne, in the early 1700s, and it later diffused. The Sun Dance is a *tribal* rather than *band* kind of religious ceremony. The band type of roots for this practice is in the individualistic techniques of fasting and self-torture to achieve a vision and supernatural power. The tribal element entered when it was done as a spectacular, communal ceremony in the summer during the great in-gathering of the tribe for carefully co-ordinated buffalo harvesting. That communal orientation produced a new tribal religion, which spread and tended to displace the earlier, more individualistic, practices.

Yet another element in the rapid development of the Plains culture was the use of the horse to open up transportation and communication links, accelerating the diffusion of cultural traits. Innovations in riding, buffalo-hunting techniques, the Sun Dance, warrior's societies, *coup* counting, and so forth quickly spread in the Plains.

The Blackfoot enthusiastically took over the horse, horse culture, and many of the Plains practices. They modified these traits very much to their own ends. For reasons that escape me, they emphasized economics, rather than religion, politics, art, or war games like the *coup* system. They became powerful warriors, but they used that power to dominate the Alberta, Saskatchewan, and northern Montana buffalo territory, rather than to get as deeply involved in the internecine warfare of the *coup* system as some of the tribes to the south did. They raided primarily for horses, which they sold to the trading posts. The men's age-grade societies became commercialized. Bride price was paid to a girl's father. The number of wives was increased to prepare buffalo skins for sale to the American fur companies. This economic orientation has persisted. The Blackfoot are among the most successful entrepreneurs among the Canadian Indians in ranching, petroleum, mining, and even in manufacturing prefabricated houses.

CHAPTER 8

PACIFIC COAST
Kwakiutl:
Political Economy of a
Fishing Chiefdom

Pacific Coast

IN MANY RESPECTS the Pacific Coast cultures were unique, not only in Canada but in the world. They were the only primitive societies in historic times to achieve the evolutionary level of a wealthy, socially ranked chiefdom without an economic base of food production—that is, without agriculture or pastoralism. Of the societies that depended on gathering food from nature and that were observed at this labor by literate peoples, the Pacific Coast societies were the richest in the world. There are archaeological indications that other rich pre-agricultural fishing societies existed earlier in a few places in the world, such as on the Dordogne River in France and the Mississippi River in the U.S. None of these, however, seems to have matched the spectacular developments of the British Columbia coast. The B.C. coast had an aboriginal population of about 50,000, making it the most densely settled region in Canada. The major language groupings—Tlingit, Haida, Tsimshian, Wakashan, and Salish—all had populations of several thousand people.

The Pacific Coast culture was an indigeneous development out of an earlier Plateau-based fishing culture along the Thompson and Columbia River systems. It seems to have spread south from the mouth of the Columbia at Portland to Cape Mendocino in California and north from the mouth of the Fraser at Vancouver to Yakutat Bay in southern Alaska. This dissemination took thousands of years, and there was a great amount of social interaction and cultural borrowing up and down the coast. By European contact times, the spread had not yet reached the limits of the natural ecological zone along the coast where intensive fishing was feasible. The culture type had filled the central part of the area where stream fishing and close-in ocean fishing by primitive methods would support large permanent populations. Still the culture type could have gone farther, south throughout the San Francisco Bay-Sacramento River area and north along the shore of southern Alaska. In the north the Eyak and Chugamiut of southern Alaska were only skimming off a minor part of the great marine resources of their areas. Drucker (1965) and McFeat (1966) published books on the area as a whole and the major works for our case material on the Kwakiutl are by Boas (1966), Drucker and Heizer (1967), and Ford (1941).

The Pacific Coast culture area extended over 1,500 miles along the coast and went inland only along the rivers. The culture was highly oriented to rivers and oceans, where the abundant runs of salmon and other fish sustained elaborate cultures. The natural abundance, combined with an environmentally appropriate technology and organization of work, provided an energy level equivalent to rich horticulture. Natural abundance alone, of course, does not by itself produce rich cultures. Thus we find that the west coast temperate marine area of South America was rich in natural resources but poorly utilized.

The Pacific Coast was cut off from many of the cultural influences of the rest of North America by the Rocky Mountains, the high dry interior basin and plateaus of the far west, and the coastal ranges of mountains. Thus when agriculture and the complex of related traits such as pottery spread north from Mexico, it penetrated westward only into the southwestern fringe of California and into the river systems into the Plains. Agriculture societies never came closer than several hundred miles from the Pacific Coast societies; these two spheres of high development in North America remained out of communication with each other. The relative isolation of the coast contributed to the continuing uniqueness of the coastal cultures. Internal communication along the coasts, particularly by boats, caused some homogeneity of the cultures within the area.

Food

Salmon fishing, particularly of the summer spawning runs with large pole and basketry fish weirs, was important throughout the area. First-salmon rites were performed by a local chief to welcome the arrival of the first fish each year. The fish spirits were addressed as honored guests and given offerings. One type of weir channeled the fish as they swam upstream through a funnel into a large trap made of poles. Another type set below a rapids or falls caught the fish that fell back from their jump. Yet another type stranded the fish at low tide by a barrier of boulders and poles. When the fish were concentrated in a weir they were taken out with a dip net; leister, a fish spear with a central spike to kill the fish and prongs on each side to grip the fish; gaff; or harpoon. Some fish were eaten fresh, but most of the salmon catch was quickly split and dried in smokehouses built near the weirs and then packed into baskets or boxes for use during the rest of the year. Literally tons of fish were taken in a single run of a week or so at some of the important weirs.

Herring were taken when they schooled up with dip nets or "herring rakes," poles with a long row of bone spikes that impaled the fish when swung through the water. Schools of smelt were fished with dip nets offshore and in baskets when they ran to the beach to spawn. Olachen, called the "candlefish" because of its high oil content, were taken in great quantities in their river runs from the Fraser northward by dip nets or herring rakes, or with long tubular nets with a flared opening. Salmon, as well as such large fish as cod and halibut, were also taken by hook and line using such things as cuttlefish as bait. Seals and sea lions were hunted by harpoon along the shore, porpoises and sea otters at sea. These and such land mammals as deer and mountain goat were largely hunted for their skins. Many other kinds of sea foods were gathered, such as clams, mussels, abalone, crabs, a variety of sea weeds, and herring eggs.

The women gathered berries and roots (lily, lupine, and fern) and, among the Kwakiutl, tended individually owned and enclosed beds of clover for its edible roots. There was a food tabu against mixing land and sea animals. Smoked fish and meat could be eaten without further preparation. Other foods were grilled over a fire, boiled in a wooden trough or box with heated stones, or steamed in an earth oven. Olachen were decayed for a week in a trough or canoe, and boiled with heated stones until the oil would separate, rise to the surface, and be skimmed off. It was used as a general cooking and eating oil. This oil was usually stored in natural kelp bottles which in turn were kept in wooden boxes. The oil was so widely used in eating that shredded bark was passed around at meals for people to wipe the oil from their hands.

Woodworking

The B.C. coast had the finest woodworking in the New World and probably the finest in the world for a primitive culture. Both the technical craftsmanship and artistic elements were excellent. The coastal Indians worked the straight-grained woods, particularly red cedar, with such tools as the adze made of stone, shell, or horn; chisel, wedge, maul, and knife. Small amounts of iron were used in some tools, presumably acquired through a long trade chain from the Siberian iron mines.

Trees were cut and then were split with wedges. One technique to split a tree lengthwise was to adze a deep side cut near the top of a standing tree, start the long cut with wedges, and slip a long pole into the cut. The workers would then leave the tree, knowing that the swaying of the wind and the weight of the pole would continue to split the tree. For house planks they split off one plank after another.

For a canoe the workers selected a particularly straight and internally sound tree from a dense part of the forest where there were no low branches which would create knots. It was felled on the side with the fewest knots, its "belly." During the work the canoe-maker followed a pattern of prayers and magical rituals and avoided sexual intercourse. He did not comb his hair because it might magically make the ends of the wood split. He painted the sides of the canoe with a frightening face that scared away the spirits of dead canoemakers who might split his canoe.

The top of the log was split off and then the center of the log was burned and adzed out until the hull was as thin as possible. At first there was a rough burning and adzing job done where the tree was felled, to reduce the weight before it was hauled to a work area by the shore. Then the sides were cut to about the thickness of a forefinger and the bow, bottom, and stern the thickness of two forefingers. One technique to ensure that the hull was of the right thickness was to drill a set of tiny holes into it and insert charred sticks into the holes to the exact depth of the hull thickness. When the adzing cuts from the inside revealed the ends of the charred sticks the adzing was stopped, the charred sticks were pulled out, and the tiny holes were sealed with shredded bark and pitch. The hull was then expanded by heating water inside it, warming it with a fire from below, and pressing springy sticks inside. Once the hull was expanded to the right width, permanent cross braces were put in. Professional canoe builders took three or four weeks to make a canoe.

Several kinds of canoes were made. The most common were a small, slender hunting canoe and a large, broad, transport and war canoe, with attached prow and stern pieces to break the ocean waves. The war canoes were manned by a team of steersman and rowers. The canoes were stored on the beach above the high-water mark. In hot weather they were filled with water and covered with mats so that they would not crack in the sun.

Houses

Large, rectangular, multifamily plank houses were used in the winter villages. The basic form had an oval doorway, a high (15–20 feet) double ridgepole, posts and roof timbers carved with aesthetic rows of adze fluting marks or more rarely zoomorphic sculptures, planks tied on the house frame walls and laid on the gabled roof, and a low central pit. The ground plan was laid out with considerable engineering knowledge, by stakes and precisely measured ropes (Boas 1966:33). Sophisticated machinery using a pivot, lever, beam guide, and support pole was used to raise and place the huge roof beams. Teams of men, coordinated by work chants, cooperated in raising the roof beams. Among the Kwakiutl the roof boards were sometimes adzed to have a curved cut down the center and then overlapped, alternately concave and convex to fit together and provide a waterproof roof.

Earth banks about one yard high and two yards wide were built along the inner sides of the houses. The families slept, stored their goods, and cooked on these platforms around the walls. They slept on beds of cedar branches covered with deerskin, and used perhaps the skin of a mountain goat or a bear for cover in cold weather. Pillows were made of skin filled with bird down. Above the family fireplace there was often a fish-smoking rack and nearby there would be a hammerstone and wooden wedges for splitting wood, tongs for handling the hot stones used in cooking, and food boxes.

In the north among the Tlingit, Tsimshian, and Haida the houses were smaller, about 40' by 40', usually had a board floor, a central fireplace that was used on a daily basis, and a permanent central smokehole in the roof. In the south among the Kwakiutl, Nootka, and Salish the houses were larger, with an earth floor, and the central fireplace was used only occasionally for community rituals while the several individual families had their own daily fires. The Kwakiutl house was like a large room, 30' wide and 50' to 140' long. The Salish type was a long low building with a single pitched roof.

Small huts were made at the summer fishing camps and were covered with bark slabs, woven mats, or even planks temporarily taken off the winter village houses. All the chiefdoms occasionally used small stockades in times of war. There were also huts where women stayed when they were menstruating, to prevent ritually contaminating the main house.

Large troughs were carved for food vessels, especially from alder because it neither splits easily nor gives the food an unpleasant flavor. Square storage boxes were used, their four sides made from a single piece of wood that was grooved and bent to form the corners. The ends were beveled and sewn together. Then the sides were precisely fitted with a mortise joint and pegs to the bottom of the box. The top was a snugly fitted board or another box that was slipped over the base box. A wide variety of platters, bowls, and chests were also made.

Villages

The B.C. coast has the topography of a flooded mountain chain: many islands, inlets, and a generally steep-walled, vertical landscape. There was little level land for village sites. The villages were commonly perched on some little ledge between a great forest-covered mountain and the sea. Other factors in the selection of a village site were shelter in a bay or inlet from ocean waves, proximity to good places to set up fish weirs, and defensibility. Because these factors have existed for thousands of years, the locations of winter villages have been very stable. Many of these sites have been consistently used for over 4,000 years.

Villages usually ranged in size from several to thirty houses, two hundred to seven hundred in population. Aboriginally, there were some 25 major winter villages among the Kwakiutl. The houses were arranged close to each other, usually in one row, facing the water, each with its totem poles in front to signify the lineage crest of the house. The Kwakiutl often painted their house fronts with huge totemic designs. Sitting and working platforms were often erected across the front of the houses. There was a wide, leveled street in front of the houses, often supported and protected from storms by an embankment of logs. Rows of steps in front of each house led down the embankment to the beach and to the canoes and menstrual huts belonging to the house.

Below the high water mark were the latrines. These were holes dug in the beach. To defecate, the Indians would squat on flat rocks next to the holes, and clean themselves with pieces of bark. These latrines, built below the high tide line, would be regularly flushed by the sea.

Clothing

While working on warm days the men were often completely nude. Clothing was not tailored. A loin cloth was used by men and an apron by women. Ordinarily the material was made of shredded, twisted, and woven cedar bark. Both men and women wore long rain capes of woven bark. The men wore them loosely over one shoulder and the women wore them more tightly like a poncho with holes for the head and the arms. Chiefs' robes were trimmed with sea-otter or other furs. Ceremonial robes were occasionally made from furs or woven from the wool of dogs or mountain goats over a warp of twisted bark. Basketry hats were commonly worn by both sexes. The hats of chiefs were elaborately shaped and painted. The people generally went without footgear of any kind, although moccasins were occasionally used, especially in the north. Shell necklaces, earrings, and nose pieces were worn by both sexes. Tattooing, body paints, and aesthetic head deformation were common in the area, especially for the nobles.

Calendar

The annual cycle was more precisely known on the Pacific Coast than in the rest of Canada by the use of a dawn light calendar. Each day a mark was made where the first ray of the rising sun struck the inside of the western wall after it passed through a hole in the eastern wall of the house. The marks together formed a line that slowly moved from winter solstice to summer solstice and back again. Thus the year was conceived as not just an annual swing of temperatures, moons, and other events in nature, but as a cycle in which each *day* had a precise position. The new year began with the second day of the first new moon after the winter solstice. The Kwakiutl knew that the solar year was longer than twelve lunar months, and made the appropriate adjustment.

The Kwakiutl divided the year into two basic parts: *baxus*, summer, when they were dispersed in food gathering activities; and *tsetseqa*, winter, when they lived in permanent villages and had the annual social rituals. The coming of the spirits from the north at the start of *tsetseqa* was ceremonially portrayed by "spirit whistles" coming into the northern part of the village. The sun and long days of *baxus* brought the great fish runs while *tsetseqa* had short days and the fish diminished in numbers. In *baxus* the secular social ranking was followed while in *tsetseqa* life was ordered in a theocratic style.

Childhood

Charles Nowell told of growing up as a Kwakiutl boy around Fort Rupert in the 1870s (Ford 1941). The children played group games. Gangs of boys about the same age marched around in long lines; played follow-the-leader and racing and jumping games; sang songs; went begging food from house to house; took turns seeing who was the bravest, the second bravest, and so on, by progressively pushing a peg with their mouths toward a fire or burning their arms with glowing charcoal. The boys masturbated together and played at being married with the girls, building little houses in the woods, and having sexual intercourse with the girls. They played war games, attacking and taking slaves, naming their groups after Kwakiutl groups that really warred against each other. They would strike at each other with stinging nettles, whip each other with spruce boughs until they cut into the skin, and have fights throwing dirt clods or clamshells at each other. They played tricks on adults, like pushing over the household bucket of urine. Older teenage boys had mock bow and arrow warfare with shortened arrow tips, but the arrows could still cut the skin.

Boys were taught early how to paddle and steer boats, spear and hook fish, and shoot birds with a bow and arrow. They would cut and haul firewood and haul water. The children were taught the names and crests of the lineages, villages, and the ranked positions and the history of their people. The children were admonished not to be bad because if they were, "The Cannibal will come after you." The Cannibal would be sent around to scare little boys in their homes, and the boys said respectfully, "Sir, I am your friend" or pleaded, "Sir, I am just a little boy." Then the Cannibal would go away.

The boys took turns at sponsoring play feasts for each other, and at playing the role of chief. The play potlatch was somewhat more serious with the boys in the gang replicating the wider society; there were a boy as sponsoring chief, older boys playing the ranked roles and giving speeches, real gifts, songs, and new names.

Boys usually began a mild form of ritual training with daily baths around ten years of age. A more severe training began around the time of puberty when a boy's voice changed, with fasting, seclusions, and a concerted quest for a vision and powers from a spiritual being to guide him through life. Boys sat cross-legged when they ate and girls squatted on their haunches.

The girls, as generally is true in North America, had an even more distinct and more socially validated puberty ceremony at the first incidence of menstruation. This involved four days of seclusion in a menstrual hut, abstinence from most foods except for some smoked salmon, drinking only through a tube, and scratching herself only with a special stick. She was not permitted to sit near a fire. When she left the hut she wore a special hat to protect her eyes from sunlight. It ended in purifying rituals of bathing, wearing new clothes, a new hairdressing, a public symbolic cleansing, and a public feast.

Later in life women returned to live in a menstrual hut during the times of the flow of menstrual blood. Menstrual blood was considered dangerous and was carefully collected in cedar bark and buried. This blood was the center of a pattern of beliefs: It could contaminate fishing and hunting equipment, it could make men sick if they had sexual intercourse with a menstruating woman, and it could be used in a positive way to poison supernatural monsters. Female kinfolk routinely brought water and prepared food to an individual staying in the menstrual hut.

Marriage

The arrangement of marriages by parents was very common in North America. The B.C. coast, however, was extreme in the care and negotiation they used in marriage arrangements because of their emphasis on social rank and transfers of property and other wealth. Noble children in particular had little to say about whom they were married to. The groom's family negotiated a bride price in terms of wealth items, such as carvings, furs, a canoe, and perhaps a large copper crest shield. The marriage in effect became legal when the bride price was paid to the bride's family. Wealthy families would reciprocate with gifts to the groom and with titles and privileges that were meant to be passed on to the children of the marriage. Even lowly commoners were supplied with a modest bride price and given a marriage feast by the lineage chief. There was also a practice of paying back the pride price, gradually and particularly after the birth of a child, that in some ways had the effect of dissolving the marriage and allowing the woman to marry someone else. However, the groom usually perpetuated the marriage by starting a new cycle of gifts to his in-laws.

The Kwakiutl marriage ceremony had features common to other cultures around the world: the reinforcement of incest prohibitions, the ideology that marriage takes place between people of different villages, and the venting of the feeling that marriage involves an emotional break of the spouse who leaves home and goes to live in the household of strangers. Among the Kwakiutl this was done through the re-enactment of a drama in which the man took his bride by force from another village. The marriage ceremony included a sham battle between the relatives of the bride and the groom. The groom's party were then subjected to tests to show that they could not be vanquished. Women also had a feast and gave speeches of advice to the bride.

Religion

Ritual training by adults was followed by eating a sparse diet of dried foods, bathing, and by avoiding sexual intercourse. Ritual training at regular monthly or seasonal intervals put men in a religious state favorable to aid by supernatural beings. In this state of ritual purity the spirit might reveal itself to the trainee, whereupon the trainee would attempt to control and take powers from the spirit for use in hunting, warfare, and curing. A shaman was a person who went more deeply into these religious practices and often apprenticed under another shaman. A curing shaman specialized in dramatic performances that (1) returned a person's lost soul; (2) cast out disease-producing objects such as bone objects, claws, or pebbles, that had been intruded into a patient's body by a malevolent spirit or an evil shaman; or (3) cured a spirit disease that was caused by breaking a tabu or being possessed by a dangerous spirit. Men and women of low or intermediate status became shamans, ostensibly to gain wealth through payments for cures. They still had to do routine work as well and the wealth they received was usually given up to the lineage when a potlatch was planned. Like being an accomplished war leader, canoemaker, or carver it was just another path to prestige outside the usual inherited ranking system.

Witchcraft was performed by taking things associated with the victim, such as excreta, hair, or clothing and giving it such special ritual treatment as placing it in a grave or tying it to a piece of human bone. Some witches put the object into a frog's mouth, sewed the mouth shut, and played the frog at the end of a line in a stream, where it jerked— causing convulsions and death to the victim. It could be put in the body of a dead snake and placed where the sun would strike it or in a tree where the wind would blow it. When the sun struck the object, the victim would have a fever. When the wind swayed it, the victim would grow dizzy and faint. As it decayed, the victim would die.

The Kwakiutl had three main male dancing societies: (1) Shamans— involving monsters that induced violent behavior; (2) Those Who

Descend from the Heavens—usually peaceful sky and sea spirits called by magical songs and portrayed with elaborate masks; (3) The Dog Eaters— who become possessed by wolf spirits that killed and ate dogs raw on stage. They all emphasized the compulsive and obviously inhuman behavior of those possessed by spirits. Each had an exclusive membership and an exclusive time of the year for their annual performance—the Shamans in the early winter and Those Who Descend From the Heavens in early spring. The roles in the first two societies were strictly ranked. They mixed comic and serious performances and staged dramatic magical events, seeming to cannibalize a person on stage (with a dummy and a bladder filled with blood), totally burning a box with a performer inside (with trap doors), making birds fly through the air in a controlled way (with carved birds pulled on strings), causing voices to speak from within a fire (with speaking tubes under the house), and so forth.

The performers re-enacted the acquisition of supernatural powers in the original formation of the society. In the process the performers were possessed or at least inspired by the spirits. The performers used masks, names, songs, dances, and magical acts that were owned by the specific society.

The Shamans' Society had several ranked performers: Cannibal was usually first in rank and typically a high chief, Grizzly Bear, Warrior, Warrior Fool, Fire Thrower, and so on to the low-ranked dancers. When three or four villages concentrated in the towns of recent historic times, there would be multiple Cannibals, Grizzly Bears, etc. The performers were kidnaped and hidden by the spirits and then appeared back publicly possessed and behaving like their spirits. In a state of possession, Cannibal might bite pieces of flesh from the spectators' arms or appear to kill and eat parts of a human on stage. Some spectators really were bitten but this required prior approval and payment from the Cannibal's victim. Grizzly Bear and Warrior would crash around and destroy valuable objects, having already secretly paid for them. These were rich men putting on a grand public show, albeit with genuine religious significance. A dancer who made mistakes in his steps or songs was grabbed by high-ranking dancers who made the audience believe that the dancer had been killed for making errors. A day or two later the "dead" dancer was brought back in another performance.

Political Economy

The Pacific coast had the only societies to reach a chiefdom level of cultural evolution in aboriginal Canada. Thus, the important theoretical lessons for the Pacific region have been largely related to its chiefdom institutions: the centralized organization of economic production and distribution, the elaboration of social ranking, and sponsorship of elaborate public art and religious ceremonies. Many of the traditional features of society were integrated through the *potlatch* ceremonies. These ceremonies were seen as wasteful and as a block to the assimilation of Indians into Canadian society, and were outlawed in Canada between 1884 and 1951 though they continued to be practised in secret.

The basic units of social, political, and economic life were small lineages—groups of kinfolk who lived in the same village, owned specific food-gathering sites and other privileges, and worked together. The principal of descent behind these lineages was matrilineal in northern B.C. (Tlingit, Tsimshian, and Haida) and bilateral with a patrilineal bias in southern B.C. (Kwakiutl, Nootka, and Salish). The lineage owned a set of names for persons, houses, canoes, etc.; the right to paint and carve certain zoomorphic totemic, heraldic crests; and dances, songs, and rituals.

The totemic animals were not worshipped, or tabued as food, or ever regarded as literal ancestors, but they were the special source of the supernatural power and historical distinctions of the lineage, a kind of transference of the individualistic guardian spirit relationship to the kinship group as a whole. The lineage sponsored a wide variety of ceremonials for birth, puberty, marriage, and death; first fruits rites; and, most importantly, the great ceremonial feasts called *potlatches* that validated the transfer of names, titles, and privileges. Each lineage had a tradition that accounted for its name and major privileges, and this history was regularly dramatized through speeches, songs, and costumed dances.

Lineage members were somewhat gradated in terms of social status, privileges, and political and economic powers from the chiefs and their noble families through the commoners. In addition, some 10 to 20 per cent of a village's population were usually slaves, owned by the various lineages of a village. Among the Kwakiutl, primogeniture and sequence of birth in the male line was the primary determinant of the inheritance of titles and privileges. All the children of a chief were considered nobles and given deference in speech and manners by those of lower social rank. The chief's family lived in the higher status parts of a house, particularly along the rear wall. People of high rank directed activities, such as constructing a weir. In daily dress the ornaments and trim of their clothing signalled their higher status. On ceremonial occasions they dressed in fine clothing and played the major roles. They were fishermen like everyone else, but young noblemen would also be trained somewhat as speech-makers, warriors, and dramatists in privileged secret societies.

As the social distinctions operated primarily within a small, cooperating kinship group of usually only two or three dozen families, a sharply defined noble class did not separate out. Among the Kwakiutl a serial ranking of noble positions developed, particularly in regard to an official sequence of seats at potlatches. Each lineage had 6 to 42 hereditary, named, and ranked positions. Thus, for example, the Ground Shakers lineage (*numaym*) had 32 positions in 1895. The name of the highest position was "Four Fathom Face," the fifth was "From Whom Property Comes," the fifteenth was "Whose Body Was All Wealth," and so on. Some men held more than one position and occasionally women held a position and behaved in the ceremonial context as if they were men. Beyond these were the wives, children, and most other relatives of the "seated nobles." Lower still were the "worthless people": illegitimates, orphans, refugees, tramps, neglected black sheep relatives, and possibly some freed surplus slaves. At the bottom and outside of normal society were the slaves.

There was a strong tendency for the nobility to marry within its own ranks. Female children of chiefs could acquire some wealth and privileges directly from their father, but their primary security was through marriage to high-ranking men, who in turn received wealth and privileges from their wealthy fathers-in-law to pass on to their children.

The primary wealth of lineages was the ownership of sites for villages and camps; fishing, sealing, clam gathering, seabird egg gathering, and hunting areas; and forests for timber and bark collection. These areas were precisely defined by natural landmarks. An outside person had to ask permission to fish, hunt, or gather there from the chief of the owning lineage and he would usually charge a proportion of the catch for the use. The members of the owning lineage survived on the produce of those sites, but the chief, who was usually the nominal owner of the site, took the surplus of that production for the sponsorship of trade; warfare and defence; payments to professional artists, canoe-makers, totem pole makers, and shamans; and for the ceremonies of the lineage. Because of the historical movements of lineages a patchwork of ownerships prevailed, rather than simple large blocks, but lineages of a winter village would usually control the region of the village. Powerful chiefs monopolized the trade in their regions by refusing the passage of foreign trading canoes through their coastal waters. Captain James Cook, who visited societies all around the world, said that he had never met a people with such strict and exclusive rights to property as the Nootka.

The acquisition, displays, inheritance transfers, and public giving of wealth were a major preoccupation along the B.C. coast. Sharing was basic to the economy of the household and the lineage and it was a pervasive ideal in society. Thus leaders were obliged to materially support all their lineage members. If a chief failed to support his own people they could shift residence and alliances to another lineage. In this sense the Kwakiutl were ambilineal, emphasizing either lineage, because a man could take his family and live with and support his mother's lineage or even his wife's lineage if dissatisfied with life in his father's lineage. A good leader supported his people well, acquired a reputation as a generous man, and gave out titles and privileges to tie his followers into the local social status system. There was also a religious side to leadership, not only in keeping up the community religious rituals but in maintaining a favored relationship with the spirit world. Since self-indulgent and stingy men were deserted by their spirits, their fortunes turned bad, their followers abandoned them, and relatives pressed their claims through inheritance and potlatching to the misers' titles.

Slavery

Slaves were primarily taken in warfare although there was also some debt slavery in the south. If their lineage was wealthy they would be ransomed back, the amount depending on the status of the person. Slavery was considered to be a disgrace to both the captives and their relatives. Captives were not very welcome to come back by escape. It was much more honorable to be handsomely ransomed back. Even then there was an elaborate purification ritual with bathing to wash off the stigma of slavery. Some poorly defended villages suffered for generations under the stigma as a place where many slaves had been captured. Even today the oral histories of the coast are laden with stories about how *our* family, lineage, village, and chiefdom were nobles and those *other* families, lineages, villages, and chiefdoms were lower class or slaves.

If no ransom was offered, the slaves were usually traded from one village to the next until far enough from their home village to be unable to escape and return home. Thus Salish taken in the Vancouver area ended up as slaves to the Tlingit in southern Alaska. Slaves lost all rank, wealth, and titles they might have had, and were usually required to cut their hair short. They were given the drudgery work such as gathering firewood, digging clams, and carrying goods around; and received the leftover food. They were neglected when sick, and when they died they were not buried or given funerals: their bodies were taken out to sea and thrown overboard. Their masters were free to sell them, give them away, or even have them killed as a funeral offering to a dead chief or just as a dramatic demonstration of conspicuous consumption. The Canadian government once burned down a village as punishment for the killing of a slave as part of the drama in a winter ceremonial. When a slave was sold it was usually with a warranty; if the slave died within a year, about half the price was refunded.

The background of warfare, slavery, and monopolistic controls of trade within regions was not conducive to long-distance trading. Therefore this became a specialized enterprise. Trade between villages was usually carried out under the protection of the institution of trading partners, chiefs who established a fictive brother relationship with each other. They stayed at each other's house, exchanged gifts and ceremonial names, and traded under the protection and in the sanctuary of each other's house. These chiefs became experts at judging the qualities of goods. They studied the articles closely and bargained down the barter rate on any defect they could find.

Alliances and Warfare

A winter village might be composed of one or several lineages. If there were more than one they had some ranking. The highest-ranking chief of the highest-ranking lineage in the village had some functions as a village chief, such as settling inter-lineage disputes, arranging village defences, and scheduling potlatches and other ceremonies. A few villages within small regions formed small confederations that reciprocated in holding potlatches for each other and that were allied in warfare. The villages too were typically ranked for the purpose of potlatching. In historic times large confederations were formed at Forts Simpson, McLoughlin, and Rupert.

The coastal chiefdoms were oriented to fishing, wealth, and to their secret societies, not to warfare. Still, their warfare was even more destructive, more territorially oriented, and less of a ritualistic summer game than the aboriginal warfare of the Iroquoian and Plains areas. There are many cases in the oral history of villages that were destroyed and of large-scale slave raids. There are a few cases of systematic genocide and enslavement. The introduction of guns contributed to this destructiveness. However, unlike the Iroquoian and Plains areas, the coastal chiefdoms were not oriented to warfare in historic times. They intensified potlatching instead. They used the new iron axes to make even larger, more spectacular totem poles, and they put on more elaborate dramas.

Witchcraft and murder were the most serious offences against society. Witches were usually put to death in an indirect way that would not react on an executioner. A witch might be tied to a stake at the water's edge at low tide to be drowned when the tide came in. Murder was quickly rectified by the group the *victim* came from on the group the *killer* came from to protect the good reputation of the victim's group. This could be (1) the selective killing of a person of the same social rank as the victim from the killer's group, (2) a mass attack on the offender's village, or (3) a blood payment in wealth arranged through a neutral go-betwen.

In one case two men were competing suitors of the same woman. While in a battle in a foreign village one shot the other in the confusion to make it look as though the enemy had shot the man. The injured man survived and held a feast to denounce his attacker in public. At the feast the attacker's older brother paid off the attack with a canoe and forty blankets.

War leaders were hereditary, but usually low-ranked, nobility, something like younger brothers of chiefs. Becoming a warrior was a somewhat distinct occupation. Warriors might rub their bodies with snake's blood and wear a pouch around the neck, containing charmed objects such as parts of a snake, frog, and grizzly bear. They might make a necklace of a snakeskin or of the toenails of a dead person. Warriors cut themselves with sharp bone points, thus leaving many scars on their bodies. They were taught to be cruel, to avoid soft beds, accumulating property, or marrying while young. They were expected to maltreat boys and to seduce girls. They "walked with stiff, jerky motions . . . expressive of their ill humor. They had to avoid laughing. Their right hand was always free so that they were ready for a fight. They carried stones in their hands with which they attacked people who displeased them" by doing something that annoyed them such as staring, or touching a wound (Boas 1966:106).

The warriors were more organized than anywhere else in Canada. They were trained in running, swimming, firing and dodging arrows, in hand-to-hand combat with clubs and knives, and in the techniques of attack and defence. There was no torture, as among the Iroquois, or counting coups of bravery, as among the Blackfoot. Raids were usually planned for August or September, after the summer foods were gathered and stored, and in a period of foggy weather to avoid detection. Raids were meticulously planned right down to the assignment of specific enemy warrior victims to each fighter, including information taken from captives and spies on the house and the place within the house where that intended victim slept. For four days before an expedition the warriors purified themselves, then usually painted their bodies black, preferably with charcoal from a lightning-struck tree. Even their wives, who stayed behind, followed a strict regimen before and during the battle.

The canoes were usually beached away from the village such that the village could be quietly approached through the forest. Ideally, the warriors would all creep to their assigned victims and kill them at the time of the war cry signal of the war leader. The successful warriors tied up the captives to be taken as slaves, looted and burned the houses, and returned home in triumph where they displayed the heads of their victims in front on poles. There were a few variations in tactics. They might enter enemy territory dressed as women or as harmless travelers. They might have a frontal attack in daylight, bringing their war canoes quickly up on the village beach and fighting into the village. A frontal attack might be just a diversionary attack while a larger force came into the village from the forest. They might declare a peace, invite their enemies to a feast, and attack them. Defensive tactics were to relocate villages to easily defended sites, build log palisades with watch towers and shooting platforms, post watches, or scatter and hide in small camps in the forest. Some houses had underground escape tunnels in case of attack.

Their warfare was not very rational in the sense of systematic attacks against the same enemy. For example, according to one version of a battle, around 1857 a Kwakiutl woman stole a valuable ceremonial whistle from a Bella Coola when families from the two societies were briefly camped together in summer. The incident became an unresolved insult to the entire Bella Coola. That fall, the Bella Coola attacked the Kwakiutl village of Gilford in revenge. They destroyed the entire village, spearing—but for seven, who escaped—all the men, women, and children; took the valuable property and the heads of the male victims; and set fire to the houses. The Kwakiutl confederation at Fort Rupert organized a retaliation war party with 36 war canoes, but they said they could not find the enemy, who were prepared and had barricaded themselves in their houses. However, the Kwakiutl did encounter a convoy of canoes from still another society (Heiltsuk or Bella Bella) and killed them instead (Rohner and Rohner 1970: 87–88). The Bella Coola, who speak a Salish language, attacked a Kwakiutl village. The retaliation was accidently deflected onto the Heiltsuk, who speak a Kwakiutl dialect. Warfare among groups speaking the same language was not uncommon; for example, Nootka groups also fought each other.

Boas (1966) recorded a version of this battle; the Kwakiutl battle speech included the following: "Now we will soar up and catch in our talons the Bella Coola. We are going to be the great Thunderbird. We shall revenge our fathers, our uncles, our aunts . . . I call upon you to make war on the Bella Coola, for they have our names and our red cedar barks. Take great care, else we may not recover our dancing masks . . . Now, you men, go tomorrow morning, bathe and rub your bodies with hemlock branches; and you women, go to another place and do alike, for we shall meet in sham fight." Wives threw a kelp ring necklace at their husbands. If the necklace broke, the husband would not go because he would be killed if he went. Then the men and women had a sham fight as a preparation for the battle.

One chief said, "Now take care warriors, else we may not get any heads. Let us start in the morning. I shall be your guide, for my ancestor was the killer whale. Therefore I am not afraid of anything, neither of war nor of potlatch." On the second day of travel they met the Heiltsuk canoes and attacked them. The Kwakiutl lost "names" (lives of titled people) to the Bella Coola, but they considered themselves successful because they had gained some of the "names" of the Bella Bella.

People were sometimes killed simply to "make others wail" or to procure a "pillow" for the death of a relative, and the person was sometimes a randomly selected scapegoat, a slave or any stranger. In one case a chief's son died. The father, half brother, and uncle went out looking for people to kill as a "pillow" for the dead boy. They pretended to go hunting sea otters, sought shelter at a village, were hosted by a family, and then killed the man and wife who hosted them. In a Nootka case, a man in a foreign village was selected by a chief to die in honor of the death of his daughter. His own village decided not to defend him. The chief sent three war canoes to the village and beheaded the man.

Early Indian–White trade relations were semi-hostile, with the Indian capture of several White ships and Whites taken as slaves. (See McFeat [1966: 8–16] for selections from the account of John Jewitt, a White who was enslaved by the Nootka.) Whites quickly learned to allow only a few Indians on board ship at any one time and to demand noble children as hostages until the trade was completed.

The Potlatch

The potlatch was a ceremonial at which gifts of wealth goods were given, usually by a chief and his lineage or village to another lineage or village; but the chief might start the process by potlatching his own people first to "make a road in the village" on which the invited lineages and villages would walk. The goods given outside the lineage were such things as furs, woven robes, carved objects, canoes, slaves, and large copper plaques in the form of shields. The potlatch usually included hosting, feasting, and entertaining the guests with songs, dances, and dramas; but the essence of the potlatch was the gifts of wealth goods. There were many feasts but few potlatch feasts. The stated purpose of the potlatch was the public announcement of a major social event around high-status people: marriage of nobility, birth of an heir to a chief, ransom and restoration of a prominent war captive, and assumption of the titles and position of a chief.

The guests arrived in their finest clothing. They usually came to the village by sea in large war canoes, the commoners paddling and the nobility standing dramatically on platforms on the canoes. The Kwakiutl assembled on the beach to greet their guests on their formal arrival (there was sometimes an informal earlier arrival) and normally held their potlatches outdoors. The host group collectively provided for, organized, and presented the potlatches, acting as ushers, speakers, food servers, gift recorders, singers, and dancers, among other roles. The nobility were ceremoniously seated, spoken to, fed, and given gifts according to a strict protocol of politeness and respect for their places in their ranking system. The ushers seated the highest-ranking guests, in order of precedence, at the appropriate places of honor. The highest-ranked was given the first gift and so on down the line of major statuses. The lineages had individuals who specialized in knowing the etiquette of the potlatch, the ranking of the guest, and the traditions. Each gift was recorded and its quantity counted and remembered by a tallyman with equivalent bundles of sticks. This information was important to both sides, host and guest, because potlatches were part of the oral history of lineages and there were some long-term obligations of reciprocation when the current guests would have their turn as hosts.

The hosts gave speeches about the event that was taking place and about the legendary history of their group, particularly as it pertained to the right to use and transfer the titles and privileges involved. This history was often dramatically re-enacted by costumed actors for the audience. The gifts to the guests were given in the name of the new recipient of the title and, like marriages, legally validated a social contract with the guests as witnesses. Guests reciprocated with speeches after each major gift and, usually, with a few minor gifts to their hosts. At the end the ranking guest or his speaker gave a general speech of thanks that reviewed the gifts, the display of titles and privileges, and had the new recipient of privileges presented to the guests.

Historical Changes in Potlatching

In historic times, there were some spectacular elaborations on the system of accumulating wealth and potlatching. At the same time that a wave of new Western wealth entered the Indian economies through the sale of fish and furs to Whites, there were severe epidemics of disease and destructive wars with guns. The Native population fell to about 30 per cent of its aboriginal size (from 50,000 in 1820 to 15,000 in 1920). The ethnographers in the late 1800s and early 1900s were describing the lives of people who, though a fraction of society that had survived, were yet prospering, giving lavish feasts and potlatching each other in claims to nobility and titles left wide open by so many deaths. The Canadian government had stopped inter-chiefdom warfare and slavery; people traveled much more freely and the trade between Native people expanded. Many of the villages abandoned their old wintering sites and concentrated around the growing coastal towns. The concentration stimulated potlatching and created a new need to work out relative social statuses among the bands, which was achieved in part through potlatching. The Fort Rupert–Gilford region Kwakiutl had more titled positions (658) than there were adults 16 years of age or more (637) in 1898. Rich commoners competed for noble titles in a period of intensive competition.

Loans were made at steep interest, up to 100 per cent, in order to accumulate wealth for potlatches. Spectacular rivalry potlatches were held among related competitors for the same titles. In rivalry potlatches goods were often destroyed to humiliate the rival through greater conspicuous consumption. Each claimant to the title would try to outdo the other by hosting the nobility of the region until they supported one claimant over the other or until one claimant went bankrupt.

Carried on in the oral traditions there is what might be called the "Guinness Book of Kwakiutl Potlatching." The maximum number of an item exchanged at a single potlatch from 1729 to 1936 was as follows: 3 coppers, 6 slaves, 8 canoes, 54 dressed elk skins, 2,000 silver bracelets, 7,000 brass bracelets, and 33,000 blankets. The most seals ever eaten at a Kwakiutl feast is fifty.

Hudson Bay Company blankets became currency units in the historic trade and they were given back and forth by the thousands. Finally money itself was given away (and occasionally burned in displays of abundant wealth) by the hundreds of dollars. The value of the old copper shield made from pounded nuggets of copper became inflated, equivalent to several thousand blankets in value. Whites made and sold coppers similar to the hand-made ones, but they did not undercut the value of the old ones. Each of the old ones had a grand name, such as "The One of Whom All Are Ashamed" or "Takes Everything out of the House." Each had a distinctive history. The wealth system focused even more on these old coppers because they were unique to the old potlatching system, irreplaceable with the new wave of wealth. When some of the coppers were confiscated by the police because potlatching was illegal, they were placed in museums. To the Natives this still did not affect the ownership—which was still transferred at potlatches while the physical objects continued to accrue value, in part because they were safely stored away. Some were returned to the Kwakiutl in 1973 to be placed by them in their own museum.

Purchase of a Copper

Canadian Indian public ceremonies have certain things in common, whether Iroquoian wampum-alliance ceremonies, a Blackfoot pipe ceremony, or a Kwakiutl purchase of a copper. The speech itself has a definite introduction of the speaker and the subject ("You all know me. I am the man who . . ."), body of speech, and a brief, formal conclusion ("Now I have finished"). The body uses analogies in a systematic way. The pipe is smoked in four directions and each direction implies a different spiritual relationship. The gifts or parts of a public prayer among the Iroquois are often given the analogy of a trip, with individual prayers given "to prepare food for the journey," "to clear the trail," "to carry you over the rivers," and so forth.

In the Kwakiutl purchase of a copper the price is paid in a sequence of payments. The first is to "make a pillow" or "make a bed" for the copper. There is talk of great feasts given, the great house, the ancestral chief and how he received his name in the beginning of the world. There is singing of village songs and feasting. Then the purchase is dramatically negotiated in the midst of speeches and a continuing flow of gifts. Boas (1966: 84–92) described a purchase: "I know how to buy coppers; I always pay high prices for coppers. Now take care, Kwakiutl, my tribe, else you will be laughed at." The speech included work chants that signified the lifting of the supposed heavy copper from the ground with the flow of wealth. Then there was a presentation of dancing by young women. Blankets were stacked in piles of 1,000. "This is the weight of my name. This mountain of blankets rises through our heaven. . . ." Then the *seller* said, "Long life to all of you, chiefs of the Kwakiutl. I can not attain to your high name, great tribes . . . You great mountain from which wealth is rolling down . . ." There were little dramas, theatrics in the giving process. The *buyer* asked for the final price. The *seller* lay down and covered his face with a blanket and nobody spoke for a long time. Meanwhile the assistants kept bringing out blankets by the hundreds, then boxes for the blankets, and, finally, canoes to carry everything away in.

Potlatch Variations

The people were innovative in thinking up new ceremonies; for instance, the purchase of a copper became a ceremony with many potlatch features, though instead of a gift it was an extremely lavish and dramatic form of negotiating and paying for the object. There were also play potlatches by children, by women, by the men against the women, and so forth. Potlatches were given as a penalty for a breach of a tabu, such as stumbling or laughing in a performance at the winter ceremonials. They might be given to save face from an embarrassment to one's self or a family member, such as the birth of a deformed child or capsizing a canoe.

In a competitive potlatch a guest could be offended if his name was called in the wrong order, or olachen oil was spilled on him, or if a gift was thrown to him instead of given with appropriate respect. In this case, the offended guest might retaliate by destroying that which had been given or by giving an obviously lavish reprimand gift to the host. The host could make restitution for the offence by giving the guest a gift double the value of the reprimand gift.

The play potlatch was usually in honor of something minor, such as giving a child a new name, and there was a lot of joking. People might take turns pretending they were some kind of animal, to get others to laugh. They might pretend they had captured someone who spoke a foreign language and they would play out the drama with one imitating the foreign speech, such as a Kwakiutl imitating Haida or Chinese, and the other translating into Kwakiutl. There would be gifts of common items such as dishes and toys.

The social upheavals of the population decline, the new wealth, and the cosmopolitan world of the White towns gave people more distance from their own traditions. That skepticism, combined with the love of drama among the coastal peoples, led to the development of essentially a new art form, the feigned rivalry potlatch. Two chiefs, in the context of some real potlatch transfers related to a birth, marriage, or death, would secretly arrange a hidden agenda of conflicts, coming out equal in their reciprocal gifts. There would be the lavish giving, boastful speech making, wealth destruction, and implications of violence as in the rivalry potlatch, but the whole affair would be organized primarily as an artistic entertainment, a drama.

Finally, the last step in the evolution of the potlatch has been the modern revitalized potlatch presented as an ethnic cultural event. There has been some continuity of the stories, songs, and dances, but there has also been much loss of tradition. Thus today, Native people are studying the old costumes in museums and trying to duplicate them. They are studying early recordings and photographs to increase the authenticity of their potlatches. 'Ksan at Hazelton, B.C., has an excellent reconstructed village with a museum, craft sales, and a drama and dance corps.

As demonstrated above, the potlatch evolved in four basic forms: (1) a ceremony of succession, (2) rivalry over succession, (3) feigned rivalry, (4) the drama of a modern ethnic group.

This is how the law against potlatching and the winter dances read when revised to be more specific in 1927: "Every Indian or other person who engages in, or assists in celebrating . . . any Indian festival, dance or ceremony of which the giving or paying back of money, goods, or articles of any sort forms a part . . . or who engages or assists in a celebration or dance of which the wounding or mutilation of the dead or living body of any human being or animal forms a part . . . is guilty of an offence and is liable on summary conviction to imprisonment for a term not exceeding six months and not less than two months."

Historical Transition

Whites had a hard time finding goods to trade with the Indians in exchange for the valuable sea otter pelts and other furs. At first the Indians desired iron for arrow points, chisels, adzes, and knives, but that market was soon glutted. Then there were fluctuating demands for such things as Western clothing and crockery, firearms, sugar, rum, and Native articles such as tanned hides and Indian slaves.

Some captains rigged sails for a chief's canoe, and the use of sails spread rapidly along the coast. Iron cutting-tools allowed some increase in the production and grandeur of carving. Firearms contributed to an intensification of warfare. Western dress was quickly incorporated into certain costumes of the dancing societies and potlatch performances. The direct trade between ships and village chiefs, however, went through a boom-and-bust cycle as the sea otters were cleared out almost to extinction by the 1820s. Then several permanent trading forts were established in the 1820s and 1830s to take in furs of all kinds in exchange for stable commodities.

White missionaries came in and were generally successful in establishing Christian churches and schools. Whites tended to support social and political ranking and chieftainship as a political and economic institution, but they attacked warfare, slavery, plural marriage, shamanism, witchcraft, the winter ceremonials, and the potlatch. By the late 1800s the chiefs were generally in favor of acculturation to White customs while retaining as much social integrity as possible for their Native communities. When British Columbia was confederated with Canada in 1871 the Indians were in effect declared Canadian subjects— but not citizens. Their land was taken away, they were not allowed to vote, and their lives were increasingly regulated by government agents and missionaries. The provincial government insisted that only the lands the Indians used for such things as village sites and fishing stations should be recognized as Indian land. Even after initial reserve allotments were made, tens of thousands of acres of the more valuable Indian lands were arbitrarily "cut off" from their reserves.

The Nishga in the Nass Valley and the Haida of the Queen Charlotte Islands have both had longstanding land claims against the government. In 1883 the Nishga expelled provincial land surveyors who had been sent to give the people small parcels of their lands as reserves. In 1887 their leaders were sent to the provincial government in Victoria to reaffirm that they had never ceded or extinguished their aboriginal title. That appeal failed and Whites continued to take their lands. In 1909 they hired a Vancouver lawyer to appeal for them to the British king. In 1913 the leaders themselves went to London. Then they took their case through the Canadian courts where they lost to the province in 1969, to the B.C. Court of Appeals in 1971, and finally lost in a split decision before the Supreme Court of Canada in 1973.

The B.C. coastal Indians in the late 1800s and early 1900s had unity and cohesiveness through their hereditary chiefs and chiefdom heritage; they therefore had more solidarity in labor relations than the Whites. They unionized early to protect themselves from displacement by immigrant Japanese fishermen and cannery workers who were being imported in large numbers by the canning companies. In 1893, 1900, and 1901 the Indians participated in violent strikes. Indian Affairs tried to force the Indians back to work, but they refused.

The strikes generally failed because of over-competition among the fishermen and rapid depletion of fish stocks. The Pacific Coast Native Fishermen's Association was formed in 1936 by the Kwakiutl and then amalgamated in a broader alliance with the Native Brotherhood of

British Columbia in 1942. The Brotherhood had been formed in 1931 as a social and political organization, but was turned by the Kwakiutl into more of an economic agent. The amalgamation occurred out of a common opposition to a new requirement that Indians must pay income taxes, but when the fishermen dominated the Brotherhood they turned it into their official bargaining agent in 1945.

The B.C. coastal societies were chiefdoms, societies with elaborate public institutions somewhat similar to those of the state societies of the Whites. With similar institutions their acculturation experiences were less traumatic than those in the other parts of Canada. Massive deaths occurred in epidemics of the Old World diseases, but that was a biological phenomenon outside the cultural processes and common to all Native North American societies. The systematic differences in the inter-societal relationships is that, under conditions of conquest by states, bands tended to be passive, tribes militant and reactive, and chiefdoms easily co-opted and integrated.

In chiefdoms, people tended to be more obedient to authority; that obedience could be transferred through a strong and hierarchical Native leadership and through missionaries, government agents, businessmen and others, to the state society. The tribes were the major originators and carriers of tradition-oriented reactions to foreign conquest, military resistance, and then religious revitalization movements. Even in the twentieth century tribal-heritage peoples such as the Iroquois and Blackfoot carry on their nineteenth century revitalization movements, such as The Longhouse Society and the Sun Dance. Chiefdoms were the major source of modern-oriented, integrative, Native movements. Thus, the B.C. coastal Indians started such modern social forms as the province-wide political organization called the brotherhood; Indian labor unions; Indian land claims against the government; and Indian women's organizations. It is no accident that the first Indian food restaurant in Canada was started in Vancouver and had Haida women doing the cooking. The institutional innovations in B.C. were social forms that drew from the experiences of operating elaborate chiefdom institutions, such as running a large and well-organized village, arranging potlatches, and putting on the winter ceremonials. People could easily move from doing things like that to fighting governments in the courts for compensation for their land and fighting fish canneries for better wages through unions.

Eventually other provinces copied the modern, integrationist, social forms of B.C. and created their own brotherhoods and their own land-claim cases. That diffusion eventually worked its way through all the band heritage societies in Canada; and, like new converts, these societies have become the most organized, militant, and innovative. The band-heritage societies are creating entirely new social forms, such as the semi-sovereign forms emerging in Arctic Quebec, Nunavut under Inuit Tapirisat, and western N.W.T. under the Dene Nation.

The B.C. chiefdoms laid much of the foundation for all modern Canadian Indian movements. The economy of the chiefdoms was not only more productive than that of the band and the tribe, but it had mechanisms that distributed goods and services beyond the multi-family household units. There was something of a permanent structure of economic support for the aged, orphans, and the sick; and for long-distance trade, public art and religious ceremonies, and warfare and defence. Feasting, concentration of wealth in valuables, transfer of wealth between lineages and villages, and other customs redistributed goods within a region and thus provided some security against occasional local scarcities, such as in the years when a salmon run was poor in a stream where a lineage built its weirs.

They were the first Indians the British met who had sufficiently similar concepts of property and law that their land could not be taken through treaties; thus the British did not make treaties and took their land without legal pretensions. As the resources the Indians were after were primarily in the rivers and the ocean, their residences occupied very little land. Therefore there was not an intensive competition with Whites over residential land, and the B.C. Indians were not displaced as much as other Indians in Canada. Thus B.C. has a large number of small reserves: 70 per cent of the reserves in Canada (1,624 of 2,301), 34 per cent of the bands (193 of 570), 19 per cent of the status Indian population (54,000 of 289,000 in 1977), and only 13 per cent of the reserve acreage (840,000 of 6.4 million acres, not including the new agreements in northern Quebec, Saskatchewan, or the western Arctic).

The Kwakiutl today have 16 bands, including two Haisla and one Heiltsuk, and a population of about 6,000, probably less than the aboriginal population. The Kwakiutl still perform the old songs and dances, wear their carved masks and button-blanket robes, but the performances are no longer exclusive. The old nobility has been democratized. The dances today are shortened versions of old dramas that each took an hour or so.

Commentary

The intensive battles, both aboriginally between Indians and historically between Indians and Whites, were over fishing rights. The Indians emerged from the recent battles with a few exclusive rights for fishing for personal subsistence purposes, including in rivers where commercial fishing is banned. That was a reaffirmation of an 1894 law that guaranteed the rights of Indians to fish for their food.

Their economic background allowed the B.C. coastal Indians to integrate into a market economy more easily than other Canadian Indians; thus they had some prosperity when the fishing and fur trapping was good. Now they are struggling merely to survive, as many other B.C. fishermen, most of whom do not have the capital to buy the large fishing boats necessary to prosperity in that competitive industry.

Though bands and tribes were generally egalitarian, the B.C. chiefdoms had more social ranking, from hereditary chiefs to slaves, than even modern Canadian society. The B.C. chiefdoms were also more aesthetic and artistic than other Native Canadians, especially in their skills in carving, weaving, costume making, and participation in public dramas. They also had more time for enjoying life than the Canadians who outlawed their potlatches.

CHAPTER 9

Modern Issues

Historical Transitions

We turn now to a brief review of Canadian-wide patterns during White contact times. The first PH.D. dissertation in Canada (1900, University of Toronto) was on the Huron Indians of the Moose River Basin; now there is a wealth of historical material on Indians (Crowe 1974, Fisher 1977, Jaenen 1976, Leacock and Lurie 1971, and Patterson 1972, provide regional histories).

Whites learned the Native bush survival techniques and a new kind of egalitarianism along with a nature-oriented ideology. The Whites also learned corn, bean and squash agriculture. This Native influence on British and French cultures in North America becomes apparent when we compare them with the kind of cultures that the Europeans developed in their other colonial areas, such as China, India, and Africa, where the colonialists were eventually forced out; and even with Australia, New Zealand, and the Pacific, where the colonialists have stayed. None of these cultures is much like the British and French cultures of Canada today, in part because of the Native influence in Canada.

The movement of Whites was from east to west, and later from south to north. The stages of (1) exploration, (2) trade and Christian missionizing, and (3) White settlement and Indian displacement, moved like waves across the continent. The initial contacts with Whites in the 1600s and 1700s were usually brief meetings with the explorers, traders, warriors, and missionaries. The Indians usually got the worst of these dealings through military defeats, European diseases, and the destruction of their aboriginal ideologies by missionaries; however, some useful tools, such as axes and guns, were also acquired. Because of this foreign invasion, military conquest, and colonization the Natives became a lowly minority in their own land.

Canadian Indians, however, have tended to survive better than U.S. Indians both as a population and in culture. Several Indian groups in southern Canada today came from the U.S., usually because they were forced out of their homelands: Iroquois (in 1784), Potawatomi (in 1841), Oneida (in 1849), and Sioux (in 1862 and 1876). The major reasons for the greater survival of Canadian Indians seem to lie in ecology and evolution, rather than the difference between Canadians and Americans. The land was large enough to allow retreat from European expansion, except in Newfoundland, where all the Natives were killed. The European settlement, owing to a harsh climate, was slower and less populous than in the U.S., and concentrated in the warm southern fringe of Canada, leaving most of the northern country open to the continuance of the Native way of life into the twentieth century. Indians in the south were enclaved in small reserves and held as irrelevant to the development of Canadian society. In the north they were drawn into the fur economy of the Whites, which made for a conservative colonial relationship between Whites and Indians that preserved much of traditional Indian ways.

The evolutionary fact that promoted survival in Canada is that the Native Canadians were mostly from band or chiefdom societies, rather than from tribes as in the U.S. *Under conquest by a state society bands tend to be peaceful and willing to retreat, as in the Arctic and Subarctic; tribes tend to fight back with violence, as in the case of the Iroquois and the Blackfoot; chiefdoms work out a political compromise, as along the British Columbia coast.* At the latitudes of the U.S. the Europeans fought their way westward in the East and the Plains through one tribal society after another, until they came to the peaceful band societies of the Great Basin.

Most early Europeans attributed their convictions, that Indians were culturally inferior, to obvious racial differences: Some early British settlements in North America passed laws against Indian–White marriages. Europeans were nationalistically allied to broad European cultural groupings, such as the British, French, Spanish, and Dutch. The broad ideologies, such as the racism and nationalism of the Europeans, were in sharp contrast to Native ideologies, which emphasized primary loyalty to small-scale social systems in which people were known personally—by lineages, clans, and tribes. Only now, in the late twentieth century, are the Indians forming large-scale racially and nationally based political organizations to lobby and negotiate with the powerful White governments.

The British created treaties on the model of state-to-state legal relationships, imposed them on the small Indian societies, and used these documents to rationalize the displacement of Native people from their land. The French, by contrast, made only a few treaties of peace, trade, and military alliance. Both the French and British maintained military alliances with the Indians. The Micmac, Malecite, Ojibwa, and Hurons were allied with the French, and many of the Iroquois were allied with the British.

The French (1) emphasized the fur trade, (2) often came as single men, (3) more often took Indian women in marriage, as the women were found useful in a bush frontier setting as translators and in the wide variety of bush skills. The British (1) came more for farming, (2) often brought their families along, and (3) brought wives in from Europe for farming and household skills needed in the European type of farming. The British needed wives who could milk cows and help with the farm chores, as well as run the house, and the Indian women did not have those skills.

The French were convinced of the superiority of French civilization and paternalistically assimilated Indians into their society through marriage, religious conversion, and formal education. It is quite understandable that the first Indian Catholic nun (Kateri Tekawitha, who became a nun in 1679) and the first college-educated Indian (L.V. Sabatannen, who graduated from Dartmouth in 1782) both had a tribal heritage and a French elementary education. The British were more racially prejudiced, convinced of the biological inferiority of the Natives, than the French. The British alienated and segregated Indians by treating them as legally separate subjects to be handled at a distance through formal government bureaucracies. Thus there were only a few registered marriages between the British and Indians while there were many between the French and Indians. These policies of greater integration between the French and the Indians have led to situations in which we now have a large French-Indian population and a generally more humane treatment of Indians in French-Canadian society.

Almost every index shows that the Indians are better off in Quebec than in any other place in Canada. They have the highest average incomes of Indians in Canada. They have the lowest rates among the Indians of Canada for such things as murder, suicide, arrests, and convictions for indictable offences. With ethnicity and language constant at Cree in comparisons, it appears that these indices get progressively worse westward. Indices of the Quebec Indians resemble those of the northern Whites in Quebec. Things get poor in Ontario, and terrible in the Prairies.

Indians in Quebec have taken the strongest stand among Indians in Canada against allowing alcoholic beverages on their reserves. They also have the lowest level of Indian political activity in Canada. The Red Power movement came very late to Quebec and is having only a mild effect, except among the Iroquois, and the Natives in James Bay, the two groups of Indians in Quebec who have had the greatest contact with the English and who usually speak English rather than French as a second language. Several thousand Indians live in Montreal. In view of the size of this ethnic population, we would expect some proliferation of Indian ethnic associations in the city. There is almost none, presumably because

TABLE I
Status Indian Data by Province
(Dec. 31, 1976)

	Population			
	Number	*National Proportion*	*Proportion of Area Population*	*Off-Reserve Proportion*
P.E.I.	467	.2%	.4%	36%
Nova Scotia	5,364	1.8%	.6%	27%
New Brunswick	5,060	1.7%	.7%	24%
Quebec	31,079	10.7%	.5%	18%
Ontario	63,191	21.9%	.8%	32%
Manitoba	42,311	14.6%	4.1%	25%
Saskatchewan	43,318	15.0%	4.7%	29%
Alberta	34,277	12.0%	1.9%	21%
British Columbia	53,776	18.6%	2.2%	36%
Yukon	2,746	1.0%	13.1%	—
N.W.T.	7,349	2.5%	19.3%	—
Totals	288,938	100.0%	1.3%	28%

	Land			
			Reserves*	
	Bands	*Reserves & Settlements*	*Acres 1,000's*	*Acres Per Person*
P.E.I.	2	4	2	3.6
Nova Scotia	12	39	29	5.4
New Brunswick	15	24	43	8.5
Quebec	39	40	192	6.2
Ontario	114	183	1,728	27.3
Manitoba	57	98	528	12.5
Saskatchewan	68	137	1,376	31.8
Alberta	41	99	1,631	47.6
British Columbia	193	1,624	840	15.6
Yukon	13	23	1	—
N.W.T.	16	30	34	—
Totals	570	2,301	6,404	22.2

*The 66 "settlements" on crown lands are not included here so the land areas are slightly higher. Also the vast new areas designated in the James Bay agreement and the Saskatchewan agreement are not included.

French Canadians who happen to have some Indian heritage are mainly involved in the French dimension of their identity.

The Indian Act

The first Indian act was passed in 1876 and was modified over the years. The last major revision came in 1951. The Act begins with various legal definitions.

A *band* is an administratively defined group of Indians who are given the right to use specified crown lands, called *reserves*, and who are given money to administer their community. The number of bands and reserves slowly changes over the years through reorganization. It is possible to follow these and other Indian administrative activities through the *Annual Reports* and *The Indian News* (a monthly newspaper) of the Department of Indian Affairs and Northern Development. There are 570 bands that control 2,301 "reserves" and 66 "settlements" with a total of 6.4 million acres of land. The bands manage their own affairs following the laws of the Indian Act, the Department of Indian Affairs administrative procedures, and the guidance of local *Indian agents* employed by the Department. Table I is a summary of population and land data.

Persons entitled to be *registered* and to have *status* under the Indian Act are those who were registered in 1874, their direct descendants in the male line, and the wives and children of such persons. About half of the Indians in Canada are not registered and are ineligible for the programs of the Department of Indian Affairs. They are usually called non-status Indians or Metis.

Persons may be taken off the list of Indian registration and become *enfranchised* if they receive "half-breed lands or money script," or if an Indian woman marries a person who is not a registered Indian. This latter rule is in effect an anti-miscegenation law that strongly discourages Indian–White marriages. The Supreme Court upheld this law in a court case in 1973, even though it promotes racism and discrimination against women, on the grounds that the government had the right to create for Indians special laws that violate the Bill of Rights.[*]

Individuals may elect to be removed from the list of registered Indians and become enfranchised. If they do this they are entitled to (1) one per capita share of the capital and revenue moneys held by Her Majesty on behalf of the band and (2) a payment equal to the next twenty years of payments under any existing treaty. This is usually no more than a few hundred dollars, and few people have sold out except women who, by marrying men that were not status Indians, were about to lose their status rights anyway.

---

[*]Changes to Indian status due to marriage were eliminated in 1985. Those who lost their Indian status through marriage can now be reinstated.

Individual Indians do not possess land on reserves except in the form of allotments by the band council. However, once a person builds a house on a plot of reserve land, he has the usual rights of lease, sale, and inheritance (to other band members). Reserve lands are not subject to seizure under legal process and therefore cannot be used to acquire a loan through mortgage. A person who trespasses on a reserve is guilty of an offence and is liable to a fine up to fifty dollars or to imprisonment up to one month or to both fine and imprisonment. Bands regulate the sale and barter of produce from their reserves, and maintain their own roads, bridges, and fences. Non-Indian government agencies may take reserve lands only with the consent of the Governor in Council, and must make compensation.

A broad range of legal, financial, and administrative matters are directed by the Minister of Indian Affairs and the Governor in Council: descent, wills, mental competence, guardianship; land and band management on such things as timber, mines, cultivation, sand and gravel permits; and loans. There are special regulations about such things as fish and game preservation, weed and insect control, vehicle traffic rules, control of places of amusement, housing, fencing, and band elections. In addition to these rules the bands can create their own bylaws and work like a municipality:

86. No Indian or band is subject to taxation of land or property on reserves, including succession, inheritance, or estate taxes if the property passes to an Indian.

106. Indian agents may be *ex officio* justices of the peace.

108. (2) An Indian woman who marries a person who is not Indian and her children become enfranchised.

115. The Minister may require attendance of Indian children at school between the ages of six and sixteen.

120. Where the majority of the members of a band belong to one religious denomination the school established on the reserve . . . shall be taught by a teacher of that denomination. Where there is no majority of band members in the same religious denomination, the band electors may decide on the religious denomination of the teacher.

The Minister is appointed by the Prime Minister of Canada to administer the federal laws of status Indians. He has tremendous powers over band affairs. Still, within the Act, the individual bands have powers which they often do not fully assume. For example, under section 120, they could probably designate that teachers in schools on reserves be of an Indian rather than a Protestant or Roman Catholic religious denomination.

The imposition of the European-derived patrilineal customs throughout the Act tends to be destructive of social arrangements within matrilineal and bilateral Indian societies and to be supportive of the social integrity of the patrilineal Indian societies. This is seen particularly in the loss of Indian status by women who marry non-status men and in the assumption of female dependency on males. The racist and ethnocentric assumptions that Indians are financially incompetent, alcohol-prone, and need to be taught how to farm, etc., which give the Minister and his local agent, the supervisor, vast powers over band affairs, should be eliminated.

There is very little in the Act that is positive, that is culture-enhancing. Where are the sections directing the Minister to promote Indian language, literature, religion, arts, dance, traditional crafts? It is oriented to assimilation into White society and to the minimization of problems to White society. It does not begin with the values of the humanistic enhancement of Indian people.

Racism

A journalist, Heather Robertson, surveyed Indian-White relations in Manitoba. "I was shocked by the reserves and Metis communities, shocked by the destitution, the squalor, the chaos, the brutality, the apathy. Worse, however, was the people's fear, servility and hatred, and the knowledge that these feelings were based on the color of my skin, as my fear was based on the color of theirs." She picked up these kinds of comments from Whites in the mid-latitude town of The Pas:

Businessman—"Sterilize them. Don't give them any money, just food. They're children. It's all the fault of welfare."

Mayor—"Indians can stand a lot of cold. It's their big salvation."

Tourist—"The Pas smells different at night, when the Indians come in" (Robertson, 1970).

Indian Affairs spends over $4 million annually on research and conferences, yet seems to avoid the politically sensitive issue of White racism as a cause of Indian problems. The causes they choose to investigate are those that flow from White middle-class ideologies: poverty, low work incentives, poor education in formal White schools, lack of management skills, etc. Beyond D.I.A.N.D. there are now over thirty federal agencies that have Indian programs, and a variety of provincial programs are being instituted for Indians. In spite of all this activity, very few people have faced up to the important facts of the destructiveness of widespread anti-Indian racism in Canada.

Native people seem to have (1) the most humane treatment by the French-Canadian culture of Quebec, (2) worse treatment by British-Canadian cultures in most of the country, (3) yet more-severe treatment in the Prairie provinces, and (4) the most extreme racism in the towns in the northern part of the provinces. The middle-latitude towns are urban points in the frontier region of Canada where Natives and Whites tend to live in highly separated communities while farther north there is more pressure for Natives and Whites to live closer to each other and to cooperate. In the north there is something of a shifting pattern of dominance in social relationships that is uncommon in the south, depending on the extent of the continuing relevance of Native skills, the size of populations, and whether the interaction context is in an Indian community or a White town. This shift is evident at the local level in certain occupations, areas, etc. Thus, Native people tend to be respected and receive very little anti-Indian racism in the frontier bush or country where Native skills are still useful for survival, but they are commonly discriminated against in the towns. There are a greater frequency of Indian–White interactions in the north and divided opinions about the legitimacy of Indian land claims and northern development issues, but there is also a strong element of mutual respect. Discrimination becomes particularly severe in the southern part of the frontier (the northern part of the provinces) where many of the Indians live on reserves and come only occasionally into the towns. That is, there is less anti-Indian discrimination in the far north because Native skills are still respected there, Natives are more often numerically dominant, and Natives and Whites live closer and are thus forced into cooperative interactions. Proximity over long periods of time tends to dissolve racism, as when children of different races go to the same schools and grow up together.

There is a compelling general correlation between the *proportion* of Indians in a population and the amount of local anti-Indian racism in the non-Indian population. The eastern provinces have low proportions (0.4 per cent to 0.8 per cent) status Indians and generally low racism, the northern territories have very high proportions (13 per cent to 19 per cent) and low to moderate racism, and the western provinces have moderate proportions (1.9 per cent to 4.7 per cent) and moderate to high racism. There are many exceptions—communities with large numbers of Indians and very little racism—but these are mainly outside the Prairies and in southern Canada.

Indian arrest rates are high in the middle latitude towns: Small places in northern Ontario such as Kenora and Thunder Bay have much higher arrest rates than the southern cities of Hamilton and Toronto. Ethnographies by Braroe (1975), Elias (1975), and Stymeist (1975) support this hypothesis about the locations of problems.

The status-Indian communities in the Prairie provinces are statistically different from those of the other provinces in several important respects (Gerber 1977). The Prairie bands are:

1. Larger in population.
2. Higher in population growth rates.

3. Poorer in road access to cities.
4. Higher in the proportions of their needs that are met within their group boundaries and in self-governance.
5. Less involved with off-reserve work.
6. Poorer in quality of housing.
7. Higher in retention of Native languages.
8. Lower in integrated schools.
9. Lower in high school enrolment.
10. Lower in average incomes.

Indian Attitudes

The Department of the Secretary of State did a national survey of Indians in twelve urban Indian friendship centers across the nation (Robbins 1977). The greatest discrimination in shops and stores in the whole survey was found in Regina, where 50 per cent of the informants said that Natives were generally not accepted in shops and stores. The Regina sample, however, was highest (83 per cent) in their sense of acceptance by government offices. Fort McMurray and Toronto were poorest in lack of acceptance in government offices. Discrimination was seen as the primary problem only in Fort McMurray, Alberta. I have abstracted some of the results of that survey on Val d'Or, Quebec; Toronto, Ontario; and Regina, Saskatchewan (see Table II). The Regina sample is the poorest educated and moderate in mobility and job satisfaction.

The Prairie provinces have recently become active in the Native movement, though historically they lagged behind B.C. and Ontario (Whiteside 1973) in forming Indian associations. Saskatchewan seems to be the most active province in Canada in establishing Native studies within elementary and secondary schools. Thus, for example, in a 1971 national survey of Indian school committees, Saskatchewan had 44; Alberta, 33; Manitoba, 30; and Ontario, 28; B.C., 21; Maritimes 20; and Quebec, only 8 (D.I.A.N.D., 1972:16).

Quebec has little Indian ethnic revitalization, Red Power movements, Indian periodicals, urban Indian centers, etc. The province has 11

TABLE II

	Regina	Toronto	Val d'Or
Education, 9 or fewer years	40%	8%	23%
Lived in more than one town in childhood	67%	79%	34%
Moved more than once within the city in the last five years	20%	64%	18%
Very satisfied with my job	58%	33%	73%

per cent of the status Indians in Canada but only 5 per cent of the Indian associations and 6 per cent of the Indian periodicals (Price 1978). Indians there tend to be uninterested in marches, demonstrations, occupations, or the revitalization of Indian religions. They express their uniqueness in commercial and socially integrated ways. Thus, for example, the Abenakis of Odanak, Quebec, have a museum. The Montagnais of Sept-Iles run a $9 million shopping center. There are a fiber glass canoe manufacturer near Trois-Rivieres that makes some 2,000 canoes a year, a lacrosse stick factory at St. Regis, a fish processing plant at Mingan; and Loretteville manufactures canoes, snowshoes, and moccasins.

Intermarriage

The Indian racial component in French-Canadian society is so strong that it tends to be accepted rather casually. French-Canadian Indians accept their Indian heritage and dismiss it as an interesting but not very relevant dimension of their identity, social organization, or daily life. Thus many Quebeckers with an Indian racial component identify themselves as French-Canadian, and thus do not join Metis associations. A problem with comparing Indian statistics in Quebec with those of other provinces, especially in relation to Metis and non-status Indians, is that many people who are *racially* Metis in Quebec are *culturally* French-Canadian.

Swartz (1977) reported on a nation-wide survey of Metis and non-status Indians. The Quebec sample had the highest provincial proportion (81 per cent) of those who had lost their status through intermarriage. The sample in Saskatchewan lost their status predominantly (53 per cent) by the historic lack of treaty rights for Indians. That is, these Saskatchewan Indians would usually be called non-status Indians, because Metis implies a racial mixture.

Driedger and Peters (1977: 169) had students at the University of Manitoba fill out social distance scales. The percentages of those who were willing to marry people of various racial and ethnic groups are as follows: British, 80 per cent; German, 64 per cent; French, 62 per cent; Ukrainian, 60 per cent; Italian, 48 per cent; Jewish, 42 per cent; Negro, 27 per cent; *Canadian Indian, 24 per cent*; East Indian, 23 per cent; Chinese, 23 per cent; and *Eskimo, 20 per cent.*

White Attitudes

Pineo (1977) surveyed a national sample of adults in their ranking of ethnic and racial groups. English-speaking informants ranked English Canadians at the top score of 83, ranked western and northern Europeans in the 46–57 range, Mediterranean and central Europeans in the 36–48 range, Japanese at 35, Chinese at 33, *Canadian Indians at 28*, and Negroes at 25. French Canadians ranked Indians four points higher than the English Canadians did, in a cluster with Greeks and Eastern Europeans, but still fairly low on the scale.

In a second national survey, Bibby (1978) tested to see the number of people that would agree with the anti-Indian statement "It's too bad, but in general Canadian Indians have inferior intelligence compared to Whites." The level of agreement with this statement ranged from a national low of 11 per cent in Quebec, through 20 per cent in Ontario, 21 per cent in B.C., and 22 per cent in the Atlantic provinces; to a national high of 24 per cent in the Prairie provinces. Note that the big increase is from French Quebec to the English-speaking provinces. The more prejudiced were less educated (22 per cent with high school or less agreed) and older (more than 28 per cent 50-plus years agreed). In the national sample, 25 per cent did not approve of marriages between Whites and Indians, 10 per cent felt that they would feel uneasy just to be in the presence of Indians, and 6 per cent say that Indians have too much power. Again, Quebec and Ontario were pro-Indian on this last question (only 3 per cent said "too much" power), B.C. was intermediate (9 per cent), and the Atlantic (13 per cent) and Prairies (14 per cent) were the most anti-Indian.

Gibbons and Ponting (1977, 1978) reported a third nation-wide survey. They asked, "If we were to compare Native Canadian Indians with other Canadians, in your opinion what would be the major differences between them?" The responses commented on such differences as cultural background and educational achievements. Francophones significantly more often mentioned cultural differences (44 per cent of the francophones to 22 per cent of the anglophones), prejudice and discrimination against Indians (23 per cent to 16 per cent), and that Indians appreciated the environment more than non-Indians (9 per cent to 3 per cent). Anglophones more often mentioned personal deficiencies (laziness, etc.) (25 per cent to 8 per cent), lack of economic opportunities and unemployment (21 per cent to 3 per cent), and differences in government treatment (13 per cent to 6 per cent).

Personal deficiencies, the code closest to anti-Indian racism, were mentioned in the following regional frequencies: Quebec, 7 per cent; Atlantic, 12 per cent; B.C., 21 per cent; Ontario, 23 per cent; and Prairies, 32 per cent. Responses to the question "What would you say are the *main problems* faced by Canadian Indians today" were most regionally different in mentions of alcohol-related problems: Quebec, 1 per cent; Atlantic, 7 per cent; B.C., 12 per cent; Ontario, 13 per cent; and Prairies, 28 per cent.

A "sympathy index" was constructed from ten questions, with a regional ranking similar to earlier questions: from very high sympathy in Quebec; progressively down through B.C., Ontario, Manitoba, Atlantic, Alberta, and to the expected national low in Saskatchewan. This index varied by age: younger people were more sympathetic. There were also variations by political affiliation—low among Conservative, higher among Liberal, higher yet among N.D.P., and highest among Social Credit party supporters. Local scores must be treated with caution because of the possibility of sampling errors, but they give us insights into the diversity within regions and core-frontier comparisons. In Table III I have arranged the 41 English interview locations from Quebec to B.C. according to "sympathy scores," from greatest to least sympathy toward Indians.

Arrest, Conviction, and Prison Rates

In 1961 the per capita arrest rate for Indians was 5.4 times greater than for the general population (Canadian Corrections Association 1967). This ratio varied by area: 1.2 in Quebec; 3.0 in the Maritimes and northern territories; 4.3 to 4.9 in most southern provinces; and 11.7 in Saskatchewan. In 1967, felony conviction ratios of Indians to Whites ranged from 0.7 in Quebec to 6.0 in Saskatchewan and 7.7 in Alberta; the national ratio was 4.6 (Judicial Statistics 1968).

The following percentages of the inmates were Indians in the federal penetentiaries on January 30, 1973: Quebec, 0.3 per cent; Ontario, 3.5 per cent; New Brunswick, 4.1 per cent; Nova Scotia, 6.0 per cent; B.C., 13.1 per cent; Alberta, 19.7 per cent; Manitoba, 24.8 per cent; and Saskatchewan, 25.3 per cent (Heumann 1973). Thus the Indian:White federal prisoner ratios were 0.5 in Quebec, 4.4 in Ontario, and from 5.4 to 7.3 in the west. An Indian in a province such as Saskatchewan has a chance of being arrested, convicted, and serving a prison sentence that is several times greater than for a White in Saskatchewan.

Indian Collective Actions

Frideres (1975) did a content analysis of newspaper reports of collective actions by Indians in Canada. He sampled nine major newspapers in three-year sequences from 1950 to 1974. His data include the usual patterns of regional differences in recent Indian–White relationships: peaceful in Quebec, moderate conflict in Ontario and British Columbia, and high conflict in the Prairies. His data also suggest distinct histories of Indian obstructive militance, perhaps correlated with the phases of urban ethnic institutionalization: little ever in Montreal, a variable and moderate level in Vancouver, a single strong wave in Toronto in the 1950s, a strong wave in Winnipeg from 1959 on, and late waves in Regina and Calgary in the 1970s.

In the past twenty years the provincial governments in the Prairie provinces have developed more programs and seem to have been more sympathetic to Indian problems than the other provinces, which usually have left Indian matters to the federal government. The B.C. government, for example, has neglected Indian problems, though the Indians of B.C. are progressive and the racism is relatively tempered. The Quebec government, as well, has generally left Indian problems to the federal government and to an attitude of benign neglect, until Quebec nationalism began to force taking over the powers from the federal government.

The reason for the greater activity for provincial programs in the Prairies seems to be that Indians became a significant political force in the Prairies after the Indians were made citizens and allowed to vote in 1960. Since then, there has been a marked increase in Indian programs of all kinds, but particularly in places where they constitute a significant part of the electorate. They have the votes and they react politically to abrasive social relations.

Urban Adaptations

The Indians of Canada are the most rural large ethnic population in the country and there are strong anti-urban, pro-rural traditions within Indian society today. The best projections we can make about the future of the Indian through the next century include the continuation of a large rural population. They have a relatively inalienable land base in the reserves and have certain other special hunting and fishing rights. Many still have the knowledge and skills of bush life, which will continue to be invaluable in the use of Canadian resources. And they have the Department of Indian Affairs and Northern Development, which provides a rural network of social services specifically for Indians. There are a few groups comparable in their rural orientations to the Indians,

TABLE III

High	Middle	Low
1. Kitchener, Ont.	14. London, Ont.	28. Medicine Hat, Alta.
2. Ottawa, Ont.	15. Penticton, B.C.	29. Camrose, Alta.
3. Montreal, Que.	16. Kingston, Ont.	30. Red Deer, Alta.
4. Bracebridge, Ont.	17. Moose Jaw, Sask.	31. Portage La Prairie, Man.
5. Chilliwack, B.C.	18. Dauphin, Man.	32. Frobisher, Sask.
6. Sudbury, Ont.	19. Prince George, B.C.	33. Nanaimo, B.C.
7. Victoria, B.C.	20. Calgary, Alta.	34. Wadena, Sask.
8. Peterborough, Ont.	21. Edmonton, Alta.	35. Prince Albert, Sask.
9. Toronto, Ont.	22. Weyburn, Sask.	36. Regina, Sask.
10. Oshawa, Ont.	23. Brandon, Man.	37. Grand Prairie, Alta.
11. Hamilton, Ont.	24. Kelowna, B.C.	38. Saskatoon, Sask.
12. Vancouver, B.C.	25. Windsor, Ont.	39. Sault Ste. Marie, Ont.
13. Winnipeg, Man.	26. Eastend, Sask.	40. Owen Sound, Ont.
	27. Sarnia, Ont.	41. Timmins, Ont.

such as the Amish, Mennonites, Hutterites, and Doukhobors, who chose
to live in sustained enclaves and live a traditional way of life for religious
reasons.

The rural character of Indians shows up in their occupations. For
example, we see an inverse correlation between the occupations of Jews,
the most urban ethnic type, and of the Indians, the most rural ethnic
type. One rarely finds Jewish farmers, loggers, fishermen, trappers,
hunters, or miners, as indicated in Table IV (Forcese and Richer 1975:
188–9).

In Indian society today there are many currents of thought and action
oriented to retention of traditional bush life, with even some active anti-
urban movements. These might be characterized as Golden Age
Movements based on a desire to go back to the way of life that existed
before Whites disrupted everything. Indians across Canada are involved
in hunting or fishing or wild plant gathering, and occasionally gardening
or ranching, usually in a seasonal pattern that combines with activities of
the urban world, such as wage work, formal education, and so forth.
Recent northern development projects and land claim cases have
stimulated research on current land use, with the rationale that if Native
people are genuinely harvesting the resources of the land, they will be
deeply affected by industrial developments there; and that claim cases are
strengthened by the demonstration of active use. The data presented
show an intensive use by the Native people of the whole range of
traditional bush resources. In fact, over-use and local depletion of desired
large game is pervasive around northern Native communities. Most of

TABLE IV
Occupations of Indian and Jewish Males in Canada

	Indians	Jews	Canada Total
Managerial	1%	39%	10%
Professional & technical	1%	14%	8%
Clerical	1%	7%	7%
Sales	1%	14%	6%
Service	8%	3%	8%
Transport & communication	4%	3%	7%
Farmers & farm workers	19%	—	12%
Loggers	12%	—	2%
Fishermen, trappers & hunters	17%	—	1%
Miners & related work	1%	—	1%
Craftsmen & production workers	18%	16%	29%
Laborers	14%	1%	6%
Not stated	3%	3%	3%
	100%	100%	100%

the northern communities have probably exceeded the carrying capacity of their natural environments in terms of wild foods.

An important pressure for Indian urbanization seems to have come simply from the growth of the rural Indian population and the stasis or, more commonly, decline, in the supply of wild food resources. The Indian population growth rate is currently about 1.9 per cent per year (double the Canadian rate), but any consistent increase in Indian communities would eventually overpopulate those areas in terms of the fixed amounts of wild resources. While the bush and rural side of Indian life appears to be an important part of any future projection, a continuing urban migration and the development of urban-based Indian cultures are also inevitable in that future.

The urbanization of Indians is a novel, creative process involving some difficulties for individual Indians and some unanticipated stresses and costs for society. In Canada (and the U.S.) government services became a federal responsibility. The services have been rural-oriented. In general, the urban system of social services has been incompetent in helping people so unprepared for urban life as Indians.

The skills and expertise developed for rural Indians, principally by the Department of Indian Affairs and Northern Development and the Health Service, have not been used when the Natives migrated to towns and cities. The urban migrant thus not only leaves a place of inalienable land rights, a home community, the local domain of one's cultural heritage, and a rural way of life, but also leaves the special support of federal services. Those federal services may be negative in their paternalistic and colonial aspects, but they have provided the only pool of expertise in social services for Indians.

When we study demography we see that the greatest push for urban migration is usually from rural overpopulation in terms of available resources. When we do questionnaire surveys and ask Indians their reasons for migrating to a town or city they usually tell us they came for a job, or, occasionally, to attend school or receive medical services. When we probe with interviews into the backgrounds of those who migrate we find they have stronger ties to the urban world than those who stayed: such ties as marriage to a White person, higher formal education, friends or relatives to turn to in the town or city, and so forth. When we investigate cultural geography we see that the urban proximity of the reserve to towns and cities is correlated with migrations and with the influence of urbanizing the reserve itself.

The rural push can be alleviated by careful and thorough harvesting of the fish, game, and fur-bearing animals and by an expansion of modern-type job opportunities for Indians in their rural communities. They have the bush skills on which there is every reason to build by the employment of Native people where they live—particularly by continuing the programs that help Native people run resource development and tourism companies where practical in Native areas. Indians ought to consider the development of programs that promote migration from overpopulated and under-employed reserves to the more prosperous reserves or new pioneer reserves in potentially good economic areas. The migration possibilities should not be just rural to urban, but rural to rural as well. The average of 22 acres of reserve or crown land per status Indian is fairly large. The land, however, is often in a poor location. It is necessary to make these points about the continuing rural presence of Native people both to explain the context of Native urban migration and to emphasize that programs for urban migrants should include vocational- and professional-level training relevant to the rural areas that the migrants came from.

Canadian Indians are slightly more stable in living in the same local areas than Canadians in general. The 1971 Canadian census showed that 80 per cent of the Indians and 75 per cent of a general Canadian sample had remained in one area for the previous five years. The residence of the Indians can be classified as follows: reserve 62 per cent, rural non-reserve 16 per cent, small urban centres (under 100,000) 11 per cent, and large urban centres (100,000 or more) 11 per cent.

The 20 per cent of the Indians who migrated were somewhat unusual in cross-cultural comparisons. More Indian women (54 per cent of the migrants) migrated than men, while the usual rural-to-urban migration pattern around the world is mainly by men. Indian women tend to go a little farther in school than Indian men and they usually take low-paying but steady, and inside, jobs in towns and cities; men tend to take higher-paying, cyclical, outside jobs, such as construction.

Recently, there have been drastic changes in the Indian population growth rate and in reserve life that support a more stable life on reserves. The natural rate of increase fell from 3.5 per cent per year in 1965 to 1.9 per cent in 1974 (Statistics Canada 1977:282). Earlier concerns of extreme reserve over-population and out-migration have been eased. Also, there have been marked improvements in housing facilities on reserves. Between 1963 and 1973 there was the following shift in proportions: (1) 5 or more rooms per house—25 per cent to 53 per cent; (2) electricity—45 per cent to 82 per cent; (3) running water—14 per cent to 42 per cent; (4) indoor toilet—9 per cent to 37 per cent; (5) indoor bath—7 per cent to 33 per cent; and (6) telephone—10 per cent to 28 per cent (Statistics Canada 1977:289).

Successful Urban Adaptations

In the case of Canadian Indians we recognize that many urban migrations are individual searches for life experiences and educational adventures, and that many Indian people have experienced city life and found the rural way of life to be better for them. We commonly find that first-generation urban migrants develop a lifetime pattern of commuting between their rural home area and the town or city they work in. This commuting may be on weekends; seasonal, with short-run city jobs; or just during summer vacations. In ideology and social relations we commonly find strong rural connections and in economic matters we find urban connections; the migrant has a dual orientation. He has an ancestry and ownership of band land on the rural side, kinship and friendship networks that reach between the rural and urban poles, and a desire to experience and participate in the urban world.

Successful urban adaptations depend on the personality and preparedness of the individual for urban life and on the nature of the town or city that the individual migrates to. Any poorly prepared individual from a rural background will undergo cultural shock and trauma on migrating into a city, unless there is an excellent system of institutions to receive and educate that person in urban culture. This individual preparedness can be somewhat predicted according to the evolutionary level of the societal heritage of the individual Indian. There are, of course, widespread non-evolutionary elements that influence this preparedness as well, such as historical elements (e.g., the length of White contact); ecological elements (e.g., urban proximity); and the urbanization of reserve life through the incorporation of reserves in nation-wide networks of transportation, communication, education, health services, and so forth.

The band-level hunters and fishers, such as the Inuit, most of the Dene, and most of the Algonquians, were semi-nomadic aboriginally, had a difficult time settling down into towns and cities historically, and are largely the groups that are having the most troublesome urban adjustment problems today. This has nothing to do with value judgements about these cultures, other than that they are very different from and have inherent conflicts with urban cultures. These groups have recently become politicized and are organizing to solve these inherent conflicts in order to cope in a more satisfactory way with the urban world.

The tribal and chiefdom societies have been more sedentary and have lived in large, fairly urban village settlements for at least several hundred years. Thus, there was an aboriginal rural–urban and evolutionary continuum in Canada that helped to pattern the nature of historical Indian–White relationships and continues into the present. The tribal societies (Blackfoot, Piegan, Blood, Sarcee, Assiniboine, Huron, and Iroquois) and the chiefdom societies (coastal B.C.) have been more successful at urbanizing than the band-level societies. Interior B.C. societies, the Plains Cree, Salteaux, and Ojibwa stood somewhat in a band-tribe transitional position.

In the last decade there has been a prolific growth of an urban Indian ethnic culture. The maturity of the local segments of that culture across Canada is extremely uneven, depending on the specific history of Indian settlement in the various cities. However, these differences become very important for new arrivals: While they provide social support and recreation for the long term residents, the urban ethnic institutional structure contributes strongly to the basic adaptive patterns of new arrivals, by providing a fundamental education about such things as getting a job, avoiding arrest, and getting along with others in the urban area. This means that the success or failure of an urban move by an individual can depend simply on the urban area that is selected.

The sophisticated political ability of the B.C. Indians in dealing with Whites, along with the marine orientation of the coast and the lateness of intensive contact, contributed to their relatively successful resistance of displacement by Whites; and they are still largely rural. Thus the B.C. coastal Indians are more widely scattered in the same settlements that they had aboriginally than Indians in any other densely settled part of Canada. The Canadian government recognized the unusual political abilities of the B.C. Indians and were more repressive with them than with any other Indians in Canada; for example, there were no recognition of treaties, the institution of the notorious potlatch law of 1884–1951, and the outlawing of the raising of funds by Indians for political purposes in 1927 in reaction to the Nishga Petition.

The B.C. coastal chiefdoms set many national patterns for modern Indian institutions. However, the development of urban Indian institutions in B.C., outside the sophistication of reserve life itself, has been limited to Vancouver until the past decade or so. The same predominating role in Ontario can be said for Toronto, but the ethnic institutional structure has become even more elaborate in Toronto with early waves of Iroquois and southern Ojibwa moving into the city during and after World War II.

Areas Ranked in Terms of Successful Urban-Indian Adaptations

1. The Quebec towns and cities probably rank the highest, particularly for French-speaking Indians. This is true in spite of Quebec's lacking the cushion of elaborate and mature Indian ethnic institutions. The Iroquois in the south have consistently led the Indians of Quebec Association. The northern Cree and Inuit have recently formed very effective organizations that will serve an important role in the north. The remaining Indians in the province (Naskapi, Montagnais, Algonkin, Huron, and Metis) have been under more French than British influence and the French have generally been more humane to Indians than the British. This greater humanity seems to have undercut the necessity for protective ethnic institutions.

2. Southern Ontario, southern Alberta, and the Vancouver area. Within the British sphere of influence these are the best places for the urban adaptations of Indians in Canada. The aboriginal cultures were mostly chiefdoms and tribes; the historical integration between White and Indian cultures was more complete and there has been less social distance. These factors have coincided with the greater urbanization and industrialization of these parts of Canada; the reserves were in proximity to towns and cities and thus highly influenced by urban life. Industrial employment has predominated over the harvesting of wild resources. These regions have less anti-Indian racism than the rest of British Canada, and they have the most mature urban Indian ethnic institutions in Canada.

3. British Columbia, Yukon, N.W.T., and the Maritimes.

4. Northern Alberta, Saskatchewan, Manitoba, and northern Ontario.

Voluntary Associations

Voluntary associations seem to be the essence of an ethnic culture within a state society. Voluntary associations were absent in band societies and usually existed as curing, warfare, or food-increase fraternities in tribes. Chiefdoms usually also had associations that helped to validate social ranking and titles. States, in addition, usually had commercial, legal, and priestly associations.

There has been a significant continuity from aboriginal times in the extent and kinds of voluntary associations that were formed. Thus people with a band heritage tended not to form voluntary associations at all in the historic period, but in the 1970s became the most enthusiastic of all: attending the Ecumenical Conference in Alberta, Inuit Tapirisat has been active since 1971; the occupation of Anicinabe Park in 1974; the Dene Declaration and the James Bay Agreement in 1975, and so forth. People from band societies have been entering the continental Native movement in the 1960s and 1970s with increasing commitment. This is their first significant experience of organized protest and they have become particularly enthusiastic once involved. They are more politically organized than they have been in their entire history.

The tribal heritage societies, such as the Iroquois and Blackfoot, went through some two hundred years of military protest, then religious revitalization, and finally modern accommodation and integration with White society. Historically they developed the most reactive voluntary associations, but they now resemble Whites in education and economic activity.

The chiefdoms of British Columbia had an extensive and relatively trouble-free integration with Canadian culture. Their aboriginal culture prepared them for the most sophisticated accommodations. Instead of the passivity of bands or the military and religious reactive pattern of tribes, their associations had instrumental orientations to the dominant society through legal, unionized, and political means. The first example of various kinds of modern Indian institutions has usually been in British Columbia: the first union, the first legally formulated land claim case (Nishga in 1912), the first provincial Indian Brotherhood (1931), the first authentically reconstructed village museum ('Ksan in 1958), the first Indian elected to Parliament (Len Marchand in 1968), and the first Indian restaurant (Muck-a-Muck House in 1972, now closed because the Indians joined a labor union).

For two reasons, reserves have not been particularly creative environments for voluntary associations. First, the small scale of the cultural world on reserves satisfied to a large extent the universal neurological needs for limited social enclaves and "territories," and ideological significance. Second, the colonial dominance of reserve institutions by White society displaced Native leadership, incentives, and means of separate associations. When many Natives moved off their reserves .to towns and cities, however, they were at once freed from colonial dominance and found a need for a new social enclave and a reworking of their ideologies in the new urban circumstances. They then created new urban-based associations.

The creation of urban-centered institutions usually involves more than the simple transfer of rural institutions into an urban setting, though there are a few cases of such transfer; for example, that of tribal dance groups. In the urban center Indians from *different* societies come together and tend to form *inter-societal Indian associations*.

Several things regularly happen in this evolution of urban Indian institutions because the predominant patterns of needs and urban adaptations spread like slow waves through each town or city: specializing, filling an increasing diversity of needs, including those of both a poor newly arriving downtown population (jobs, legal aid, housing, family counseling, etc.) and a stable middle-class suburban population (youth clubs, crafts, recreation, etc.). The number of bars used by a predominantly Indian clientele starts at zero, builds up to several (the maximum depending upon the size of the Indian population and, probably, the extent of racial segregation in the city because this phenomenon is uncommon in French Canada where there is little French–Indian segregation), and then declines over the years back down to two, one, or even zero.

The urban Indian voluntary associations correlate with the later stages of urban development of ethnic institutions, each characterized by certain dominant institutions: (1) bar cliques and social service agencies,

(2) kinship-friendship networks and urban ethnic centers, (3) voluntary associations, (4) academic, entrepreneurial, and professional services.

When reserve Indians migrate to a particular city, they first tend to relate to agencies designed to help Indians, and to the development of their own social cliques in skid row bars. In time they develop longer-lasting kinship-friendship networks and often some of the work of the service agencies is channeled and given a more Indian character through an urban ethnic center. As the institutional structure matures there is an increasing design and control of institutions by Native people. The Indian bars and their cliques become less important as social contacts are transferred more to settings that are private or of voluntary associations, such as youth clubs, craft groups, dance groups, and so forth. Finally, the fourth order institutions emerge, designed and staffed by Native people but offering services to the public as well as to the ethnic group: arts and crafts sales, entertainments, restaurants, Native studies, etc. The various towns and cities of Canada are at different stages in their development of Indian institutions; the particular place that an Indian goes to live in will have an important influence on whether he ends up drinking on skid row or socializing through a voluntary association.

The number of Indian adults in formal Indian voluntary associations is low in Edmonton (9 per cent in one survey), and moderate in Toronto (22 per cent), Winnipeg (25 per cent), and Vancouver (26 per cent). This rate of membership is something of an index to the institutional character of ethnic life in the various cities. That is, we would expect the Indian bar culture cliques to be prominent in Edmonton with few advanced Indian ethnic institutions.

The large Indian bar culture described by Brody (1971) for Edmonton and found thriving today in cities in the Prairies and certain other parts of Canada seems to be a temporary stage that disappears when a more functional and mature Indian institutional structure is built up in the city. The Prairie cities are experiencing the kind of Indian bar culture that was around fifteen years earlier in Toronto; a culture that has shriveled, in Toronto, to a few new migrants, usually from distant places, who do not have a stable network of friends and relatives in the city.

Winnipeg probably has the largest Indian skid row area in Canada, but it also has a very elaborate Indian ethnic institutional system. The first urban Indian friendship center in Canada, for example, started in Winnipeg. Toronto's Indian skid row has virtually died out, with only some minor patronage of the Silver Dollar bar—mostly by newly arrived young Indians from the north. With about 27,000, Toronto has the largest population of Indians of any city in Canada and it has been a consistent national leader in the development of urban Indian institutions. Vancouver, however, has more per capita participation in associations by the Indians in the city. They are more active and committed to their Indian institutions, while in Toronto a high proportion (78 per cent of adult Indians surveyed) belong to formal *non-Indian* organizations.

Stanbury and Siegel (1975; secondary analysis by Don N. McCaskill) reported on a 1971 survey of status Indians over 16 years of age who lived off their reserves in British Columbia. The Vancouver part of that survey gives us some idea of Indian life in a large city. They tended to be young (median age, 28), single (47 per cent), recently arrived (median time of arrival 4 years earlier), moderate in level of education (median 8 years), and low in income (average family income in 1970 was about $3,570). Most (71 per cent) knew Indians and some (41 per cent) knew non-Indians in the city when they first came to Vancouver. Most (62 per cent) could speak an Indian language: Salish, 24 per cent; Kwakiutl, 15 per cent; Tsimshian, 10 per cent; Athapascan, 7 per cent; Nootka, 4 per cent; and Haida, 3 per cent. However, only 18 per cent used their Indian language in their home, 6 per cent in combination with English, and 12 per cent exclusively. This level of ability to speak an Indian language is similar to that among Indians in other Canadian cities: Edmonton, 70 per cent; Winnipeg, 73 per cent; and Toronto, 62 per cent.

The following proportions had these life style traits in Vancouver:

Watch television	87%
Read a Vancouver newspaper	72%
Listen to radio	70%
Read an Indian publication	63%
Bank account	56%
Driver's licence	36%
Life insurance	28%
Credit card	23%
Own a house	11%

Commentary

Nunavut

The direction of traditional Inuit flexible adaptations shifted in historic times from the physical environment to the new cultural environment of a dominant state society with its missionaries, traders, police, and educators. They are now coping with the imposed environment of Canadian institutions through creating their own ethnic institutions. The most important organization is Inuit Tapirisat of Canada, which is pressing for political control over their aboriginal territory in the Northwest Territories, which they called Nunavut, "Our Land" in Inuktitut. The I.T.C. claim is for outright ownership of 250,000 square miles of land selected in such a way that each community has at least 2,500 square miles. The remaining 500,000 square miles north of the treeline would be surrendered, though the Inuit would retain exclusive hunting, fishing, and trapping rights and a royalty of 3 per cent of the revenue from the sale of natural resources.

The Inuit are quite capable of administering Nunavut as a Territory of Canada, but it is against the principles of modern government to have a racial or ethnic requirement to land ownership and enfranchisement. Canada itself violated this principle and refused to enfranchise Native people in general until 1960, but that discrimination should not be reciprocated now by Native discrimination. The accommodation to the conflict between the cultural and personal values of the Inuit and the legal and political values of the Whites might be to allow Nunavut the degree of sovereignty that other territories have, ensure that all races and ethnic groups have equal rights of participation in Nunavut government, and ensure that those who have voting rights must really know about the Arctic and thus become eligible to vote only after a residency of about two years.

In July 1978 the 2,500 Inuit of the Western Arctic reached a tentative agreement on land claims. They will renounce all claims to 168,000 square miles; will exclusively own 5,000 square miles; will own but must honor the existing leases on another 32,000 square miles; and will receive $45 million compensation or about $18,000 per Inuit, tax free. A separate 5,000 square miles will be set aside for a national wilderness park on the international border to adjoin a similar park in Alaska. The Inuit choice of lands are to be made in terms of traditional hunting, trapping, and fishing or future tourism, but not of those areas proven to have gas and oil reserves. Only Inuit who have lived in the area for at least ten years will be eligible. Inuit companies will be created to receive and manage the benefits.

Toward True Multiculturalism

In both the U.S. and Canada the reserves were generally not important labor pools for exploitation by metropolitan centers until the twentieth century. They were enclaves that Whites assumed would be eliminated by the assimilation of their people to the naturally superior White culture. The government, the school system, the missionaries, the R.C.M.P., the Hudson Bay Company or other traders tried to systematically eliminate Indian culture and replace it with White European culture. What they did instead was deculturate and bureaucratize the Indian people. They pressured them into becoming an ethnic minority with a very low level of power, privilege, and prestige. Reserves became the base of modern poverty, welfare, and protest on one hand, and the common experience of all Indians on the other. From a condition of extreme diversity the Indians have been drawn into the uniform experience of government-administered reserves. This then became the foundation for the creation of a new culture—the U.S. and Canadian Indian ethnic culture.

Diamond Jenness, an early anthropologist, said that parliament voted just enough money to meet Canada's treaty obligations and then forgot the Indians and Inuit because their numbers were small and they had no influence in politics. The Indian administration was so involved in the routine of its administration that it forgot the purpose of its custodianship. The Native people, however, have the highest population growth rate of any ethnic group in Canada. When we include the non-status Indians, there are about 600,000 people with a Native heritage in Canada, or about 2.5 per cent of the total population. Since the time of Diamond Jenness they have become a significant political voice. They are the majority of the population in the Northwest Territories and almost half of the population in Yukon Territory.

We hope that Canada will recognize the special historical status of the Native people, will recognize their aboriginal and treaty rights, and will allow them the diverse accommodations to life in Canada that are called for by the diverse cultural backgrounds described in this book. Some will choose to move toward the urban side of life and some will choose to retreat to as much of a traditional life as possible in the northern bush country. We have seen several recent moves by Native people that are supportive of a traditional way of life and the resumption of more control over their land and their lives.

1. In 1968 Chief Robert Smallboy led 143 Indians from the Hobbema Reserve in Alberta back into the wilderness to return to a traditional way of life. That year the National Indian Brotherhood was formed, Len Marchand became the first Indian elected to the House of Commons, and the CBC radio program "Our Native Land" went on the national network.

2. In 1969–70 the federal government's Indian policy White Paper, that favored the assimilation of Indians into the general society and the transference of Indian programs from the federal to the provincial government, was widely rejected by Indians. Harold Cardinal's book *The Unjust Society* became a best seller.

3. In 1970 the first Indian Ecumenical Conference was held on the Crow Reservation in Montana and then in later years on the Stoney Reserve in Alberta. This is the major institution of religious revitalization among Native Canadians. In the same year Inuit Tapirisat of Canada was formed.

4. In 1971 a Chipewyan group left Churchill, Manitoba and went back to Tadoule Lake to live in the traditional way.

5. In 1974 Native people in Kenora, Ontario forcibly occupied some park land that had been taken from them. In the same year the Heritage Stoney Wilderness program began teaching traditional Indian ways to Whites.

6. The Cree and Inuit of northern Quebec negotiated supports for a traditional way of life in the James Bay Agreement, signed in 1975. The Dene Declaration of Indian "nationhood" was made in the Northwest Territories in the same year.,

7. In 1975 to 1977 the Cree and Dene of the Northwest Territories effectively delayed the construction of the Mackenzie Valley Pipeline by at least ten years in order to develop their land claim case and to find ways to protect their traditional culture.

8. In 1978 the federal and provincial governments and the Federation of Saskatchewan Indians agreed to settle outstanding claims from 1871 and 1906 treaties by transferring ownership or revenue sharing on about one million acres of land to provincial Indians, some 128 acres per capita.

We hope that Canada will recognize the value of a true multicultural policy which allows the continuation of sustained enclaves of these different kinds of Native societies. These enclaves will invariably have many strands of integration with the nation as a whole, but the Native people should be allowed to contribute in that integration from the wealth of their own cultural heritages.

1981 Census Data

	Population X 1,000	Speak A Native Mother Language	Average 1980 Income X $1,000
Status Indians	293	38 %	7.6
Non-Status Indians	75	9.5%	9.9
Metis	98	13.9%	9.5
Inuit	25	74.1%	8.3
Total Native	491	28.7%	8.6
Total Canadian	23,592	---	13.1

Population

	Native	Canada
British Columbia	16.8	11.3%
Prairies	40.2	17.4%
Ontario	22.4	35.4%
Quebec	10.7	26.4%
Atlantic	3.7	9.2%
Territories	6.2	0.3%
	100	100%

High school or higher level education, adults:
   Natives 28.7%   Canada 52.8%

In 1987 Natives are struggling with the development of the institutions for economic, political, and social self-determination. In Metropolitan Toronto, for example, there are several Indian businesses and such urban Indian ethnic institutions as (1) hostels for both men and women; (2) one housing company for Indian families and seniors and another one for Metis; (3) a skid row drop-in centre and soup kitchen; (4) an Indian centre run by middle class Indians that provides services such courtworkers, inmate liaison, speakers bank, and youth groups; (5) Association for Native Development in the Visual and Performing Arts; (6) an artisans association; (7) a Native mental health service; (8) a women's centre; (9) Ontario Indian Education Council; (10) Ontario Native Council on Justice; (11) a residential alcohol and drug treatment centre; (12) a thrift store; and (13) an elementary school with a Native staff and curriculum.

Bibliography

Chapter 1: Race and Prehistory

The major publication series on archaeology in Canada is the Papers of the Archaeological Survey of Canada, National Museums of Canada. There are also provincial museum publications and the Bulletins of the Canadian Archaeological Association.

BORDEN, CHARLES E.
  1975   *Origins and Development of Early Northwest Coast Culture to About 3000 B.C.* Ottawa: National Museums of Canada.
BUREAU OF NUTRITIONAL SCIENCES
  1975   *Nutritional Canada: The Indian Survey Report.* Ottawa: National Health and Welfare.
CHOWN, B. and M. LEWIS
  1958   *Blood Groups in Anthropology: With Special Reference to Canadian Indians and Eskimos.* Ottawa: National Museum of Canada, Bulletin 167.
DEWDNEY, SELWYN H.
  1967   *Indian Rock Paintings of the Great Lakes.* Toronto: University of Toronto.
DUFF, WILSON
  1975   *Images Stone B.C.: Thirty Centuries of Northwest Coast Indian Sculpture.* Toronto: Oxford University.
HEIDENREICH, CONRAD
  1971   *Huronia: A History and Geography of the Huron Indians, 1600–1650.* Toronto: McClelland & Stewart.
HUGHES, DAVID R. and EVELYN KALLEN
  1974   *The Anatomy of Racism: Canadian Dimensions.* Montreal: Harvest House.
JOHNSTON, RICHARD
  1968   *The Archaeology of the Serpent Mound Site.* Toronto: Royal Ontario Museum.
MACDONALD, GEORGE F.
  1968   *Debert, A Paleo-Indian Site in Central Nova Scotia.* Ottawa: National Museums of Canada.
MCKAY, ALEXANDER G., editor
  1977   *New Perspectives in Canadian Archaeology.* Ottawa: The Royal Society of Canada.

MACNEISH, RICHARD S., editor
1973   *Early Man in America.* San Francisco: W.H. Freeman & Co.

MARTIN, PAUL S. and H.E. WRIGHT, editors
1967   *Pleistocene Extinctions: The Search for a Cause.* New Haven: Yale University.

MEADE, EDWARD
1971   *Indian Rock Carvings of the Pacific Northwest.* Sidney, B.C.: Gray's Pub. Co.

NOBLE, WILLIAM C.
1972   *One Hundred and Twenty-Five Years of Archaeology in the Canadian Provinces.* Canadian Archaeological Association Bulletin, No. 4.

QUIMBY, GEORGE I.
1966   *Indian Culture and European Trade Goods: The Archaeology of the Historic Period in the Western Great Lakes Region.* Madison: University of Wisconsin Press.

SHEPHARD, ROY J. and S. ITOH, editors
1976   *Circumpolar Health.* Toronto: University of Toronto.

STEWART, T.D.
1973   *The People of America.* London: Weidenfeld & Nicolson.

SUCH, PETER
1978   *Vanished Peoples: The Archaic, Dorset, and Beothuk People of Newfoundland.* Toronto: NC Press.

WILLEY, GORDON R.
1966   *An Introduction to American Archaeology.* Vol. 1. Englewood Cliffs, N.J.: Prentice-Hall.

WRIGHT, JAMES V.
1972   *Ontario Prehistory: An Eleven-Thousand Year Archaeological Outline.* Ottawa: National Museums of Canada.
1976   *Six Chapters of Canada's Prehistory.* Ottawa: National Museums of Canada.

Chapter 2: Language

The Ethnology Mercury Series of the National Museums of Canada includes descriptive monographs on Canadian Indian languages such as Sarcee, Mohawk, Inuktitut, and Kwakiutl; and linguistic conferences on Iroquoian, Algonquian, and Dene languages. The major journal with articles on Canadian Indian languages is *International Journal of American Linguistics.*

BASSO, KEITH
1972   Ice and Travel Among the Fort Norman Slave: Folk Taxonomies and Cultural Roles. *Language and Society,* Vol. 1, No. 1.

BLOOMFIELD, LEONARD, editor and translator
1930   *Sacred Stories of the Sweet Grass Cree.* Ottawa: National Museums of Canada.

BOAS, FRANZ
1911   Introduction. *Handbook of American Indian Languages.* Washington: Bureau of American Ethnology. Reprinted in 1966 by University of Nebraska.

CARROLL, JOHN B., editor
1956   *Language, Thought and Reality: Selected Writings of Benjamin Lee Whorf.* New York: John Wiley and Sons.

CHAMBERS, J.K., editor
   1978   *Languages of Canada.* Quebec City: Centre Educatif et Culturel.
COOK, EUNG-DO and JONATHAN KAYE, editors
   1978   *Linguistic Studies of Native Canada.* Vancouver: University of British Columbia.
DARNELL, REGNA
   1970   The Kaska Aesthetic of Speech Use. *Western Canadian Journal of Anthropology,* Vol. 1, No. 1.
DENNY, J. PETER
   1974   Semantics and the Teaching of Elementary Grades in Native Languages. *Proceedings, Canadian Ethnology Society.* Ottawa: National Museums of Canada.
DEPARTMENT OF INDIAN AFFAIRS AND NORTHERN DEVELOPMENT
   1970   *Linguistic and Cultural Affiliations of Canadian Indian Bands.* Ottawa.
ELLIS, C.D.
   1973   A Proposed Standard Roman Orthography for Cree. *The Western Canadian Journal of Anthropology,* Vol. 3, No. 4.
SAPIR, EDWARD
   1921   *Language: An Introduction to the Study of Speech.* New York: Harcourt, Brace & Co.
SWADESH, MORRIS
   1951   Diffusional Cumulation and Archaic Residue as Historical Explanation. *Southwestern Journal of Anthropology,* Vol. 7, No. 1.
TOMKINS, WILLIAM
   1969   *Indian Sign Language.* New York: Dover.
VOEGELIN, CARL and F.M. VOEGELIN
   1966   Map of North American Indian Languages. Seattle: American Ethnological Society.

Chapter 3: Cultural Dynamics

The major bibliography is *Ethnographic Bibliography of North America,* Vols. 1-5, 4th edition, George P. Murdock and Timothy J. O'Leary, editors (1976, New Haven: Human Relations Area Files). The publication series with the most material on the ethnology of Canadian Indians are (1) publications of the National Museums of Canada, (2) *Anthropologica,* and (3) *The Western Canadian Journal of Anthropology.*

ANDERSON, ROBERT
   1976   *The Cultural Context: An Introduction to Cultural Anthropology.* Minneapolis: Burgess.
CARNEIRO, ROBERT L.
   1968   Ascertaining, Testing, and Interpreting Sequences of Cultural Development. *Southwestern Journal of Anthropology,* Vol. 24, No. 4.
COX, BRUCE, editor
   1973   *Cultural Ecology: Readings on the Canadian Indians and Eskimos.* Toronto: McClelland & Stewart.

CROWE, KEITH J.
1974   *A History of the Original Peoples of Northern Canada.* Montreal: McGill-Queen's University.

DRIVER, HAROLD E.
1969   *Indians of North America,* 2nd edition. Chicago: University of Chicago.

FISHER, ROBIN
1977   *Contact and Conflict: Indian-European Relations in British Columbia, 1774–1890.* Vancouver: University of British Columbia.

GEOGRAPHIC BOARD OF CANADA
1913   *Handbook of the Indians of Canada.* Ottawa: King's Printer. Reprinted in 1971, Toronto: Coles.

GRAHAM, ELIZABETH
1975   *Medicine Man to Missionary: Missionaries as Agents of Change Among the Indians of Southern Ontario, 1784–1867.* Toronto: Peter Martin Associates.

HEARD, J. NORMAN
1973   *White Into Red: A Study of the Assimilation of White Persons Captured by Indians.* Metuchen, N.J.: Scarecrow.

HEARNE, SAMUEL
1795   *Journey From Prince of Wales Fort in Hudson's Bay to the North Ocean in the Years 1769–1772.* London. Reprinted in 1958 by Macmillan of Canada.

JAENEN, CORNELIUS
1976   *Friend and Foe: Aspects of French-Amerindian Cultural Conflict in the Sixteenth and Seventeenth Centuries.* Toronto: McClelland & Stewart.

JENNESS, DIAMOND
1932   *The Indians of Canada.* Ottawa: National Museums of Canada. Reprinted in 1977 by University of Toronto.

KANE, PAUL
1859   *Wanderings of an Artist Among the Indians.* London: Longman, Brown et al. Reprinted in 1968 by Hurtig.

KROEBER, ALFRED L.
1934   Native American Population. *American Anthropologist,* Vol. 6, No. 1.

LEACOCK, ELEANOR and NANCY O. LURIE, editors
1971   *North American Indians in Historical Perspective.* New York: Random House.

MCLEAN, JOHN
1889   *The Indians: Their Manners and Customs.* Toronto: William Briggs. Reprinted in 1970 by Coles.
1896   *Canadian Savage Folk: The Native Tribes of Canada.* Toronto: William Briggs. Reprinted in 1971 by Coles.

MEALING, S.R., editor
1963   *The Jesuit Relations and Related Documents.* Toronto: McClelland & Stewart.

NAGLER, MARK, editor
1972   *Perspectives on the North American Indians.* Toronto: McClelland & Stewart.

OBERG, KALVERO
1973   *The Social Economy of the Tlingit Indians.* Vancouver: J.J. Douglas.

OSWALT, WENDELL H.
1978   *This Land Was Theirs: A Study of the North American Indian,* 3rd edition. Toronto: John Wiley & Sons.

OWEN, ROGER C. ET AL., editors
1967   *The North American Indians: A Sourcebook.* New York: Macmillan.

PATTERSON, E. PALMER
   1972   *The Canadian Indian: A History Since 1500.* Don Mills: Collier-Macmillan.
PATTERSON, NANCY-LOU
   1973   *Canadian Native Art.* Don Mills: Collier-Macmillan.
PRICE, JOHN A.
   1973   The Superorganic Fringe: Protoculture, Idioculture, and Material Culture. *Ethos,* Vol. 1, No. 2.
   1975   Sharing: The Integration of Intimate Economies. *Anthropologica,* Vol. 17, No. 1.
   1978   *Native Studies: American and Canadian Indians.* Scarborough: McGraw-Hill Ryerson.
SERVICE, ELMAN R.
   1971   *Primitive Social Organization: An Evolutionary Perspective,* 2nd edition. New York: Random House.
   1975   *Origins of the State and Civilization: The Process of Cultural Evolution.* New York: W.W. Norton.
TEDLOCK, DENNIS and BARBARA TEDLOCK, editors
   1975   *Teachings From the American Earth: Indian Religion and Philosophy.* New York: Liveright.
TERRELL, JOHN U. and DONNA M. TERRELL
   1976   *Indian Women of the Western Morning: Their Life in Early America.* Garden City, New York: Anchor.
UNDERHILL, RUTH M.
   1965   *Red Man's Religion: Beliefs and Practices of the Indians North of Mexico.* Chicago: University of Chicago.

Chapter 4: Arctic

BALIKCI, ASEN
   1970   *The Netsilik Eskimo.* Garden City, New York: Natural History Press.
BIRKET-SMITH, KAJ
   1959   *The Eskimos.* London: Methuen.
BOAS, FRANZ
   1888   *The Central Eskimo.* Washington: Bureau of American Ethnology. Reprinted in 1974, Toronto: Coles.
BRIGGS, JEAN L.
   1970   *Never in Anger.* Cambridge: Harvard.
BRODY, HUGH
   1975   *The People's Land: Eskimos and Whites in the Eastern Arctic.* Markham, Ontario: Penguin Books of Canada.
DAILEY, ROBERT C. and LOIS A. DAILEY
   1961   *The Eskimos of Rankin Inlet.* Ottawa: Northern Coordination and Research Centre.
DAMAS, DAVID
   1973   Environment, History, and Central Eskimo Society. In *Cultural Ecology,* edited by Bruce Cox. Toronto: McClelland & Stewart.
HONIGMANN, JOHN and IRMA HONIGMANN
   1965   *Eskimo Townsmen.* Ottawa: The Canadian Research Centre for Anthropology.

HUGHES, CHARLES C.
  1965   Under Four Flags: Recent Cultural Changes Among the Eskimos. *Current Anthropology,* Vol. 6, No. 1.

JENNESS, DIAMOND
  1928   *The People of the Twilight.* Chicago: University of Chicago.

METAYER, MAURICE, editor
  1966   *I, Nuligak.* Toronto: Peter Martin Associates.

MOWAT, FARLEY
  1954   *People of the Deer.* Toronto: University of Toronto.

  1959   *The Desperate People.* Toronto: University of Toronto.

PRYDE, DUNCAN
  1971   *Nunaga: Ten Years of Eskimo Life.* New York: Walker.

RASMUSSEN, KNUD
  1931   *The Netsilik Eskimos.* Copenhagen: Reports of the Fifth Thule Expedition, Vol. 8.

SWINTON, GEORGE
  1956   *Eskimo Sculpture.* Toronto: McClelland & Stewart.

VALENTINE, VICTOR F. and FRANK G. VALLEE, editors
  1968   *Eskimo of the Canadian Arctic.* Toronto: McClelland & Stewart.

VALLEE, FRANK G.
  1962   *Kabloona and Eskimo in the Central Keewatin.* Ottawa: Northern Coordination and Research Centre.

WILLMOTT, WILLIAM E.
  1960   The Flexibility of Eskimo Social Organization. *Anthropologica,* Vol. 2, No. 1.

Chapter 5: Subarctic

BAILEY, ALFRED G.
  1969   *The Conflict of European and Eastern Algonkian Cultures, 1504–1700.* Toronto: University of Toronto.

BALIKCI, ASEN
  1963   *Vunta Kutchin Social Change: A Study of the People of Old Crow, Yukon Territory.* Ottawa: Northern Coordination and Research Centre.

BIRKET-SMITH, KAJ
  1930   *Contributions to Chipewyan Ethnology.* Report of the Fifth Thule Expedition, Vol. 6, No. 3.

BISHOP, CHARLES A.
  1974   *The Northern Ojibwa and the Fur Trade: An Historical and Ecological Study.* Toronto: Holt, Rinehart and Winston of Canada.

BOCK, PHILIP K.
  1966   *The Micmac Indians of Restigouche: History and Contemporary Description.* Ottawa: National Museums of Canada.

CHANCE, NORMAN A., editor
  1968   *Conflict in Culture: Problems of Developmental Change Among the Cree.* Ottawa: Canadian Research Centre for Anthropology.

DENSMORE, FRANCES
  1929   *Chippewa Customs.* Washington: Bureau of American Ethnology.

DUNNING, ROBERT W.
1959   *Social and Economic Change Among the Northern Ojibwa.* Toronto: University of Toronto.
FORT GEORGE, QUEBEC
1971   *Traditional Indian Recipes.* Cobalt, Ontario: Highway Book Shop.
FUMOLEAU, RENE
1973   *As Long As This Land Shall Last: A History of Treaty 8 and Treaty 11, 1878–1939.* Toronto: McClelland & Stewart.
GUEDON, MARIE-FRANCOISE
1974   *People of Tetlin, Why Are You Singing?* Ottawa: National Museums of Canada.
HELM, JUNE
1961   *The Lynx Point People: The Dynamics of a Northern Athapascan Band.* Ottawa: National Museums of Canada.
HELM, JUNE and NANCY O. LURIE
1961   *The Subsistence Economy of the Dogrib Indians of Lac La Martre.* Ottawa: Northern Affairs.
HENRIKSON, GEORGE
1973   *Hunters in the Barrens: The Naskapi on the Edge of the White Man's World.* St. John's: Memorial University of Newfoundland.
HILGER, INEZ
1951   *Chippewa Child Life and Its Cultural Background.* Washington: Bureau of American Ethnology.
HONIGMANN, JOHN J.
1946   *Ethnography and Acculturation of the Fort Nelson Slave.* New Haven: Yale University.
1954   *The Kaska Indians: An Ethnographic Reconstruction.* New Haven: Yale University Publications in Anthropology, No. 51.
JENNESS, DIAMOND
1935   *The Ojibwa Indians of Parry Island, Their Social and Religious Life.* Ottawa: National Museums of Canada.
1937   *The Sekani Indians of British Columbia.* Ottawa: National Museums of Canada.
KNIGHT, ROLF
1968   *Ecological Factors in Changing Economy and Social Organization Among the Rupert House Cree.* Ottawa: National Museums of Canada.
LANDES, RUTH
1937   *Ojibwa Sociology.* New York: Columbia University Contributions to Anthropology.
1971   *The Ojibwa Woman.* New York: W.W. Norton.
LEACOCK, ELEANOR
1954   *The Montagnais Hunting Territory and the Fur Trade.* American Anthropological Association, Memoir No. 28.
MCCLELLAN, CATHARINE
1975   *My Old People Say: An Ethnographic Survey of Southern Yukon Territory.* Ottawa: National Museums of Canada.
MCGEE, H.F., editor
1974   *The Native Peoples of Atlantic Canada.* Toronto: McClelland & Stewart.
NELSON, RICHARD K.
1976   Hunters of the Northern Ice. In *Custom Made: Introductory Readings for*

Cultural Anthropology, edited by C. Hughes, Chicago: Rand McNally.

O'MALLEY, MARTIN
1976   *The Past and Future Land: An Account of the Berger Inquiry into the Mackenzie Valley Pipeline.* Toronto: Peter Martin.

OSGOOD, CORNELIUS B.
1936   *Contributions to the Ethnography of the Kutchin.* New Haven: Yale University.
1971   *The Han Indians.* New Haven: Yale University.

PARKER, SEYMOUR
1960   The Wiitiko Psychosis in the Context of Ojibwa Personality. *American Anthropologist,* Vol. 62, No. 4.

PRESTON, RICHARD
1976   *Cree Narrative: Expressing the Personal Meanings of Events.* Ottawa: National Museums of Canada.

RAY, ARTHUR J.
1974   *Indians in the Fur Trade: Their Role as Trappers, Hunters, and Middlemen in the Lands Southwest of Hudson Bay, 1660–1870.* Toronto: University of Toronto.

RICHARDSON, BOYCE
1972   *James Bay: The Plot to Drown the North Woods.* San Francisco: Sierra Club.

ROGERS, EDWARD S.
1962   *The Round Lake Ojibwa.* Toronto: Royal Ontario Museum.
1963   *The Hunting Group-Hunting Territory Complex Among the Mistassini Indians.* Ottawa: National Museums of Canada.
1967   *The Material Culture of the Mistassini.* Ottawa: National Museums of Canada.
1973   *The Quest For Food and Furs: The Mistassini Cree, 1953–1954.* Ottawa: National Museums of Canada.

ROWE, FREDERICK W.
1977   *Extinction: The Beothuks of Newfoundland.* Toronto: McGraw-Hill Ryerson.

SLOBODIN, RICHARD
1962   *Band Organization of the Peel River Kutchin.* Ottawa: National Museums of Canada.
1966   *Metis of the Mackenzie District.* Ottawa: Canadian Research Centre for Anthropology.

SPECK, FRANK G.
1935   *The Naskapi: Savage Hunters of the Labrador Peninsula.* Norman: University of Oklahoma.
1940   *Penobscot Man.* Philadelphia: University of Pennsylvania.

TANNER, ADRIAN
1966   *Trappers, Hunters, and Fishermen.* Ottawa: Northern Coordination and Research Centre.

VAN STONE, JAMES W.
1965   *The Changing Culture of the Snowdrift Chipewyan.* Ottawa: National Museums of Canada.
1974   *Athapaskan Adaptations: Hunters and Fishermen of Subarctic Forests.* Chicago: Aldine.

WALLIS, WILSON D.and RUTH S. WALLIS
1955   *The Micmac Indians of Eastern Canada.* Minneapolis: University of Minnesota.

Chapter 6: Iroquoia

FENTON, WILLIAM N.
   1963   *The Iroquois Book of Rites.* Toronto: University of Toronto.
FENTON, WILLIAM N., editor
   1968   *Parker on the Iroquois.* Syracuse, N.Y.: Syracuse University.
GROS-LOUIS, MAX
   1973   *First Among the Hurons.* Montreal: Harvest House.
HEIDENREICH, CONRAD
   1971   *Huronia: A History and Geography of the Huron Indians, 1600–1650.* Toronto: McClelland & Stewart.
HUNT, GEORGE T.
   1940   *The Wars of the Iroquois: A Study in Intertribal Trade Relations.* Madison: University of Wisconsin.
KURATH, GERTRUDE P.
   1964   *Iroquois Music and Dance: Ceremonial Arts of Two Seneca Longhouses.* Washington: Bureau of American Ethnology.
MORGAN, LEWIS H.
   1851   *League of the Ho-De-No-Sau-Nee or Iroquois.* Reprinted in 1954 by the Human Relations Area Files.
OTTERBEIN, KEITH F.
   1964   An Analysis of Iroquois Military Tactics. *Ethnohistory,* Vol. 11, No. 1.
SAGARD-THEODAT, GABRIEL
   1939   *The Long Journey to the Country of the Hurons.* Toronto: Champlain Society.
SHIMONY, ANNEMARIE A.
   1961   *Conservatism Among the Iroquois at the Six Nations Reserve.* New Haven: Yale University.
TAIT, LYAL
   1971   *The Petuns: Tobacco Indians of Canada.* Fort Burwell, Ontario: Erie.
TOOKER, ELIZABETH
   1967   *An Ethnography of the Huron Indians, 1615–1649.* Midland, Ontario: Huronia Historical Development Council.
TRIGGER, BRUCE G.
   1969   *The Huron: Farmers of the North.* New York: Holt, Rinehart & Winston.
   1976   *The Children of Aataentsic: A History of the Huron People to 1660.* 2 Vols. Montreal: McGill-Queen's University.
WALLACE, ANTHONY F.
   1972   *The Death and Rebirth of the Seneca.* Toronto: Random House of Canada.
WAUGH, F.W.
   1916   *Iroquois Foods and Food Preparation.* Ottawa: National Museums of Canada. Reprinted in 1973.
WEAVER, SALLY M.
   1972   *Medicine and Politics Among the Grand River Iroquois.* Ottawa: National Museums of Canada.
WILSON, EDMUND
   1960   *Apologies to the Iroquois.* New York: Vintage Books.

Chapter 7: Plains

CARD, BRIGHAM Y., G.K. HIRABAYASHI, and C.L. FRENCH
   1963   *The Metis in Alberta Society.* Edmonton: University of Alberta.

DEMPSEY, HUGH A.
   1965   *A Blackfoot Winter Count.* Calgary: Glenbow Foundation.

EWERS, JOHN C.
   1958   *The Blackfoot, Raiders of the Northwestern Plains.* Norman: University of Oklahoma.

HANKS, LUCIEN M. and JANE R. HANKS
   1950   *Tribe Under Trust: A Study of the Blackfoot Reserve of Alberta.* Toronto: University of Toronto.

JENNESS, DIAMOND
   1938   *The Sarcee Indians of Alberta.* Ottawa: National Museums of Canada.

KROEBER, ALFRED L.
   1908   *Ethnology of the Gros Ventre.* New York: American Museum of Natural History.

LEWIS, OSCAR
   1941   Manly Hearted Women Among the North Piegan. *American Anthropologist,* Vol. 43.
   1942   *The Effects of White Contact Upon Blackfoot Culture.* Seattle: University of Washington.

LOWIE, ROBERT H.
   1909   *The Assiniboine.* New York: American Museum of Natural History.

MACEWAN, GRANT
   1973   *Sitting Bull: Ten Years in Canada.* Edmonton: Hurtig.

MANDLEBAUM, DAVID G.
   1940   *The Plains Cree.* New York: American Museum of Natural History.

MCFEE, MALCOLM
   1972   *Modern Blackfeet: Montanans on a Reservation.* New York: Holt, Rinehart & Winston.

SCHAEFFER, CLAUDE E.
   1969   *Blackfoot Shaking Tent.* Calgary: Glenbow-Alberta Institute.

SECOY, FRANK R.
   1953   *Changing Military Patterns on the Great Plains.* American Ethnological Society, Monograph 21.

SNOW, JOHN
   1977   *These Mountains Are Our Sacred Places: The Story of the Stoney Indians.* Toronto: Samuel Stevens.

WISSLER, CLARK
   1910   *Material Culture of the Blackfoot Indians.* New York: American Museum of Natural History.
   1912   *The Social Life of the Blackfoot Indians.* New York: American Museum of Natural History.
   1913   *Societies and Dance Associations of the Blackfoot Indians.* New York: American Museum of Natural History.

Chapter 8: Pacific Coast

ADAMS, JOHN
  1973   *The Gitksan Potlatch.* Toronto: Holt, Rinehart & Winston.
BARNETT, HOMER G.
  1955   *The Coast Salish of British Columbia.* Eugene: University of Oregon.
  1968   *The Nature and Function of the Potlatch.* Eugene: University of Oregon.
BOAS, FRANZ
  1966   *Kwakiutl Ethnography.* Edited by H. Codere. Chicago: University of Chicago.
CODERE, HELEN
  1950   *Fighting With Property.* New York: American Ethnological Society.
CURTIS, EDWARD S.
  1915   *The Kwakiutl.* Norwood, Connecticut.
DENSMORE, FRANCES
  1939   *Nootka and Quileute Music.* Washington: Bureau of American Ethnology.
DRUCKER, PHILIP
  1950   *Culture Element Distributions; XXVI. Northwest Coast. Anthropological Records,* Vol. 9. No. 3.
  1951   *The Northern and Central Nootkan Tribes.* Washington: Bureau of American Ethnology.
  1958   *The Native Brotherhoods.* Washington: Bureau of American Ethnology.
  1965   *Cultures of the North Pacific Coast.* San Francisco: Chandler.
DRUCKER, PHILIP and ROBERT F. HEIZER
  1967   *To Make My Name Good: A Reexamination of the Southern Kwakiutl Potlatch.* Berkeley: University of California.
DUFF, WILSON
  1964   *The Indian History of British Columbia.* Victoria: Queen's Printer.
FISHER, ROBIN
  1977   *Contact and Conflict: Indian-European Relations in British Columbia, 1774–1890.* Vancouver: University of British Columbia.
FORD, CLELLAND S.
  1941   *Smoke From Their Fires: The Life of a Kwakiutl Chief.* New Haven: Yale University.
GARFIELD, VIOLA E. and PAUL S. WINGERT
  1950   *The Tsimshian Indians and their Arts.* Seattle: University of Washington.
GOLDMAN, IRVING
  1975   *The Mouth of Heaven: An Introduction to Kwakiutl Religious Thought.* New York: John Wiley & Sons.
GUNTHER, ERNA
  1972   *Indian Life on the Northwest Coast of North America, As Seen by the Earliest Explorers and Fur Traders.* Chicago: University of Chicago.
HAWTHORNE, HARRY B., C.S. BELSHAW, and S.M. JAMIESON
  1958   *The Indians of British Columbia: A Study of Contemporary Social Adjustment.* Toronto: University of Toronto.

JENNESS, DIAMOND
    1943   *The Carrier Indians of the Bulkley River.* Washington: Bureau of American Ethnology.

JILEK, WOLFGANG C.
    1974   *Salish Indian Mental Health and Cultural Change: Psychohygienic and Therapeutic Aspects of the Guardian Spirit Ceremonial.* Toronto: Holt, Rinehart & Winston of Canada.

LAVIOLETTE, FORREST E.
    1973   *The Struggle for Survival: Indian Cultures and the Protestant Ethic in British Columbia.* Toronto: University of Toronto.

LEWIS, CLAUDIA
    1970   *Indian Families of the Northwest Coast: The Impact of Change.* Chicago: University of Chicago.

MCFEAT, TOM, editor
    1966   *Indians of the North Pacific Coast.* Toronto: McClelland & Stewart.

MCILWRAITH, THOMAS F.
    1948   *The Bella Coola Indians.* Toronto: University of Toronto.

MOZINO, JOSE MARIANO
    1970   *Noticias de Nutka: An Account of Nootka Sound in 1792.* Seattle: University of Washington.

ROHNER, RONALD P. and EVELYN C. ROHNER
    1970   *The Kwakiutl Indians of British Columbia.* New York: Holt, Rinehart & Winston.

SPRADLEY, JAMES P., editor
    1972   *Guests Never Leave Hungry: The Autobiography of James Sewid, a Kwakiutl Indian.* Montreal: McGill-Queen's University.

STEWART, HILARY
    1977   *Indian Fishing: Early Methods on the Northwest Coast.* Vancouver: J.J. Douglas.

TEIT, JAMES A.
    1930   *The Salishan Tribes of the Western Plateaus.* Washington: Bureau of American Ethnology.

TURNEY-HIGH, H.H.
    1941   *Ethnography of the Kutenai.* Memoir of the American Anthropological Association.

VAN DEN BRINK, J.H.
    1974   *The Haida Indians: Cultural Change Mainly Between 1876–1970.* Leiden: E.J. Brill.

WOLCOTT, HARRY F.
    1967   *A Kwakiutl Village and School.* Toronto: Holt, Rinehart & Winston.

WOODCOCK, GEORGE
    1977   *Peoples of the Coast: The Indians of the Pacific Northwest.* Edmonton: Hurtig.

Chapter 9: Modern Issues

BERGER, THOMAS R.
    1977   *Northern Frontier, Northern Homeland: The Report of the Mackenzie Valley Pipeline Inquiry.* Vols. 1 and 2. Ottawa: Supply and Services Canada.

BIBBY, REGINALD W.
1978   The Delicate Mosaic: A National Examination of Inter-Group Relations in Canada. *Social Indicators Research.*

BOWLES, R.P. ET AL., editors
1972   *The Indian: Assimilation, Integration, or Separation.* Scarborough: Prentice-Hall of Canada.

BRAND, JOHANNA
1978   *The Life and Death of Anna Mae Aquash.* Toronto: James Lorimer.

BRAROE, NIELS W.
1975   *Indian and White: Self-Image and Interaction in a Canadian Plains Community.* Stanford: Stanford University.

BRODY, HUGH
1971   *Indians on Skid Row.* Ottawa: Information Canada.

CANADIAN CORRECTIONS ASSOCIATION
1967   *Indians and the Law.* Ottawa.

CARDINAL, HAROLD
1969   *The Unjust Society.* Edmonton: Hurtig.
1977   *The Rebirth of Canada's Indians.* Edmonton: Hurtig.

CORRIGAN, SAMUEL W.
1970   The Plains Indian Powwow: Cultural Integration in Manitoba and Saskatchewan. *Anthropologica,* Vol. 12, No. 2.

CUMMING, PETER A. and NEIL H. MICKENBERG
1972   *Native Rights in Canada,* 2nd edition. Toronto: Indian-Eskimo Association of Canada.

DEPARTMENT OF INDIAN AFFAIRS AND NORTHERN DEVELOPMENT
1969   *Mortality by Suicide, Comparison of Indian to National Rates, 1968.* Reference No. 5075.
1972   *Indian Education Program.* Ottawa.
1973   *The Canadian Indian: Statistics.* Ottawa.
1977   *Number and Acreage of Indian Reserves and Settlements by Band.* Ottawa.

DOSMAN, EDGAR
1972   *Indians: The Urban Dilemma.* Toronto: McClelland & Stewart.

DRIEDGER, LEO and JACOB PETERS
1977   Identity and Social Distance. *The Canadian Review of Sociology and Anthropology,* Vol. 14, No. 2.

ELIAS, PETER D.
1975   *Metropolis and Hinterland in Northern Manitoba.* Winnipeg: Manitoba Museum of Man and Nature.

ELLIOTT, JEAN L., editor
1971   *Minority Canadians: Native Peoples.* Scarborough: Prentice-Hall of Canada.

FIDLER, DICK
1970   *Red Power in Canada.* Toronto: Vanguard.

FORCESE, D. and S. RICHER
1975   *Issues in Canadian Societies: An Introduction to Sociology.* Scarborough: Prentice-Hall of Canada.

FRIDERES, JAMES S.
1974   *Canada's Indians: Contemporary Conflicts.* Scarborough: Prentice-Hall of Canada.

GERBER, LINDA M.
1977   *Community Characteristics and Out-Migration From Indian Communities: Regional*

Trends. Center for Population Studies, Harvard University.

GIBBONS, ROGER and J. RICK PONTING
1977   Contemporary Prairie Perceptions of Canada's Native Peoples. *Prairie Forum,* Vol. 2, No. 1.
1978   Canadians' Opinions and Attitudes Toward Indians and Indian Issues: Findings of a National Study. 48 Pp. Ms.

GOODERHAM, KENT, editor
1969   *I Am An Indian.* Toronto: J.M. Dent & Sons.

GUILLEMIN, JEANNE
1975   *Urban Renegades: The Cultural Strategy of American Indians.* New York: Columbia University.

HAWTHORN, HARRY B., editor
1966–   *A Survey of the Contemporary Indians of Canada.* Parts I and II. Ottawa: Indian
1967   Affairs and Northern Development.

HERTZBERG, HAZEL
1971   *Search for an American Indian Identity: Modern Pan-Indian Movements.* Syracuse, New York: Syracuse University.

HEUMANN, HANS ET AL.
1973   *The Native Offender in Canada.* Law Reform Commission of Canada.

HODGINS, B.W. ET AL., editors
1977   *The Canadian North: Source of Wealth or Vanishing Heritage.* Scarborough: Prentice-Hall of Canada.

JENNESS, DIAMOND
1964   *Eskimo Administration: Canada.* Montreal: Arctic Institute of North America.

JUDICIAL STATISTICS
1968   *Statistics of Criminal and Other Offences, 1967.* Ottawa: Statistics Canada.

KING, RICHARD A.
1967   *The School at Mopass: A Problem of Identity.* Holt, Rinehart & Winston.

MCCULLUM, HUGH and KARMEL MCCULLUM
1975   *This Land is Not For Sale.* Toronto: Anglican Book Centre.

NAGLER, MARK
1970   *Indians in the City.* Ottawa: Canadian Research Centre for Anthropology.

ORNSTEIN, TOBY E.
1973   *The First Peoples in Quebec.* Vols. 1–3. Montreal: Thunderbird Press.

PELLETIER, WILFRED and TED POOLE
1973   *No Foreign Land: The Biography of a North American Indian.* Toronto: McClelland & Stewart.

PINEO, PETER C.
1977   The Social Standing of Ethnic and Racial Groupings. *The Canadian Review of Sociology and Anthropology,* Vol. 14, No. 2.

PRICE, JOHN A.
1978   *Native Studies: American and Canadian Indians.* Scarborough: McGraw-Hill Ryerson.

ROBBINS, ALLAN
1977   A Survey of Migrating Native People: Preliminary Findings, Version III. Ottawa: Secretary of State.

ROBERTSON, HEATHER
1970   *Reservations Are For Indians.* Toronto: James, Louis & Samuel.

SCOTT, DUNCAN C.
  1931   *The Administration of Indian Affairs in Canada.* Toronto: Canadian Institute of International Affairs.

SEALEY, D. BRUCE and VERNA J. KIRKNESS, editors
  1973   *Indians Without Tipis: A Resource Book By Indians and Metis.* Winnipeg: William Clare.

SMITH, DEREK G.
  1975   *Canadian Indians and the Law: Selected Documents, 1663–1972.* Toronto: McClelland & Stewart.

STANBURY, WILLIAM T. and JAY SIEGEL
  1975   *Success and Failure: Indians in Urban Society.* Vancouver: University of British Columbia.

STYMEIST, DAVID H.
  1975   *Ethnics and Indians: Social Relations in a Northwestern Ontario Town.* Toronto: Peter Martin Associates.

SWARTZ, JERRY S.
  1977   Survey of Metis and Non-Status Indians. Ottawa: Research Projects Group, Native Employment Division, Employment and Immigration.

TREMBLAY, MARC-ADELARD, editor
  1976   *Les Facettes de L'identite Amerindienne.* Quebec: Laval University.

WATKINS, MEL, editor
  1977   *Dene Nation: The Colony Within.* Toronto: University of Toronto.

WAUBAGESHIG (HARVEY MCCUE), editor
  1970   *The Only Good Indian: Essays by Canadian Indians.* Toronto: New Press.

WHITESIDE, DON
  1973   *Historical Development of Aboriginal Political Associations in Canada: Documentation.* Ottawa: National Indian Brotherhood.

WUTTUNEE, WILLIAM
  1972   *Ruffled Feathers.* Calgary: Bell.

Subject Index

Name Index